THE
COASTAL
FORAGER

THE
COASTAL
FORAGER

*Wild maritime food to
preserve, cook & eat*

MARK WILLIAMS

ILLUSTRATED BY SOFIA IVA

Skittledog

Contents

The Intertidal Zone: Shellfish 217

Foraging on the coast

Foraging is in our DNA and, while it may have become hidden from many of us, buried under a few thousand years of agriculture, it is always ready to emerge if we allow it. Foraging is about recognizing abundance, knowing what to do with it, then acting on that knowledge. It is active and deeply practical, pragmatic rather than idealistic, responsive rather than controlling. It can be deeply personal and meditative, but also a wonderful social activity: the communal harvesting and processing of wild foods has nurtured human relationships for as long as we have walked the Earth.

Wild food can be the cornerstone of a diet, or just a tiny embellishment to enliven it. Such is the nutritional density of many wild foods compared to their cultivated counterparts, that even introducing small wild flourishes to meals can bring great improvements to our diets. The reasons people forage are as diverse as the things they forage for, but however it fits into our lives, the act of gathering food from the wild is an intimate act that bonds us with the land: physically, mentally, nutritionally and culturally.

'When the tide is out, the table is set' is a saying originating from the First Nations of the Pacific Northwest coast of Alaska and Canada, but it applies equally to most coastal regions where the sea is clean. Of all the habitats in which a forager might look for food, the coast is by far the most rewarding, surpassing even the richest riverbanks or most fecund forests in both diversity of edible species and nutritional density. Our hunter-gatherer ancestors knew this well, choosing to spend large portions of their year by the sea. Preserved piles of discarded shells many metres deep (known to archaeologists as shell middens) show us that seasonal gorging and preservation of shellfish such as mussels and oysters was commonplace among hunter-gatherers. Yet these tell only a small part of the story: most of the coastal diet of our ancestors left no trace.

Modern foragers don't need to see physical evidence to know that their ancestors feasted on seaweeds and coastal plants. In northern climes, the coast was the only place where large nutrient-rich wild vegetables were abundant and easily harvested, and this hasn't changed. Many of the vegetables that we have cultivated for consumption still grow free and wild in coastal habitats. Wild cabbage (*Brassica oleracea*; see page 117), for example, was domesticated by 2000 BCE and has since been selectively bred into a host of staples including broccoli, cauliflower, cabbage, kale and Brussels sprouts.

Cultivation hasn't always improved on the flavour or nutritional value of wild plants but merely made them easier to grow in straight lines or away from the sea. I once rescued some sea beet (see page 81) that had been unceremoniously dumped on the coast road by a storm and planted them in my garden. They took well enough to their new domestic setting and sprouted the following year, but their leaves – so glossy and succulent in their coastal home – were sad, flimsy and tasteless by comparison. Fortunately, having evolved to cope with their turbulent habitat, the wild colonies quickly sprung back even stronger, and I continued to thin them rather than harvest the domesticated weaklings in my garden.

The challenges and rewards of the coast

For plants, there are several upsides to growing near the sea. Springs just above the high tide line bring fresh water that is rich in nutrients leached from the land, and compared to the land, the sea is slow to cool down in the winter, lengthening the growing season and minimizing the challenges of frost. As a result, many plants, even those that haven't specifically evolved for coastal environments, thrive there – the earliest, fattest, juiciest, sweetest and most abundant berries are often found near the coast. Closer to the sea, high tides deposit an unending supply of nutrient-rich silt and dead seaweed (a brilliant compost, as every gardener knows).

In order to take full advantage of the benefits of coastal living, plants have to overcome some major challenges. Salt, tides, wind, sand and the often violent unpredictability of the sea have led to evolutionary adaptations that make coastal plants rewarding for foragers. Thick, succulent leaves with waxy coatings are pleasing to the palate and more filling than skinny inland plants. These salt-tolerant plants, or halophytes, store and excrete surplus salt using their leaves, often giving them a pleasingly 'pre-seasoned' tang. Grazing insects are less of an issue on wind-swept coasts, so the plants that live there tend to produce fewer of the bitter or toxic compounds that foragers worry about inland. To a well-adapted plant, the coast is prime real estate.

As we drop below the high tide line, the challenges and adaptations become even more extreme. Seaweeds – which include the ancestors of all our terrestrial plants – produce slippery compounds to help them slide through crashing waves without being smashed to pieces. Two of these compounds are of particular interest to humans: glutamates give seaweeds their prized umami properties, while alginates can be used to thicken and set recipes or used as moisturizer. Alginates also slow down digestion, helping us better absorb our food. Smaller seaweeds deter grazing aquatic molluscs by producing compounds with incredible truffle-like flavours that leave gourmets chortling with joy. Many seaweeds are nutritional powerhouses, capturing and concentrating minerals from ocean currents. This isn't to say that they are all worth eating: the challenge for seaweed foragers is in locating the choice species and knowing how to use them.

The gastronomic rewards of shellfish are more widely appreciated and they command a high price in shops and restaurants. With a little care and practice they can be foraged for free from any clean waters.

No wonder our ancestors spent long parts of their foraging year near the sea – the origin of life on earth, it continues to sustain us in innumerable ways. It is one of the last truly wild places on earth that we can access with ease. Beyond its many gastronomic delights, this is what makes foraging there most magical. By attuning ourselves to it, we can rediscover our place within the natural order of things. I hope this book helps you on that journey.

Right: Coastal plants have to overcome harsh challenges just to exist. To be able to thrive here, they must adapt to salty, windy conditions and the unpredictability of the sea.

About this book

Although it is defined and moulded by its proximity to the sea, the coast is not a homogenous entity, but a complex mosaic of interlocking ecosystems that are defined by their exposure to tide, wind and wave, and characterized by distinctive plant, seaweed and shellfish communities. These don't just happen to live in their habitat or ecosystem but play an active role in shaping and maintaining it.

To help you digest the complexity of the coast, I have organized this book by distinct habitats, enabling you to find and connect with the remarkable cast of edible species that help to build and populate it. A few species do well across a number of habitats, and where this is the case, I have included them under the habitat in which they are best harvested, and have noted other habitats in the text.

Given the abundance and diversity of coastal plants and marine life that can be eaten (in temperate waters, several hundred species of seaweed alone are potentially edible), and the limitations of space, I have applied the following filters:

They don't run or swim away (very quickly).
This keeps us in the gentle and benign world of foraging rather than hunting or fishing. I say 'very quickly', as some shellfish do take evasive action – I expect you can outrun a winkle, but razor clams can move at quite a pace (but they are too much tasty fun to leave out). With a heavy heart I have omitted crabs, shrimps and lobsters, as these bring us too close to hunting and fishing, but don't let that stop you rummaging in rock pools for them.

You don't need to swim to get them.
Snorkelling is a brilliant way to explore seaweeds in all their wavy, shimmering glory, but my explorations here stop at the low spring tide line – though foraging for a few of the seaweeds and shellfish may require you to get your feet wet.

They are delicious and/or nutritious, ideally both.
'Edibility' is a moveable feast: just because something can be eaten doesn't mean it's worth eating. Conversely, some things that taste great may not be especially good for us – wild food is no different from cultivated and processed food in that respect. Much of this is subjective judgement, but I've sampled, and judged, most things so you don't have to. Trust me: stranded jellyfish, sea slugs and starfish aren't worth the work.

Within these parameters, I have focused on what I consider to be the most rewarding and accessible edible species, plus a few less rewarding but very common species, and a few uncommon species that I include more for their historical and ethnobotanical interest rather than as things to pick in any quantity. I urge you to explore beyond these as your knowledge and confidence increase.

In terms of geographical range, I have focused on the temperate coasts of the North Atlantic bound by the eastern seaboard of North America from the Carolinas northwards through Canada, and the Atlantic and North Sea coasts of Europe from Scandinavia down to Northern Spain. There is considerable variation in species and their abundance across this vast area. Where possible, I have noted this in the text for each species and included localized common names. Binomial names are more helpful for doing further research and finding near relations.

Foraging is a wonderful entry point into a wider appreciation of the natural world beyond our human appetites, so I have included ecological as well as ethnobotanical notes on each species. By understanding their lifestyles and complex interactions with the wider web of life, I hope you will become a happy, kind forager, appreciative of your tiny place in the enormity of the world.

I recommend you use this book in conjunction with good general plant, seaweed and coastal fauna identification guides in order to fill the less delicious, but just as fascinating, blanks. I've recommended some of my favourites in the resources section at the back.

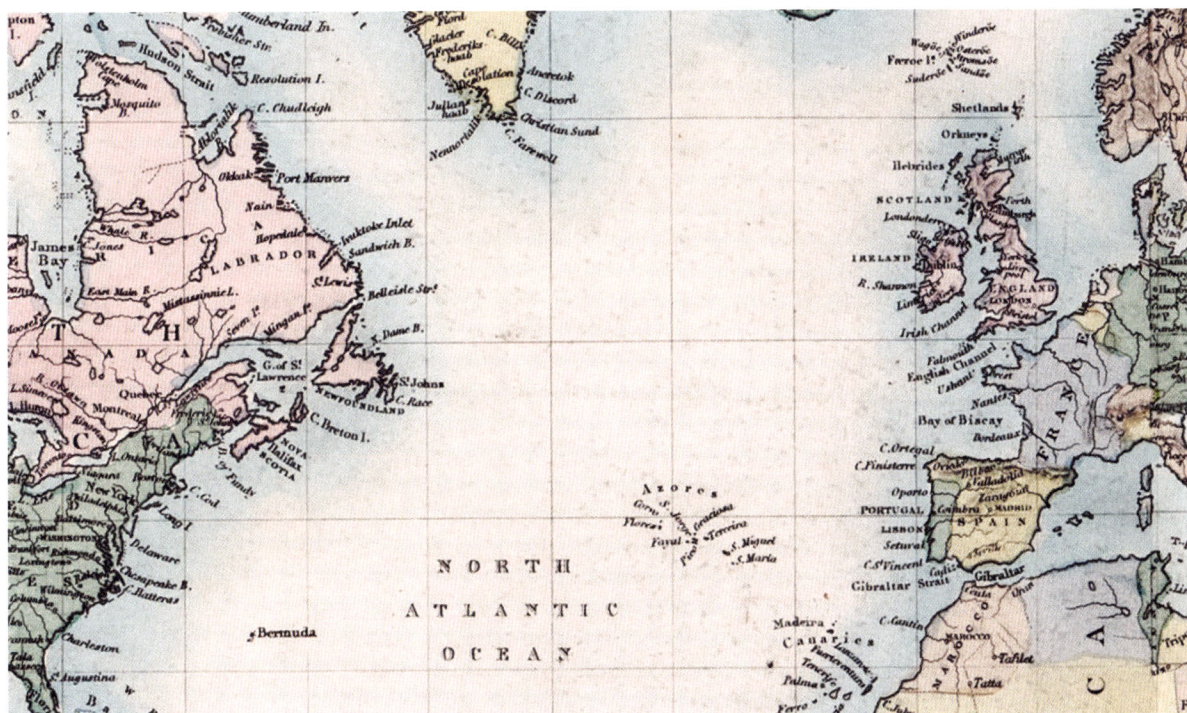

Above: The species in this book are mostly found on the temperate coasts of the North Atlantic. This vast area includes the eastern seaboard of North America and the Atlantic and North Sea coasts of Europe.

A note on the recipes

Much of my focus in this book is on general treatments, preparations and methods. My intention is to equip you with a set of skills rather than a set of instructions that will allow you to follow where nature, your taste, and the wild harvests that are abundant in your bit of the world lead you. That said, there are a few concoctions I've stumbled on down the years – some 'classics', some my own happy accidents, and others inspired by fellow foragers – that I think you might like to recreate, so I have included more focused recipes for these.

Some of my recipes recommend a range of wild seasonings and embellishments that may initially seem beyond you. Don't worry: these will either be optional or I will suggest a tame alternative. Once you get the foraging bug, however, your kitchen will soon fill with all manner of powders, potions and preserves that you will use without a second thought instead of their shop-bought inferiors.

Legal, responsible & considerate foraging

Few sources of sustenance have less impact on our planet than foraging, but this does not make it a magical panacea for our broken food system. As foragers, we must reconcile our appetites with care for the earth and its inhabitants by nurturing a foraging culture based on legal, responsible and considerate practices.

I differentiate between these because, if you stick only to the law, it's still possible to be an irresponsible and inconsiderate forager. It is also possible to forage perfectly responsibly in a way that contravenes laws, and even foraging that is legal and responsible may not necessarily be considerate of others who may value a species or habitat.

Legal foraging

Laws around foraging vary widely according to which country you live in. Your first consideration should be around access: are you legally permitted to be in the location where you intend to forage? You should have a sense of what is legal and socially acceptable in terms of access to land in your country and locale, but it is worth checking if you aren't sure. Ownership of the coastline and the intertidal zone can be particularly opaque and variable, so I have provided notes on further reading for anyone wishing to delve into the specifics of their country or region (see page 265). Wherever you are, asking a local is always a good start, and you may get more nuanced insight from a five-minute chat than a day on the Internet.

Once you have ascertained that you can legally be somewhere, you need to unpick the even more confusing world of foraging law. Laws around foraging are often vague, piecemeal and confusing because they have evolved without clear direction over centuries and are rarely reviewed or modernized. In the absence of any coherent legal framework, a combination of common sense, self-interest and self-policing generally suffices.

In most parts of the world, if you are legally allowed to be somewhere, you will be within your legal rights to gather the 'four Fs' – fruit, flowers, foliage and fungi – provided they are not deliberately being grown. If you intend to uproot anything, even for your own consumption, you should seek the landowner's permission. For reasons lost in the mists of time, seaweeds are generally not included, while shellfish tend to be governed by a host of very localized rules and regulations. Again, I recommend in-person enquiry with both the authorities and other coast-users.

Where there is a long-established tradition of wild harvesting, there may be a permissive right to foraging activities – a customary acceptance, if you will. I suspect that if push came to shove, most authorities would accept that personal seaweed harvesting falls within this category. Common sense suggests that if something has taken place for a long time without anyone being bothered about it, or even noticing, challenging it legally might be a waste of everyone's time. As foragers often value what non-foragers consider to be weeds, responsible and considerate foraging can easily eclipse the letter of the law.

That said, practices once considered normal are sometimes found to be problematic, and one person's common sense is another's pillaging. As foragers, we should be prepared to politely explain what we are doing to anyone who might enquire, impressing on them that we have given serious and careful thought to how to do it responsibly and considerately, while being receptive to new information. All foragers should be ambassadors for foraging, so it's worth rehearsing these conversations in your head, even if you rarely need to deploy them. I don't recommend mentioning your legal rights unless severely pressed – people respond better to humans than statutes.

Wherever in the world you are, you cross a significant legal and cultural boundary when you seek to profit financially from wild harvests. You will usually require permission from the landowner before harvesting anything you intend to sell or trade commercially.

Some sites will have protected status as nature reserves or sites of scientific interest. This doesn't necessarily mean that you can't forage anything there. For example, gathering sea buckthorn berries in an area where orchids are protected may well be fine, or even helpful, but you should seek permission before doing so.

Responsible foraging

The decline of biodiversity is testament to the inadequacy of the law for protecting the natural world. This is due to habitat loss, environmental degradation and commercial exploitation rather than foraging for personal consumption. Nevertheless, you will enjoy your wild harvesting a lot more if you learn how to do it well.

Glib sustainability messages such as 'Never take more than 10 per cent of what you find' (Of what? In what area?), 'Always leave plenty behind' (How do you define plenty?) and 'Always forage sustainably' are bandied about without any precise explanation or definition of terms (define 'sustainably'?). A more holistic and helpful approach is to recognize the uniqueness of each species and how it contributes to its wider ecosystem, then harvest (or not) in a way that is sensitive and appropriate to its location.

For example, sea buckthorn growing in one location may be considered a troublesome non-native species that you are encouraged to pick, while in another it may be important for stabilizing sand dunes or as a food source for over-wintering birds. Responsible foragers take an interest in all such nuances, and appreciate, above all, that they are just one of many individuals and species that are invested in the ongoing health of a plant, colony or ecosystem.

Hobby foragers tend to be much more interested in what is locally abundant than hunting down rare species. Not everything explored in these pages will be abundant everywhere this book is read, so please consider it a launchpad for getting properly intimate with your local wild harvests. I have included ecological notes and sustainable harvesting strategies, but please don't stop at them – observe and consider the effects of your own gatherings and tweak your behaviour accordingly. With this in mind, I offer only one general foraging 'rule': you are doing it well if nobody can tell you have been there.

Considerate foraging

As well as staying legal and minimizing our impact on the natural world, we should also consider our impact on other foragers and land users, and what we can give back to the wild places that sustain us.

On stumbling upon a bumper harvest, even ecologically responsible foragers may think of it as 'their' spot. This is a perfectly normal and understandable way of bonding with a landscape, but we should stop to consider that this bountiful patch of tasty, nutritious wild food may well have been someone else's patch long before we 'discovered' it. It may also be appreciated for other reasons by people with no interest in foraging. This applies most keenly when exploring new areas. Foraging is a practice that predates humans, and our current knowledge and understandings are almost always borrowed from or built upon the foundation of indigenous knowledge and practices. As foragers, we should acknowledge this gift with gratitude and pass it on with humility.

Humans, and especially those that forage, are innately territorial, but on our busy planet it is public-spirited to consider what might be our 'fair share'. By curbing our baser instincts and chatting with other nature-lovers we can, with care and good manners, share best practice and spark community rather than colonialism and rivalry.

Beyond minimizing our impact, as considerate foragers, we should find ways to support, nurture and protect the natural world. A good way to do this is to try to remove more plastic than anything else when visiting the coast, something which is depressingly easy to do. More focused efforts, such as helping to control non-native invasive species, sharing observations with botanical databases or volunteering, all contribute to a positive foraging culture.

Opposite: Sea kale (see page 67) may be scarce and protected in some areas, but hyperabundant in other locations. By only thinning abundance, foragers have minimal impact and learn to cherish and protect colonies.
Previous page: Oyster plant (see page 95) is scarce in much of its range, and harvesting should be restricted to no more than the odd leaf unless actively working to increase populations.

The good forager's checklist

LEGAL:
- Am I allowed to be here?
- Do I intend to sell or trade what I harvest?
- Do I intend to uproot anything?
- Are there any restrictions on what I can take (e.g. nature reserve, conservation area, species-specific harvesting limits)?

RESPONSIBLE:
- Have I spent time getting familiar with the area I intend to forage in?
- What is the ecological role of the species I intend to harvest?
- What is an appropriate quantity to take from this location?
- What specific harvesting strategies will ensure the ongoing health of the plant/colony/ecosystem?

CONSIDERATE:
- Might this be someone else's 'spot' already?
- Will anyone be able to tell I have been here?
- What am I giving back to this plant/colony/ecosystem?

Staying safe at the coast

The coast can seem like a generous and benign place, but it can also be a series of elaborate traps for anyone uninformed, careless or under the hypnotic spell of foraging. The treasures I describe in this book are essentially bait in those traps, so here is a summary of how to avoid mishaps. Please don't be put off – there is no danger here that a little knowledge can't defuse.

Appropriate attire

Weather changes quickly on the coast, often following its own set of localized rules that a general weather forecast will not account for. A pleasant breeze inland can feel like a stormy blast by the sea, and even if it doesn't bring rain, it is still likely to be damp and penetrating. Inshore forecasts are available in most coastal regions – make sure to check the forecast for your destination before setting out. In all but the most settled warm weather, take an extra layer that you hope not to need.

Before embarking on any serious foraging in the intertidal zone, decide in advance whether you are prepared to get wet feet. Most people's instinct is, understandably, to try to stay dry, and welly boots are fine for this. However, unless it's winter, I strongly recommend accepting wet feet not just as an inevitability, but as a positive choice.

In spring, summer and autumn my personal preference – and strong recommendation – is to wear both socks and an old pair of trainers/sneakers, and fully commit to having wet feet inside them. Combined with short trousers, this set-up will, after 30 seconds of mild discomfort on first immersion, leave you nimble, carefree, safer and the envy of anyone fretting about staying dry. But do remember to bring dry footwear to change into afterwards. You can also try wearing wetsuit-style boots inside an old pair of trainers – these are effective even in winter.

Safety checklist

The four simplest things you can do to minimize the chance of disaster are:

- Pair up. Even the most nimble, fit and experienced can slip, or trap a foot between rocks, so having someone to help or raise the alarm can be a life-saver.
- Take a well-charged phone, ideally in a waterproof case. Countless lives are saved each year by calls to the coastguard.
- Do some basic research if an area of coast is new to you, through maps, tide tables/apps, signage and (especially) talking to locals.
- If you must go alone, let someone know where you are going, and when you expect to be home.

When traversing beaches and rocks, remember:

- Seaweeds are, by their very nature, slippery. Tread between them, not on them.
- Assume that all rocks are going to be slippery, doubly so if they are wet.
- Tread in the nooks and crevices between rocks and boulders, not right on top of them.
- Barnacles are dependably non-slip, even when wet.
- Stay aware of the texture of sand and silt, and back out gently if you lose sight of your feet.
- Pay attention to signage, especially those pointing out rapid tides/currents and quicksand/deep mud.

Tides

Tides make coastal foraging both magical and challenging. Tuning into the pull of the sun and moon on our oceans tears us from the mechanical ticking of artificial time and returns us to more natural rhythms. However, it is all too easy to be lured out at low tide and get lost in the beauty of seaweeds only to find yourself cut off by the rising tide.

Fortunately, tides are predictable, and a little insight into how they work will help keep you safe while you fill your bucket with tasty things. The main influence on tides is the gravitational pull of the moon, which acts on oceans, causing them to bulge at times when it is closest, and recede as it moves further away. This oscillation means most coasts experience a low tide every 12 hours and 25 minutes. To put it another way, it takes about 6 and a quarter hours for the water at the shore to go from high to low, or from low to high. The extremes will be between 25 and 40 minutes later each day.

Tides do not ebb and flood (the correct nautical terms for going out and coming in) at an even rate throughout each cycle. Rather, the tide turns slowly, then gathers pace, before braking to make its next turn. The rule of twelfths is useful for measuring this: in the first hour after low tide the water level will rise by one-twelfth of the range; in the second hour, by two-twelfths; in the third hour, by three-twelfths; in the fourth hour, by another three-twelfths; in the fifth hour, it drops back by two-twelfths; and in the sixth hour, to one-twelfth.

For foragers, this means a nice gentle harvesting window with lots of seabed exposed around low tide but the possibility of being chased back to dry land by an accelerating flood tide. In large estuaries and sand flats, where the sea can go out for several miles over very gentle gradients, it can move faster than most people can run, turning an inconvenience into a life-threatening situation.

Timing your foray for an ebbing tide saves rushing, and provided you have noted the time at which the tide turns, you will be able to relax and explore for a few hours. But be warned: the motions of a turning tide are subtle, and it's easy to get cut off. If you are foraging on an exposed promontory, setting an alarm to remind you when the tide is turning can be helpful. If you're on a flat bit of shore, a carefully placed stone or bucket is useful as a visual reference point.

The tides' highest highs and, more importantly for foragers, lowest lows occur a day or two after a full moon, known as spring or king tides. Here, spring refers to the elasticity of the tide, not the time of year, though the most extreme do occur around the spring (and autumn) equinox. At their very lowest, these tides can afford foragers access to shellfish that usually require a lobster pot or wetsuit to access – well worth noting in your diary.

There will be a published tide table showing times and heights for designated coastal stations in your local area. These are usually available cheaply in any coastal general store or business that takes an interest in the sea. There is also a great range of tide apps available – some free (but perhaps only showing tides for the week ahead) and some paid (with a longer range and more bells and whistles) – see page 265 for my recommendations.

Currents

Provided you have paid attention to tide times, there should be no need to do anything wetter than gentle paddling to gather any of the species in this book. Occasionally, though, it is fun and helpful to gather seaweeds from deeper water. If doing so, you should be aware of tidal flows and localized currents that can rapidly sweep careless swimmers out to sea.

Currents are not the same as tides but are strongly influenced by them. While tides refer to the height of the water, currents describe the speed and direction in which the water is moving. Currents are usually at their strongest when the tide is in the middle of its range and moving fastest, and they are usually more gentle at low/high tide (or slack water, as it is often known). But don't rely on these rules of thumb: enquire locally, look out for warning signs and get to know an area before committing to full immersion.

Opposite: The island in the background is accessible on foot at low tide – but only for a few hours.

Consuming wild food

Foraging brings its own particular set of food safety challenges around correct identification, safe preparation and adverse reactions. Please take careful note of the potential issues I raise here and, above all, never munch on a hunch!

Seaweeds and shellfish

Provided they are alive and growing in clean water, the health risks of eating seaweeds are small, though there are a few things to consider, which are explored on page 157.

Shellfish are curious in the world of foraging insofar as they are all more-or-less edible, but they can present some serious health risks in terms of their condition, water quality, pollution, handling and storage. These, and how to mitigate them, are explored in detail on page 220.

Sensible precautions

- If you have a known intolerance to certain foods, check which plant family they belong to and be extra careful with their wild relations. Where something is particularly allergenic, or closely related to plants that commonly cause adverse reactions, I have noted this in the text.

- If you have never eaten something before, try only a small amount the first time, and wait an hour or two before eating more.

- It is possible to have too much of a good thing: foods that are good for you in moderation may not be if you gorge on them. Some may need to be prepared in a specific way.

Poisonous plants

The complexity of botanical chemistry inevitably throws up (pun intended) problematic compounds for foragers of plants. Often these are accidents of chemistry – with human poisoning being collateral damage in a much bigger war between plants and insects. Conversely, what is unpleasant or toxic to an insect is not necessarily problematic to humans, and may well prove delicious and tasty. Mustard, garlic and mint flavours all arise from compounds that evolved to deter insects.

Temperate coastlines are, in general, home to fewer species of plants that are troublesome to foragers than inland areas. The reasons for this aren't well documented, but it seems likely that salty, windswept coasts shelter fewer insects, so the chemical ingenuity typical of inland plants isn't as important. This doesn't mean there is room for complacency: it only takes one lapse of judgement or concentration to turn a tasty wild meal into a gastric upset or worse. That said, there is no need to let paranoia and anxiety govern your foraging experience: by learning to recognize and avoid just a few toxic species, you can nibble without fear.

Two poisonous plants that every coastal forager should know are hemlock water-dropwort and hemlock. Both are members of the carrot/parsley (Apiaceae) family and are by no means exclusively coastal, but both do quite well there. It's worth seeking them out and closely observing them over a full growing season. You'll soon be able to spot them from afar, and once they are familiar, you won't imagine them lurking at every turn and will be able to impress your friends with your witchy knowledge.

Hemlock water-dropwort

Oenanthe crocata

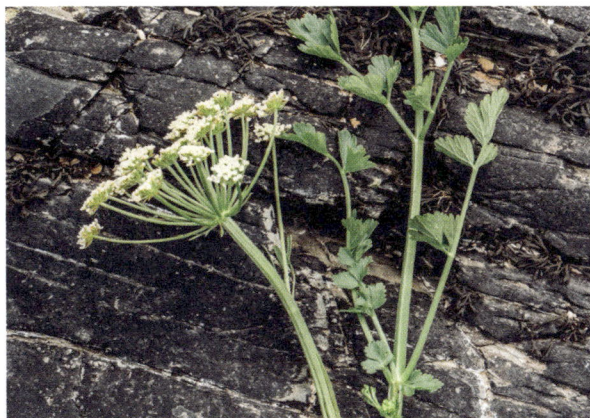

Hemlock water-dropwort is abundant and fast-growing, appearing in large colonies anywhere it can keep its roots in fresh water. Although not specifically adapted to the coast, it can tolerate some salinity and wind.

IDENTIFICATION Vigorous hairless perennial, with pinnately divided lobed leaves and umbels of white flowers in summer. Crushed leaves and broken stems smell of acrid celery.

DISTRIBUTION Common in temperate Europe, especially near the coast. In North America, the similar and equally toxic water hemlock (*Cicuta maculata*) occupies a similar niche.

SEASON January (first shoots, often visible underwater in streams, ditches, etc.) to October.

HABITAT Streams, ditches, slow-moving rivers; riverbanks; high-water springs, often emerging just above the high tide line from shingle and lining the upper limit of salt marshes.

POSSIBLE CONFUSION In this book, its leaves most resemble alexanders (page 29), but it has white flowers. Although related to Scots lovage (page 109) and rock samphire (page 105), its habitat and looks are different.

TOXICITY Every part is potentially deadly, but mostly the roots and seeds. Toxins are not destroyed by cooking. All parts are safe to handle and the surrounding water does not absorb toxins. Poisonous to all mammals, so dog owners should learn to recognize the distinctive 'dead men's fingers'; roots that are often washed up on beaches after storms.

Hemlock

Conium maculatum

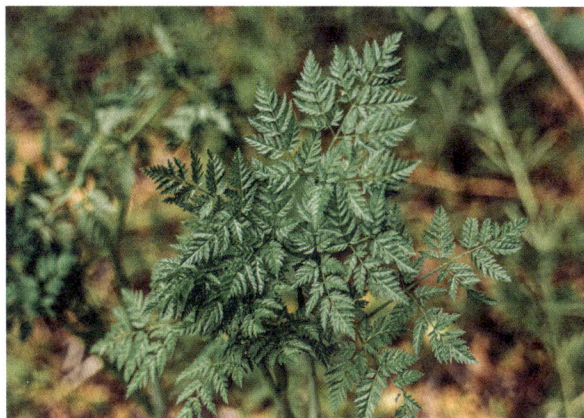

Although it is by no means a coastal specialist, where I live in south-west Scotland, hemlock *only* grows in coastal locations, where it enjoys the warming effect of the sea, less shading from trees and avoids acidic soils more common inland.

IDENTIFICATION Hairless perennial growing up to 2m (6ft), with finely divided pinnate leaves and small umbels of white flowers above. Stems have purple blotches. Crushed leaves and broken stems have a musty/ammonia smell.

DISTRIBUTION Widely distributed native of northern Europe; also well established in North America.

SEASON April to November.

HABITAT Waste ground and wind-sheltered sunny spots, often just above the beach.

POSSIBLE CONFUSION Does not closely resemble any of the edible species in this book, but take extra care when harvesting its relative, alexanders (page 29).

TOXICITY Every part is potentially deadly, though the toxins are at their most concentrated in the roots and seeds. Some reports claim that its toxins are diminished by cooking, but I wouldn't bet (my life) on it.

Maritime Woods
& Hedgerows

Plants that thrive near the coast

in a frostless land
salt sun bakes fat berries
and we lean
with
the
wind

The plant communities of maritime woods and hedgerows are hardy and adaptable enough to take advantage of its benefits, growing heavy with edible fruit and flowers. I use the term 'hedgerow' here loosely, to include all free-spirited plants that enjoy unkempt edges – the coast being the unruliest edge of all. Near my home in south-west Scotland there are long stretches of coast that are bound by a narrow strip of bent and gnarly trees. An old Scots word, *jachelt*, describes their wind-sculpted, wind-twisted growth. In testing times, the resilience of trees can be hopeful and inspiring.

Such trees are not restricted to Scotland. In German, *krummholz* (from krumm: twisted/bent and holz: tree) describes a similar upland phenomenon. I've also seen them and the mini forests they create described in North Amcrica as dwarf or elfin. Such fantastical terms seem apt – their gnarly overgrown shades often make me think of a Disney prince slashing his way through thorn-filled forests to rescue a sleeping princess. To the romantic, these are places of witchcraft, phantasmagoria and hidden treasure.

For foragers, the treasure can be very real. While not specifically evolved for life on the coast, these plant communities thrive on its upsides. They enjoy the warming effect of the sea, which makes for a longer and frost-free growing season, and occasionally sandy, free-draining soils, an abundance of mineral-rich fresh water running off the land, and less predation by insects and herbivores.

For these reasons, the earliest, biggest, juiciest and sweetest fruits tend to swell near our coasts, and also some delightful aromatic herbs, the stems and leaves of which grow fatter than those of their inland kin. These opportunists are an intrinsic part of the coastal pantry, and always available should you arrive when the tide is high.

Flower stems emerge from sheaths that often have reddish or purple stripes.

Grooved, hairless stems.

Substantial carrot-like roots.

Fruits have deeply ridged compartments, and turn from green to black as they mature.

Alexanders

Smyrnium olusatrum

Like all good plants, there are many stories and half-remembered histories around alexanders. Many sources repeat the idea that the Romans brought it from the Mediterranean to the wider world to feed their horses. It has also been suggested that it grew in northern Europe long before they arrived. Its pollen is notoriously hard to identify in paleobotanical sediments, so the debate may continue for some time yet. Its common name is attributed to Alexander the Great and clues to its uses are hidden in its binomial name: *Smyrnium* means myrrh-like, a reference to its aromatic oil, and *olusatrum* means black herb, because of its jet-black seeds. In northern Europe, it is usually within a stone's throw of the sea, but it strays further inland the farther south you go.

ALSO KNOWN AS Alisander, allsander, alshinder, alick, skit, skeet, hellroot, megweed, wild parsley, horse parsley, Macedonian parsley, wild celery, horse celery, stanmarch, black lovage.

EDIBILITY All parts are edible, with a strong, bitter, aromatic flavour: stems, roots and flower buds as a vegetable; leaves as a herb; seeds as a spice.

IDENTIFICATION Erect, grooved, hairless biennial with green stems, sometimes with purplish stripes; shiny leaves with three-toothed diamond-shaped leaflets. The lower leafstalks and nascent flower buds grow from distinctive sheaths around the stem. Small lime green to yellow flowers appear on umbels. Grows to 50–150cm (20–60in) high.

DISTRIBUTION Common in most coastal regions of the Mediterranean and Western Europe as far north as Scotland, but becoming less abundant in the north of Wales. A rare non-native in North America.

WHEN TO HARVEST Stems and leaves are best collected in winter and early spring, before the flowers open. Green seeds form in the summer, drying into black seeds by autumn, which often persist well into the winter.

HABITAT Hedgerows, clifftops, roadsides, banks and rough ground close to the sea, though it can grow inland too, where it is often an escapee from historic kitchen gardens.

SIMILAR SPECIES Alexanders is a member of the carrot (Apiaceae) family, which includes some poisonous species that are superficially similar (see page 22). However, it prefers drier soils to the wet ground and riverbanks favoured by hemlock water-dropwort, and has more broadly lobed leaves than hemlock. If in any doubt, wait for its yellow flowers to appear – its poisonous cousins have white flowers.

Harvesting alexanders

Alexanders is a biennial plant (meaning it has a two-year life cycle), so you will often find low first-year leaf growth beneath the flowering stems of year-two plants. It is one of the earliest plants to start its growth cycle, making it one of the greenest and lushest you are likely to see on coastal roadsides in February and March. The flowers secrete copious amounts of nectar early in the spring, and over 150 species of insects have been recorded enjoying the feast. Where it is established, alexanders can become extremely abundant. It is so successful in some coastal areas that it is considered a nuisance and actively controlled. Foragers can play their part in this by thinning out colonies with a clear conscience.

The principal harvests are fat stems, leaves and parcels at the stem bases, which contain nascent flowers and leaves. These should be pruned out with a knife or secateurs near the ground. Green or black seed heads can be pulled or snipped off individually, or umbellules or full umbels can be collected for stripping at home, depending on how well established a colony is. Roots are quite shallow and best dug at the end of the first year's growth, though you should have the landowner's permission to do this.

Eating alexanders

Alexanders is aromatic – some would say perfumy – with a distinctly bitter aftertaste. It resembles its carrot-family brethren celery and lovage, with perhaps a hint of juniper and myrrh – an acquired taste for dulled modern palates, but certainly one worth acquiring. Its intensity is diminished by cooking, so by starting with small amounts in cooked dishes you may come to enjoy it, especially mixed with milder greens.

The fat stems, harvested before flowering, can be chopped and used in place of celery alongside carrots and onions in mirepoix – the stock base of so many classic soups and sauces. Stems can be stringy on the outside, so peel them first if you intend to leave them in the stock.

Young roots and peeled fat stems are best steamed for 10 minutes (or longer if you wish to dilute their flavour more) then eaten as a truly eye-opening wild vegetable, perhaps with some hollandaise or a poached egg. If you get a taste for that and feel receptive to a more intense alexanders experience, unopened flower buds (rather like flimsy, intensely flavoured broccoli) can be similarly cooked in their Willy Wonka-like red-striped pyjamas and peeled at the table, or opened first and fried. A good coating of butter and a grind of black pepper (or black alexanders seeds) sets them off splendidly.

Leaves, young shoots and thin stems have a more pungent, celery-like flavour that is too much for most in any quantity, but used sparingly they add an interesting flavour to salads, especially tempered with an oily dressing. In Turkey, young shoots and leaves are cooked and eaten with yogurt – a good treatment for any intensely flavoured greens. They can also be finely shredded and used like an extra aromatic parsley in soups and sauces, or to add an exciting twist to pesto or salsa verde (see page 107)

Alexanders seeds are an excellent spice, reminiscent of black cumin. When still green they are intense and quite bitter, mellowing as they age and turn black. They contain an essential oil called cuminal, which is also present in cumin, eucalyptus and myrrh, and have less heat but more bitterness than black pepper. Toasting them briefly in a low oven or dry frying pan to ensure they are bone-dry helps with grinding and awakens their aromatics. Try adding roughly ground seeds to bread, especially rye bread. Keep some pre-ground in a pinch pot by the cooker to remind you to vary your seasonings – too often, any seasoning that isn't salt or black pepper languishes forgotten at the back of the cupboard.

Whole seeds (green or black) make excellent aromatic additions when pickling coastal plants, especially pickled marsh samphire (see page 129), and I often have animated gourmets on my wild picnics demanding to know what exotic-tasting flavour-bomb just exploded on their palate.

Lacto-fermented alexanders

The juicy, pre-flowering stems and buds of alexanders can be pickled in vinegar (see page 258), but I prefer them lacto-fermented. This process uses a weak salt solution to deter moulds and less desirable bacteria while allowing helpful *Lactobacillus* bacteria to form. These emit CO_2 and increase the acidity of the solution to below the magic pH level of 4.6 (which prevents botulism), adding a sour tang and subtle fizz to an already complex flavour (think sauerkraut or kimchi). The stems can be fermented in long sections or chopped into bite-sized pieces. I describe the basic recipe here, but it can be freely embellished with spices and other (wild or tame) harvests.

Ingredients

Buds and stems from pre-flowering alexanders

2% brine solution: 20g (¾oz) salt per 1L (1¾ pints) unchlorinated water

Cabbage leaf, for weighing down the stems

Peel the stringy outers from juicy alexander stems and place in a large glass jar or fermenting crock. Cover with brine. Use a clean weight (a smaller jar, perhaps) or cabbage leaf to keep the alexanders immersed beneath the brine and loosely put on the lid.

Leave at ambient indoor temperature for a week. After the first day or two you will start to notice bubbling. If you have put the lid on tightly, you will need to release the pressure in the jar every day or so, a process that experienced fermenters call 'burping'. While doing this, check that everything remains immersed in the brine, pushing it down with a clean spoon if necessary. The chief cause of spoilage is air. After a week, when the bubbling subsides, tighten the lid and place the jar in the fridge for another week or so.

After that, it's ready to eat. I like it in cheese sandwiches, or as a side with Thai curries. If you have any issues with the fermentation process, try adding shredded wild garlic (ramps) leaves to the brine – they deter unwanted moulds.

Alexanders salt

This is an excellent seasoning for burgers, hot dogs, tomatoes, coleslaw or coast-slaw (see page 75), and can be used in place of celery salt in a Bloody Mary cocktail. It works equally well made with Scots lovage or rock samphire. In a food processor, blitz approximately 1 part (by weight) of alexanders leaves and stems with 2 parts sea salt. Spread the mix thinly on a tray and pop it in a dehydrator on a lowish heat setting (or in a fan oven on its lowest setting, with the door propped open). You can speed up the process by breaking it up a bit halfway through. Once it is thoroughly dry, blitz it again, then store in an airtight jar. Alexanders salt is a nice seasoning to sit alongside your alexanders pepper.

Alexanders cocktail bitters

Rather than running in fear from the bitter qualities of alexanders, I prefer to embrace them. This simple infusion allows their aromatics to shine, and seasons cocktails with a very grown-up, clean, peppery bitterness. It's best to dispense it from an atomizer spray, which can be easily sourced online, but if you don't have one, a few drops stirred into a drink from a bottle is fine. It is especially good sprayed onto a martini just before drinking, but it is also a refreshing addition to a gin and tonic, fizzy water or orange juice.

Toast 2 teaspoons of black alexanders seeds in a dry frying pan. Crush them a little in a mortar and pestle, then put them into a 100ml (3½ fl oz) spray bottle. Top up with vodka (minimum 40% ABV, ideally stronger) and screw on the top. Leave for two weeks, shaking occasionally. It's fine to leave the seeds in the bottle – the bitters will get stronger with time, but just use less as it does.

Blackthorn blossoms are one of the first flowers to appear in early spring – a good indicator of where to hunt sloes in autumn.

Bark is smooth, and dark brown to black in colour.

Drupes turn from green to deep purple-blue.

Mature sloes often have a whitish bloom.

Shrivelled sloes later in autumn still have good flavour.

Blackthorn

Prunus spinosa

Blackthorn is a large shrub or small tree that does extremely well on the coast. Its hard wood, fierce thorns and dense, suckering growth habit help it to resist salty coastal winds by building its own windbreaks. Blackthorn blossoms are a valuable source of early nectar and pollen for bees in spring and its leaves are food for the caterpillars of dozens of moth species and hairstreak butterflies. The dense thickets it creates are a haven for birds. Blackbirds, thrushes and larger tits feast on sloes in autumn and in clean coastal air it is heavily colonized by many species of lichen.

ALSO KNOWN AS Sometimes called sloe, though this term really refers to blackthorn fruits, not the tree. The correct botanical term for sloes and other stone fruits is drupes.

EDIBILITY Sloes are wonderfully fruity marbles of sourness, with tannic skins and almond notes in their pits (stones). Flowers and leaves have a bitter almond flavour.

IDENTIFICATION A large thorny shrub or small tree with dark bark, up to 5m (16½ft) tall, usually less near the coast. The flowers are about 1.5cm (½in) in diameter, with five creamy-white petals, usually one of the first white flowers in spring hedgerows, making a spectacular display before the distinctive small oval leaves with finely serrated edges form. Dark purple drupes are about 1cm (⅜in) in diameter, often with a pale bloom.

DISTRIBUTION Widespread and common across Europe, but not Norway. It is less common in North America, found in dune systems on the coast between Maryland and Maine, where it is considered a non-native invasive species with the potential to undermine the native coastal beach plum (*Prunus maritima*). It looks very similar, with a slightly larger and sweeter fruit, and can be used in similar ways.

WHEN TO HARVEST Buds and blossoms in March–April; young leaves in May–June; fruits August–November.

HABITAT Hedgerows, wood edges and rough grazing; it does well on marginal farmland near the coast.

SAFETY NOTE Flowers, leaves and pits should be consumed in moderation as they contain a precursor to hydrogen cyanide. Don't be too alarmed: so do apple pips, and anything wild that tastes of almonds. Small quantities are safe, and it is denatured by heating to 70ºC (158ºF). The thorns are fierce and can cause infection if they puncture your skin and break off. Wear gloves if you aren't nimble-fingered.

Similar species

Other members of the *Prunus* genus include (in ascending order of drupe size) cherry plums, beach plum (US), bullaces, greengages, damsons and plums. All are edible and can be used in similar ways, becoming relatively less sour as the drupes get bigger.

Harvesting sloes

Blackthorn's white blossoms are the first to appear in early spring, growing before the leaves and turning the prickly black scaffold below into plump white clouds. They make a great signpost for foragers as to where to find their fruits later in the year. Spring storms can mess with this happy arrangement, however, as flowers blown off before pollination mean less fruit.

Like many fruits, sloes ripen earlier and tend to grow bigger, juicier and more prolifically near the sea, where they can be plump and dark enough to harvest as early as August. Traditionally, sloes are not harvested until after the first frost, thus ensuring full ripeness and allowing the expansion and contraction of freezing and thawing to break the skins, which helps their flavour to diffuse more readily. You can wait a long time for frost near the coast, so I recommend accumulating sloes in your freezer.

Be wary of unforgiving thorns when you are harvesting sloes – you will always end up reaching through them to hook those just-out-of-reach branches that invariably seem to have the fattest fruit. Don't dress in your expensive waterproofs; wear tough old fibres like denim and take a walking stick (perhaps made from blackthorn) or similar.

A cloth shopping bag slung around your neck leaves both hands free for picking, and you can revel in the great dexterity of your fingers (which evolved for just this sort of task), as you tease sloes from their prickly hosts. Don't be too fussy about how your sloes look: they needn't all be plump and fat. The ones that look a bit past it, with a tendency to squidge a bit as you pick them, usually make the best sloe gin and jam.

The perennial popularity of sloes is curious. They are far less glamorous looking than sea buckthorn or raspberries, guarded by fierce thorns, and too sour to enjoy unprocessed. Yet, at least in the UK, they have remained in high esteem, even with those who don't otherwise forage. The reason for this is the delightful elixir known as sloe gin. People who would never consider eating any other wild harvest will enthuse about their 'special' sloe gin recipe, then go all secretive about their harvesting spots.

It isn't the only thing you can make from blackthorn though. The blossoms and young leaves share with other members of the Rosaceae family the same bitter almond flavour profile that, with a little care, can be used to flavour all manner of syrups, desserts, preserves and ferments.

Sloes also make great jam (think membrillo), fruit cheeses, fruit leathers and wine. The Japanese have long esteemed the sour fermented cherry/plum/bitter almond flavours of sakura (Japanese cherry blossoms) and umeboshi (Japanese salt plums).

Blackthorn is used in salt making in coastal areas where sun evaporation isn't efficient. Seawater is dribbled through graduation towers densely packed with blackthorn cuttings. Coastal breezes evaporate the water and a concentrated brine drips out of the bottom.

Pickled sloes, umeboshi style

The Japanese know a thing or two about turning sour plums (ume) into delicious savoury condiments (umeboshi). This variant is excellent with sushi, rice, meat or cheese, and the sweet pickling liquor makes an excellent cordial or salad dressing.

Ingredients

1kg (2lb 3oz) sloes, or bullaces, damsons or other stone fruit

1kg (2lb 3oz) brown muscovado sugar

10 cloves, or a handful of clean wood avens roots

½ teaspoon ground ginger, or 2 teaspoons dry ground hogweed seed

300ml (11 fl oz) apple cider vinegar

1 teaspoon sea salt

Freeze the fruit, then let them defrost in a large, non-metallic bowl and set aside.

Place the sugar, syrup and spices in a pan with the vinegar and heat gently until the sugar dissolves. Pour the mixture over the sloes, cover and leave to rest for two or three days. Strain the vinegar mixture into a pan, bring to the boil, then pour over the sloes again. Leave them to rest for another two or three days.

Repeat the straining, boiling and resting process once more. Strain the vinegar into a pan and simmer until it has reduced to a thick syrup. Pack the strained sloes into sterilizd jars then pour the hot syrup over them. Let the pickled fruit mature for a few weeks before opening.

Blackthorn blossom syrup

Harvest blackthorn blossoms when they emerge in April. Layer them in a jar, half and half by volume, with caster sugar and leave for a few days. Empty the jar into a pan, then fill the jar with water, give it a swirl to rinse out all the remaining sugar and flowers, and add that to the pan. Heat very gently while stirring until the sugar is dissolved and the liquid is slightly too hot to comfortably put your finger in (this is the signal that you've reached the temperature at which hydrogen cyanide is denatured). Do not boil it – any smell in your kitchen is flavour lost from your syrup. Strain into a sealed jar and leave to cool. Freeze or keep in the fridge and use within two weeks.

In north-west Spain, sloes are used to make pacharán, which uses anise liqueur as the base rather than gin and adds a few flavours such as coffee beans and cinnamon – easy to emulate and a nice variation.

Very sloe gin

At its simplest, making sloe gin requires only that you soak sloes in gin and add something sweet (usually sugar) to balance their tartness. While I have no wish to complicate such a straightforward procedure, there are a few simple things you can do that will take your sloe gin to dangerously tasty new heights.

GO EASY ON THE SUGAR. Many people sweeten their sloe gin to the point where it tastes more like a slightly boozy syrup than a sour liqueur. If that's how you like it, then fair enough, but there is no need to add sugar at the start of the process. You'll extract more flavour more efficiently from your sloes by steeping them in unsweetened alcohol then sweetening them to taste later on.

TRY VODKA INSTEAD OF GIN. Vodka works just as well as gin, and for purists, its less complex flavour delivers a cleaner sloe flavour.

USE STRONG GIN (OR VODKA). The stronger your gin, the more quickly and cleanly you will extract the sloes' flavour. It's a waste of money to use premium gin but ensure it is at least 37.5% ABV.

FREEZE YOUR SLOES. Harvesting sloes after the first frost and/or pricking them before steeping are the traditional ways of speeding up infusion. Frosts are happening ever later or not at all in coastal areas, but you can simulate them by freezing your sloes. They burst as they defrost, which also removes the need to prick them.

DON'T BE STINGY. Three-quarter fill your jars with frozen sloes then pour over the gin. If your steeped gin becomes too fruity, you can always dilute it with more gin later.

PLAN LONG-TERM. Three months is generally considered the minimum period for infusion – but the longer you leave the sloes in the gin, the deeper the alcohol will penetrate and the more flavoursome it will become. Three years is about when the flavour ceases to improve, but up until this point there is nothing to be gained by straining out your sloes, so keep them under for as long as possible.

UP THE ALMOND. After about one year the alcohol will begin to pull delicious almondy flavours from the pits. You can accentuate this flavour by adding blackthorn blossoms and leaves during the infusion process, or better still, by adding blackthorn blossom syrup (see page 37) later. If you do add flowers, leave them in for no more than a couple of hours as the alcohol will quickly start to degrade them, leading to muddy, vegetal flavours.

TAKE CARE OF YOUR JARS. Use jars with rubber-sealed lids or you will lose some precious alcohol to evaporation (known as 'the angel's share') over a long steeping period. Keep them away from bright light and at a steady ambient temperature. Give them a wee shake every few months.

TREASURE THE JAM. When you are ready to bottle your now very sloe gin, pass it through a fine strainer into a large jug or bowl. Don't under any circumstances discard the jammy goo that will, if you have been patient, stick to the bottom of the jar – this is the best bit. Scrape it out and add it to the bowl. Now it is time to taste and, if you wish, sweeten.

DON'T RESTRICT YOURSELF TO SUGAR. Try using honey, birch or maple syrup, or, best of all, blackthorn blossom syrup. Whatever you use, add a little sweetness at a time, stir (making sure that sugar, if that is what you are using, is fully dissolved), taste and, if necessary, repeat.

A HINT OF BITTER. I like to season my very sloe gin with a few drops of alexanders bitters (see page 33) before drinking it.

Narrow, silvery leaves.

Fruits can be very densely packed on twigs.

Some strains produce fewer fruits. If there are none, you may have a male.

Sea buckthorn

Hippophae rhamnoides

Pollen grains of sea buckthorn have been found in UK soil deposits dating back almost 10,000 years, suggesting that it was part of the first wave of pioneers to repopulate post-glacial regions after the last Ice Age. Its roots spread rapidly and extensively, producing new sprouts and fixing nitrogen in surrounding soils. This also creates favourable conditions for other plants, and eventually larger shrubs and trees will shade it out. As large trees tend to be less successful in windswept sandy soils, sea buckthorn's natural home has become the coast. It has been deliberately introduced in some areas to stabilize dunes, a job it occasionally performs too well, crowding out other coastal plants. Sea buckthorn is far from the most troublesome invasive species, however, supporting diverse insect communities and providing a good food source for wintering thrushes. By thoughtfully stewarding your local patch, you can help stop it from becoming a nuisance.

ALSO KNOWN AS Sea berry (North America), sandthorn, sallowthorn, Russian pineapple.

EDIBILITY Delicious and good for you – use berries for a sour juice, and leaves, flowers and seeds for tea.

IDENTIFICATION A large shrub or small tree with alternate silvery elongated oval leaves with short stems, long thorns and distinctive bright orange berries that remain well into winter.

DISTRIBUTION Locally abundant around the coasts of northern Europe up to central Scotland, though it is increasingly being planted inland and further north. In the US, it is scarce in the wild but becoming popular in food forests and edible gardens.

WHEN TO HARVEST Fruits mature around mid-autumn, often persisting on the tree well into the following year.

HABITAT Mostly coastal, but also flourishes inland in sandy soils and can be found on embankments and in gardens.

Harvesting sea buckthorn

Sea buckthorn is dioecious, which means it has distinct male and female plants. The males produce innocuous twig-hugging flowers that distribute pollen on the wind. One lucky male can pollinate seven or more female plants, on which you will find the orange berries that are of most interest to foragers. You may find locations where only one sex is present, poor lonely, fruitless things. On happy female sea buckthorn trees, berries grow prolifically, surrounding twigs in what looks like vivid orange bubble wrap before ripening into fragile little balloons of bright orange juice.

Sea buckthorn berries are very good for you, containing high levels of vitamins and other biologically active compounds. They are also high in malic acid, the same substance that makes apples taste sour. Harvesting them presents a challenge to foragers as they are ready to burst at the slightest touch. Proficient sea buckthorn harvesters fall into two camps: 'milkers' and 'freezers'.

Milkers don old raincoats, very thick, long gloves and, if they are wise, goggles, and 'milk' the berried twigs into buckets. This technique is joyously messy – the juice will run down your arm carrying bits of leaf and twig with it. You'll end up wearing quite a lot of the juice. Do it with friends and have a giggle.

Freezers selectively prune the most berry-laden twigs (but not the new tips, as these will be where next year's berries grow), take them home, freeze them, then collect the berries cleanly and easily while still frozen (or squeeze them out at home). If done mindfully, spreading your pruning around, this has negligible effect on the plant or ecosystem. Where sea buckthorn is considered to be a problem, you may well be thanked – or even rewarded – for vigorously pruning it. I know a small business that makes two income streams from it – one through a paid contract with the local council to control it, and a second selling the juice from their trimmings.

Rule number one of sea buckthorn harvesting is to wear thick gloves. The thorns that give it its name are long, sharp and prolific, with fine tips that can break off in your skin. Where you have a large, healthy sea buckthorn colony, leaves can be easily harvested by pulling your (heavily gloved) hand along the outer twigs for making tea. This is best done in late spring and summer, before the fruits form and when the leaves are robust. This might seem a rather crude and unsympathetic way to harvest them, but these are strong and prolific plants, and they can easily spare a few twigs-worth of leaves per tree.

Eating sea buckthorn berries

Sea buckthorn berries are usually only eaten whole and raw as an occasional palate-blasting, tongue-blistering, life-affirming bullet of acidity, or perhaps if a friend with a sadistic sense of humour invites you to try a handful on first introduction. Beyond their acidity, sea buckthorn berries have a complex flavour, somewhat tropical, with hints of mango, pineapple, physalis and something that I can't quite put my finger on – cider infused with Chinese five spice perhaps? A word of warning: for some people, the juice, especially while cooking, can have a distinct waft of baby sick! If you are one of these unfortunates, try not to let it put you off. Most people find that the smell disappears during the cooking process.

Foragers are always looking for wild, local alternatives to high-food-mile staples such as lemons. To this end, I have seen sea buckthorn juice used in place of lemon juice to make ceviche, drizzled on pancakes, and added to cordials. While I applaud the notion on environmental grounds, a note of culinary caution: sea buckthorn carries more – and different – flavours and natural oils than lemons, so direct substitution doesn't always work. Do experiment, though – a big part of adapting to climate change will be retraining our cooking techniques and palates to what is local and abundant.

Chefs often pair sea buckthorn with white or dark chocolate in desserts. The berries make an excellent jelly with crab apples and a judicious amount of sugar. Sea buckthorn curd can be made by following any lemon curd recipe, substituting the lemon juice for sea buckthorn juice. Sea buckthorn sorbet or ice cream is also delightful, but I like it best in a cocktail.

Right: Sea buckthorn is often deliberately introduced to stabilize sand dunes.

Sea buckthorn and apple chutney

My friend James MacKenzie came up with this recipe. He's a serious chutney aficionado, who likes things hot. I have halved the amount of chilli he uses, and sensitive souls may wish to reduce it further. It's good with a sharp cheese on an oatcake, alongside a curry or dhal, or on a muffin with bacon. Makes approximately 1.5kg (3lb 5oz) of chutney.

Ingredients

500g (1lb) white onions

650g (1lb 7oz) peeled and cored cooking apples

1 whole chipotle

3g (½ teaspoon) chipotle powder

350g (12oz) caster sugar

450ml (16 fl oz) white wine vinegar

275g (10oz) whole sea buckthorn berries

1 teaspoon sea salt

Chop up the onions, apples and chipotle and stew over a medium heat with all the other ingredients except the sea buckthorn berries. Cook until the apples start to lose their shape. Add the sea buckthorn berries and continue to cook gently for 20 minutes, stirring as you go.

Let the mixture cool, then pour into clean jars. (If you wish, sterilize the jars first, though I don't find this necessary.) The chutney will keep well out of the fridge until you open the jar. After this, store it in the fridge.

Sea buckthorn juice

Juice is the easiest way to use and store sea buckthorn berries. Like lemon juice, which has a similar level of acidity (around pH 3), sea buckthorn juice requires tempering with something sweet or unctuous for all but the most leathery digestive tracts.

Press the debris-filled sea buckthorn milkings, or defrosted berries from pruning, through a fine sieve and collect the juice. It is sufficiently acidic to keep well in clean jars or bottles in the fridge for two weeks – freeze or pasteurize it if you need to keep it longer.

A nice, simple way to enjoy the tropical notes and sour goodness of sea buckthorn juice is to add a shot to your orange juice in the morning, or, better still, mix it half and half with carrot juice. Apart from the natural colour sympathy (you will never have seen anything quite so orange), this will prime your system with beta carotene, a great source of vitamin A, which is good for vision and eye health, a strong immune system, healthy skin and well-formed mucous membranes.

Wild whisky buck

This cocktail is a variation on the classic whisky sour, which is traditionally made with bourbon, lemon juice and sugar. The pungency of whisky moves happily into the background when mixed with sour fruit, and even those who don't usually enjoy whisky will enjoy this tipple.

Ingredients

2 parts whisky. Being Scottish, I tend to use scotch, but Irish whisky, bourbon or rye all work well too. Keep your single malts for sipping and use a cheap blend – you are going to be mixing it with the plant equivalent of battery acid!

1 part sea buckthorn juice

1 part maple or birch-sap syrup. If you have neither, a plain strong sugar syrup (2 parts sugar dissolved in 1 part water) works just fine.

Optional but highly recommended: 3 dashes of alexanders cocktail bitters (see page 33). Angostura bitters work too.

Optional: 1 egg white. This makes for a thicker, mellower, more luxurious cocktail with a creamy head and a smoother mouthfeel. If you omit the egg white, the drink will still taste delicious, though sharper, but it will tend to settle if you drink it slowly.

Ice

Optional: Garnishes – an umbellule of alexanders, Scots lovage or rock samphire sets it off a treat, and trimmed alexanders stem makes a nice compostable straw that also adds some extra aromatics to the drinking experience.

Add all ingredients except the ice and garnishes to a cocktail shaker and shake well for 30 seconds. This is called a 'dry shake' and allows the egg-white proteins to coagulate without being diluted by melting ice. Then add ice to the shaker and shake for up to 20 seconds, until the drink is chilled to your liking. Strain into a glass and garnish. Spraying a mist of bitters over the finished drink sets it off nicely.

I take pre-mixed bottles of wild whisky buck (without the egg white) on coastal foraging camps and expeditions for quick, fortifying shots at short notice.

Leaves are serrated at
the edges and have a
corrugated texture.

Fine, bristly
thorns.

Unripe hips are green
and hard.

Fully ripe hips are soft
and red all over.

Beach rose

Rosa rugosa

There are many species of wild rose, most of them dainty, subtly perfumed and associated with the symbolism and traditions of their native region. The beach rose found on the coasts of the North Atlantic is none of these things: it is a big, bold, brash interloper, brought by Victorian plant hunters from North-East Asia to Europe around 1800 and to North America 50 years later. Gardeners quickly took to its boisterous growth, fragrant blooms and disease resistance, and it became a staple of parks and gardens. From there it soon escaped to the wild, settling most happily near the sea, where its natural resistance to salt, suckering growth and liking for sandy soil gave it a distinct advantage. It is now considered an invasive non-native in some regions; in the UK it is a civil offence to cause it to grow in the wild. It is a gift to foragers, providing more intensely aromatic blossoms and bigger, juicier hips than any of its cousins.

ALSO KNOWN AS Japanese rose, rugosa rose, Ramanas rose, letchberry, beach tomato, sea tomato, saltspray rose, potato rose, Turkestan rose, beach plum.

EDIBILITY Petals and fruits (which are known as hips) are both abundant and tasty.

IDENTIFICATION Shrub, 1–2m (3–6ft) tall, forming dense thickets. Stems are covered in short, straight prickles. Leaves are serrated at the edge and corrugated (rugose), arranged in three or four pairs with a single terminal leaf at the end. Flowers are pink or white and have five petals with yellow stamens in the middle. Hips are like large cherry tomatoes, with five straggly sepals protruding from the end.

DISTRIBUTION Widely distributed and common.

WHEN TO HARVEST Flowers from early summer to early autumn; hips in late summer and autumn.

HABITAT Coastal scrub and maritime hedgerows, as well as gardens, parks and waste ground inland.

SIMILAR SPECIES All roses can be used in the same ways, though few rival beach rose for abundance, flavour and ease of harvest and preparation.

SAFETY NOTE In Scotland, rose hips are known as itchycoos on account of their small hairy seeds that irritate the skin. Minor skin irritation can be a major problem in the throat, so all recipes involving rose hips require either meticulous de-seeding before cooking or fine straining afterwards.

Harvesting beach rose

Beach rose is often so prolific, dense and prickly that it isn't possible to harvest more than a tiny fraction of its petals or hips. Where it is established in the wild, you can generally harvest freely.

Petals pull off easily, leaving the stamens intact on the bush, where it may still produce a hip. If the flower isn't yet fully unfurled, take care that it doesn't contain a bee or you'll both get quite a fright! Beach rose hips tend to ripen earlier than those of other wild roses and have a longer harvesting season. Hips that are deep red and soft may be overripe and can harbour maggots. Green or orange hips are not ripe enough. With a little practice you will get a feel for their sweet spot.

Eating beach rose

The scent of beach rose petals is of classic rose – like the smell of rose water or Turkish delight. The petals readily infuse their scent into water, and stuffing a handful in your water bottle will add a pleasant flavour in 10 minutes. Alternatively, pop a generous amount into vodka for two hours to make a fragrant schnapps. Don't leave them in any longer, as the alcohol will start to degrade them and introduce vegetal notes.

The petals also make glamorous additions to salads or desserts, especially infused into milk or cream when making carrageen pudding (see page 189). They also make a nice syrup – follow the method for blackthorn blossom syrup (see page 37). If dried very gently, beach rose petals retain a reasonable amount of their fresh flavour for use later in the year.

The hips are extremely high in vitamin C and also contain vitamins A, D and E, as well as antioxidants. When fully ripe, their flesh is quite delicious nibbled raw from the bush, provided you are careful to avoid the hairy seeds. If you make a small hole in the skin, the soft flesh can be squeezed out like toothpaste. Rose hips are widely used to make a pleasant-tasting medicinal syrup to help ward off coughs, colds and flu in the winter (you'll find endless recipes for it online). More interestingly, beach rose hips are the closest we have in North Atlantic regions to a wild tomato – less juicy, but with a nice balance of sweet, fruity and tart flavours. Unlike the slender hips of other roses, beach rose hips are plump enough to make a decent amount of sauce without spending days cleaning them, though there is still a bit of work in removing the hairy seeds.

Beach rose petal champagne

This is a nice way to capture and drink the sweet perfume of beach rose petals in a lightly alcoholic summer fizz, fermented using the natural yeasts in the air and on the flowers. You'll need a large food-grade lidded tub or bucket and four large and thoroughly cleaned plastic fizzy drink bottles. Don't use bottles with corks, as the pressure of fermentation will push the corks out. You can use flip-top glass bottles, but these make it harder to monitor pressure build-up, and they are more hazardous than plastic bottles if they explode!

Ingredients

2.25L (4 pints) cold water

325g (11oz) white sugar

1 lemon, or 2 tablespoons sea buckthorn juice (see page 44). Sea buckthorn juice gives a slightly tropical tang to the whole affair, though it does leave some orange clouds.

25 beach rose petals, or more, depending on how intense a rose flavour you like

2 tablespoons apple cider or white wine vinegar

In the tub or bucket, mix the sugar into the water and stir until dissolved. Quarter and squeeze the lemon, then add the juice and squeezed pieces to the bucket. Add the petals and vinegar and stir. Put on the lid and leave it somewhere cool for four days.

Strain the mixture through a fine sieve and use a funnel to pour it into the bottles, leaving a good few inches of air in each bottle. Screw the lids on tightly and leave at an ambient temperature for 6–14 days – how long will depend on the ambient temperature. Check the bottles after a few days by giving them a squeeze – the bottles will start to pressurise as fermentation gets underway.

Once the bottles feel tightly pressurised, carefully unscrew the lids a little to release carbon dioxide, then tighten them back up. Be ready to quickly screw the lids back on tightly before you lose precious liquid in a foamy fountain!

If the middle of the bottle bulges, or the dimples at the bottom begin to round out, you urgently need to release some pressure. It's important to check the bottles regularly – they will explode if you forget about them – but if you constantly depressurize them, your champagne will become flat, so try not to get too nervous.

When is it ready to drink? That's up to you. The champagne evolves from a light, low-alcohol tipple after a week of fermenting to a stronger, perhaps-starting-to-get-vinegary wine at about five or six weeks. For me, the sweet spot for drinking is between two and four weeks. At this stage, I put it in the fridge, which all but stops fermentation.

Beach rose hip 'tomato' sauce

This versatile sauce can be used like tomato sauce (or tomato paste if you reduce it down). It's good with sea spaghetti (see page 199) and perhaps some cockles, spread on a pizza, or used to enrich a sauce. Mixing the sauce with cooked laver (see page 181) gives it a little of the umami that tomatoes have but rose hips lack, though it will turn the lush red colour muddy.

SMOOTH SAUCE OR PASTE
This simple method gives you a smooth texture and you do not need to de-seed the hips beforehand. Top and tail the rose hips and pop them in a pan with just enough water to cover them. Bring to a gentle simmer for 15 minutes until the hips are soft. Put the hips in a food processor and blitz, then press the pulp through a fine sieve or mouli grater. Then return the pulp to the pan and repeat the process.

Pour the sauce into a clean pan and bring back to a gentle simmer. Season with salt, pepper and any herbs you like, reducing it to a strength and consistency that suits you – I make it quite concentrated, as it can always be diluted later. Depending on the ripeness of your hips, the sauce may benefit from a little sugar to offset the tartness.

TEXTURED SAUCE
This more involved method requires you to de-seed the hips. Top and tail the rose hips and chop them in half. Use a teaspoon to scrape out the seeds and any stray hairs. Place the prepared hips in a thick-bottomed pan with a little olive oil. Heat gently until they begin to break down – perhaps give them a mash with the back of a spoon. Season with salt and any herbs you like. Add a little water if they start to stick, or if you'd like a wetter sauce.

To keep for future use, freeze the sauce in large-lump ice-cube trays, then store in ziplock bags in the freezer.

Beach rose petal ketchup

Beach rose petals make a simple but pleasing condiment for drizzling on salads. If you make it with fresh petals, they retain their glamorous pinkness.

Densely pack a jar with fresh or dried beach rose petals and top up with two parts apple cider vinegar to one part water and one part sugar, and a generous pinch of salt. If the lid of the jar is metal, place cling film between it and the jar before screwing it on to avoid it corroding. Put the lid on, shake vigorously and leave for one month, agitating the jar occasionally. The petals will disintegrate into a delightfully tasty condiment.

Add minced chillis and any spices you fancy to the mix for a rudimentary but satisfying rose petal harissa that is excellent with couscous or orache grains (see page 88).

Other species of interest

Fennel

Foeniculum vulgare

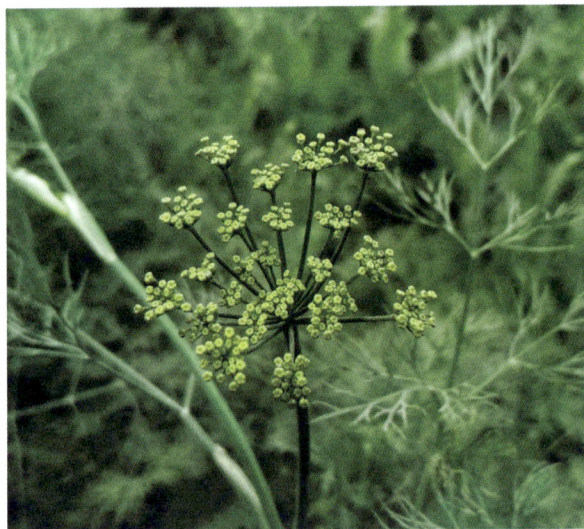

DISTRIBUTION Indigenous to the Mediterranean, but widely naturalized on both sides of the North Atlantic, especially on dry coastal soils.

This tall (up to 2m/6ft) member of the carrot family (which includes the poisonous species hemlock and hemlock water-dropwort; see page 23) is easily distinguished by its very thin, finely divided leaves, umbels of tiny yellow flowers and obvious aniseed-liquorice aroma in all parts. It is native to the Mediterranean, but naturalized on coastal roadsides and waste ground on both sides of the North Atlantic, especially in southern England.

Fennel works very well with fish (try stuffing the fronds in the belly cavity before cooking), shellfish (infused into bisque), and as a spice in pickles and curries (especially the fresh or dried seeds). A simple Pernod-like digestif can be made by steeping the crushed green seeds in vodka for a week then filtering them out.

To use the flowers and pollen, harvest umbels of fully open flowers, dry them gently but thoroughly, blitz them briefly in a food processor, then sieve out the twiggy bits. The resulting powder is a delicious and versatile seasoning for meats, vegetables and desserts.

Wild carrot

Daucus carota

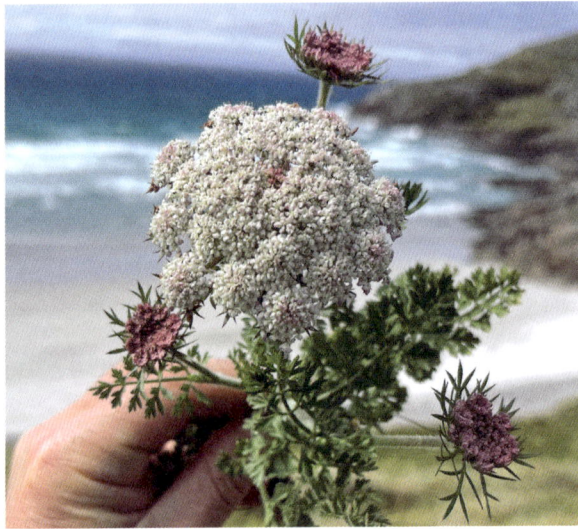

ALSO KNOWN AS Bird's nest, bishop's lace and Queen Anne's lace (US) – though that name is regularly used for other members of the carrot family.

DISTRIBUTION A common native of temperate Europe, widely naturalized in North America.

Wild carrot is not exclusively coastal, but thrives in coastal grasslands, hedgerows and stable dune systems. Distinguish it from other members of the carrot family (especially its toxic cousins on page 23), by its hairy stems/leaves, and finely divided bracts beneath the flower umbels, which later fold upwards to enclose seed heads in a 'bird's nest'. Flowers are white (perhaps tinged pink), usually with a single purple flower in the middle of the umbel. It can grow over 1m (3ft) tall, but is usually much shorter in coastal locations.

Despite being the ancestor of cultivated carrots, the roots tend to be thin and woody, only worth exploring in where they are easy to pull up. The seeds are an excellent wild spice tasting somewhere between caraway and celery seeds and can be baked into rye bread, or infused into vodka to make cocktail bitters. There is no modern science that supports their traditional use as an abortifacant, but it seems wise to avoid them if you are pregnant.

Ground ivy

Glechoma hederacea

ALSO KNOWN AS Alehoof, creeping charlie/jenny, run-away-robin.

DISTRIBUTION Common and abundant around the North Atlantic in woodlands, gardens and waste ground. In areas of the US it is considered a problematic non-native species.

A creeping member of the mint family, with hoof-shaped round-toothed leaves, later with upright shoots of dainty purple flowers that hug the square stem.

Around my home in south-west Scotland I only find ground ivy near the sea, but you may very well find it anywhere with moderately sandy soils. Feel fortunate if you do, as it is a fantastic aromatic herb. The alternative name 'alehoof' reflects its traditional use in flavouring beer and it also makes a great cordial that goes nicely in whisky cocktails. Its best use though is infused in vinegar, where it will take your salad dressings and pickles to dizzy new heights. Just give it a quick wash, then stuff a generous amount – stems, leaves, flowers and all – into (ideally cider) vinegar where it will merrily infuse its vibrant sage-citrus-geranium-mint flavours in a day or two (though there is no harm in leaving it in indefinitely). For further guidance on using it when pickling, see page 261.

Sand leek

Allium scorodoprasum

ALSO KNOWN AS Rocambole, Korean pickled-peel garlic.

DISTRIBUTION Native to northern Europe (most common in northern England/southern Scotland) and has been introduced to the west coast of North America.

This member of the allium/onion family looks like a small leek in spring, but this stage is very easy to miss. More obvious are the tall (up to 1m/3ft) flowering stems of summer topped with purple pompoms that nod in open sandy-soiled hedgerows around midsummer. These inflorescences comprise a tight cluster of hard bulbils emerging from a papery sheath with a few small flowers twisting around them.

The bulb, leek stage and bulbils are all edible and good, but as the division of bulbs is a key part of their reproductive cycle, please don't dig them up unless you are actively stewarding a patch. The flower heads can be considerably thinned from well-established locations and, once broken up a little, used like mini onions or garlic – excellent briefly fried with salt marsh greens, pickled (either as the star of the jar, or as an embellishment for something else), or studded raw through salads, especially coastal potato salad (see page 133).

Sand & Shingle

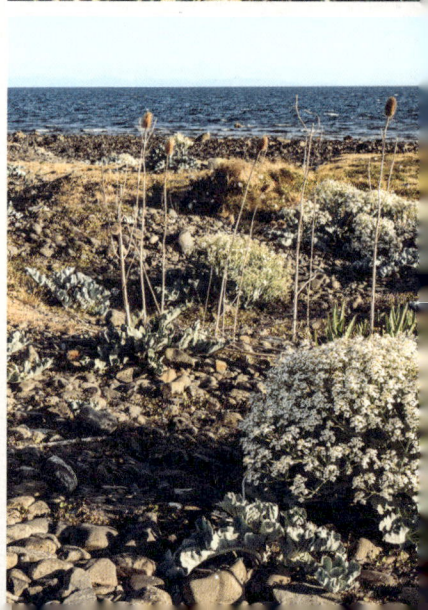

Habitat builders: Life on shifting sands

in restless edges
between chaos and order –
opportunities

Beaches are dynamic places, constantly moving and morphing as tides, waves and wind shift sand, shells and stones, lifting, grinding, sorting, depositing, then lifting again, in restless, rhythmic flux. This ceaseless ordering and reordering accounts for the textures of any given beach and the infinite variability of the ocean means no two are the same. From gentle slopes of finely ground sand that squeak as you walk on them, to those made entirely of shells, or the thunderous seething of tumbling cobbles in a steeply banked cove, every beach tells an ancient story.

There is nothing within the regular reach of tides that is dependable enough for terrestrial plants to cling to, but above the strandline – the highest extent of the waves – larger sediments begin to stabilize. On these, thousands of tons of seaweed are deposited each year to rot and leach a fecund cocktail of nutrients. Even in the driest summers, this fertile strip gets a steady supply of fresh water seeping from the land, making the foreshore prime real estate for well-adapted plants.

Ancestors of modern cultivated vegetables, including kale, beet and cabbage, make their home here, often growing bigger, tastier and richer in nutrients than their wimpy descendants. I still gasp with surprise each spring at sea kale plants larger than sheep growing from what looks like nothing but windswept pebbles. Not that size is everything – even pure sand supports, and is supported by, binding mats of tasty plants like sea sandwort. These ecosystem engineers stabilize shores and allow other plants to take hold.

Leaves grow in symmetrical pairs up the stem.

A complex network of roots stabilizes the sand and shingle.

Five-petalled flowers start to appear around mid- to late spring.

Yellow seed capsules swell in summer.

Sea sandwort

Honckenya peploides

Sea sandwort is a miracle of resilience and ingenuity, being able to withstand regular immersion by the sea, coastal exposure, free-draining sand and the ever-changing nature of its coastal home. With its perfect double symmetry, it is also rather beautiful. It plays an important role in stabilizing sand and shingle, allowing other coastal plants to colonize the foreshore, and grasses to establish themselves further inland. It provides shelter for sand hoppers and other crustaceans of the upper shore that sea birds like to feed on, and its flowers are visited by small bees, hoverflies, flies and ants. While it is usually a dioecious plant (having two different sexes), some colonies form both male and female parts on the same plant, a reproductive strategy that better suits challenging, resource-poor habitats.

ALSO KNOWN AS Sea chickweed, sea pimpernel, sea-beach sandwort, seaside sandplant (Canada) and occasionally sea purslane (though in the UK sea purslane generally refers to a different edible coastal plant – *Atriplex portulacoides*; see page 143).

EDIBILITY A delicious and versatile succulent perennial, with a crisp texture and a flavour reminiscent (in spring) of cucumber and pea shoots – a true gift of nature.

IDENTIFICATION Dense mats of small succulent shoots (5–15cm/2–6in) with triangular to oval-shaped leaves growing in symmetrical pairs up the stem. Each pair of leaves sits at right angles to the previous pair. Tiny white five-petalled flowers and pea-like seed capsules develop in the summer.

DISTRIBUTION Common, often abundant in suitable habitats all around the UK and much of northern Europe and North America.

HABITAT Semi-stable sand and shingle beaches, just above the mean high tide line, able to tolerate occasional immersion.

WHEN TO HARVEST Spring – it becomes bitter at the start of summer. In warmer southern regions, a second growth may occur in autumn, which is once more good to eat.

SIMILAR SPECIES Sea milkwort (*Lysimachia maritima*) has similar symmetrical leaf structure but is less succulent. It has pinkish rather than white flowers and is found in salt marshes. It is not toxic, but not especially worth eating, and may have a soporific effect if eaten in large quantities. Sea spurge (*Euphorbia paralias*) is superficially similar, but much larger (20–60cm/8–24in) and not carpet-forming. It has simple cup-like flowers and exudes white sap that is toxic – do not taste.

Sustainable harvesting

As sea sandwort is extremely abundant, widely dispersed, resilient and fairly fiddly to pick, it would take a lot to threaten this remarkable little plant through foraging for personal use. However, its abundance helps to maintain coastal habitats, so treat it with the respect you would any other hard-working eco-engineer.

The whole above-ground part of the plant is edible – leaves and stem – and best harvested before summer by cutting the top one third to one half off each shoot. Practice an approach of thinning abundance rather than clear-felling whole areas. It is fine to hold tufts of shoots and cut them carefully from below with a sharp knife, but don't repeat that process over and over in the same location. There is always another patch of sea sandwort nearby, so spread your picking around and harvest from the middle rather than the edge of colonies. The area around the high tide line is a plastic-waste catastrophe zone, so sadly there is usually ample opportunity to give something back by taking away more plastic than sea sandwort.

Opposite: Sea sandwort often forms extensive carpets just above the high tide line on sand and shingle beaches. Below: The crisp succulence of sea sandwort lends itself extremely well to pickling.

Eating sea sandwort

Given its name, and its home, it isn't surprising that sea sandwort requires a lot of rinsing to divest it of sand. It only takes one grain of sand to turn a pleasurable eating experience into a grim one, so rinse it thoroughly in several changes of water. Being mild tasting (at least before it flowers) and succulent, it is perfect for eating raw in salads or scattered on dishes at the last minute to add a bit of fresh, juicy crunch. Lightly steamed, it can be eaten as a vegetable, perhaps dipped in hollandaise or wild garlic mayo.

Sea sandwort isn't an aromatic plant – its flavour is locked deep in its flesh, so I think of it as an 'eater' not an 'infuser'. However, its stunning good looks, buoyancy and cucumbery flavour profile make it irresistible as a garnish for cocktails   especially gin-based ones.

The bitterness that sea sandwort develops on flowering can be tempered by blanching it for a minute or so before use, but for me it's always there in the background. I prefer to eat it as a spring treat or live off harvests preserved in the spring by blanching and freezing (see page 83). Better still, its juicy inner and waxy skin makes it ideal for pickling, as the leaves don't break down in the acidic pickling solution like less fleshy inland greens. See my guidance on pickling on page 258. It's particularly good pickled in ground ivy vinegar with sea lettuce.

Creeping stems sucker
and form new plants.

Shoelace-like roots
can grow up to
30cm (12in) long.

Silverweed

Potentilla anserina

On windswept northern coasts, silverweed is often the only nourishing wild plant to be found in any quantity. In his 1777 work *Flora Scotica* on the native plants of Scotland, John Lightfoot observes silverweed roots in the Western Isles as being: 'much esteemed in answering in some measure the purposes of bread' and notes that '...they abound in barren and impoverished soils, and in seasons that succeed the worst for other crops, so they never fail to afford the most seasonable relief to the inhabitants in times of greatest scarcity.'

ALSO KNOWN AS *Argentina anserina*, common silverweed, silver cinquefoil, *brisgean* (Scots Gaelic).

EDIBILITY Roots are nutritious and tasty, though rather fiddly to harvest. They can be eaten raw but are better cooked. Leaves are extremely dry and tannic, not worth eating.

IDENTIFICATION Rosettes with 10cm (4in) stems with paired silvery green serrated leaflets alternating with pairs of small leaflets and bright yellow five-petalled flowers. Don't mistake the thin red above-ground creepers for roots.

DISTRIBUTION Very common and often abundant in suitable habitats all around the UK and much of northern Europe and North America.

HABITAT Semi-stable sand and shingle beaches, just above the high tide line, on poor soils among grass and open ground, most often near the sea but also further inland, especially along the edges of heavily gritted roads.

WHEN TO HARVEST Roots are best gathered in early autumn or early spring. They are good in winter, too, but hard to locate as the leaves die back.

POSSIBLE CONFUSION The leaves and their arrangement in rosettes resemble sea radish (see page 73), and they often grow close together. Sea radish lacks the silvery leaf colour and is rougher and more fleshy. The related creeping cinquefoil (*Potentilla reptans*) has similar flowers but palmate, non-silvery leaves. It is edible but not worth foraging for.

Eating silverweed

Those of us fortunate enough to live in times and places where carbohydrates are easily come by tend to overlook optimistic and ubiquitous silverweed. Its stringy roots are often described as a 'famine food' – a wild food eclipsed by seemingly more convenient introduced plants. In fact, nutrient analysis reveals that silverweed roots contain 31g of assimilable carbohydrate per 100g (1oz per 3½oz), more than cultivated potatoes. They are also higher in minerals.

As well as carbohydrate, the roots contain tannin, starch and resin, and are best prepared by parboiling then roasting. This produces a small but not unpleasant mouthful with nutty, Jerusalem artichoke overtones. First Nations of the Pacific Coast of North America esteemed it highly enough to cultivate it in raised beds. In Scotland it was considered an important enough crop in crofting communities to have been clearly allocated harvesting lots on otherwise common ground – and woe betide you if you should harvest your neighbour's *brisgean*!

Don't be tempted to eat the leaves. While not toxic per se, they are extremely drying, immediately robbing your mouth of all moisture! This astringent property is employed by herbalists – applied externally to treat piles, or as a tea to ease diarrhoea, gastrointestinal cramps and irritations of the stomach.

Should you feel inspired to go and dig some silverweed roots in preparation for the collapse of our agricultural system, remember two things. First, you should obtain the landowner's permission before uprooting any plant. Second, don't overlook the extremely important job that silverweed is doing in binding together loose sand, preventing coastal erosion and allowing other plants to grow – spread your harvesting around.

Opposite: Silverweed can make its home in almost any poor, salty soil – usually near the coast but also fringing gritted roads inland.

*Broccoli-like
florets.*

*As the leaves grow
they turn blue-green.*

*Purple fronds
emerge in
early spring.*

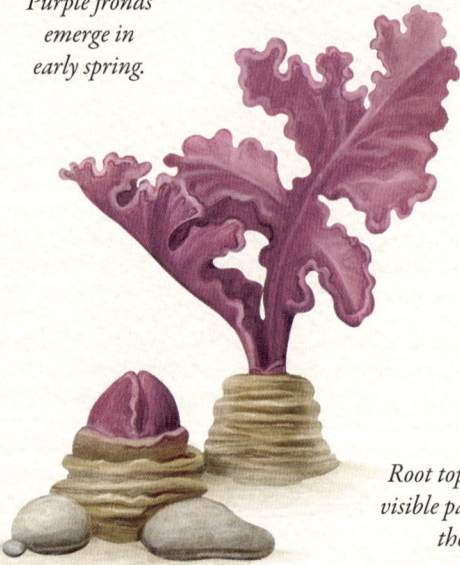

*Root tops are the only
visible part throughout
the winter.*

*Seed capsules are
1–2cm (½–1in) in
diameter, initially
green and tender,
soon becoming corky.*

*Four-petalled white
flowers smell of honey
and taste of peas.*

Sea kale

Crambe maritima

Even if it wasn't edible, sea kale would still be my favourite plant. Its alien-looking purple shoots, sculpturesque leaves and nodding white flowers are works of high art to intoxicate the senses and marvel the mind, always looking quite improbable emerging from their gravelly, windswept home. It also happens to be delicious and nutritious in almost every part, providing some sort of food for most of the year. Sea kale produces hermaphrodite flowers that both self-pollinate and are cross-pollinated by insects, flies and bees, and a colony of mature sea kale in full flower buzzes with life, even in windswept locations. Each year fully grown plants can produce 1,000–10,000 seeds in a pea-like casing that can float in the sea for several months, taken by tides to new locations.

ALSO KNOWN AS Crambe, blue seakale, sea-colewort, halmyrides.

EDIBILITY Young shoots are excellent vegetables, raw or cooked; older leaves are less good but enormous. Budding flower heads (florets) can be eaten like broccoli; open flowers are delightful in salads. Young seed pods can be cooked and eaten like peas. Roots have carbohydrate value but tend to be woody.

IDENTIFICATION Distinctive at every stage, with strange purple shoots growing into large, thick, squeaky green-blue leaves up to 50cm (20in) long, with honey-scented cruciferous white flowers and pea-like seed pods.

DISTRIBUTION Widely distributed as individual plants, small groups or, where shingle beach is extensive and semi-stable, large colonies.

HABITAT At and just above the spring high tide line on shingle and occasionally boulder beaches. Extensive shingle beaches are increasingly rare habitats and often protected, so do some local research before harvesting.

WHEN TO HARVEST Shoots and young leaves in early spring to summer. Florets (unopened flower heads) from mid-spring to early summer. Seed pods in summer, with only a two-week period of succulence. Roots are available all year but should not be dug up.

Sustainable harvesting

Sea kale is a protected species in the UK but quite how this relates to the careful harvesting of a few shoots from a healthy colony isn't clear. The Botanical Society of Britain and Ireland notes that the main threat to sea kale comes from sea-defence works that destroy their shingle habitats. In large colonies, 'nursery beds' of immature plants often occupy a slightly lower position on the shore than larger flowering specimens. This lower location is more susceptible to tidal movement and erosion, so there is a higher turnover of plants.

It also falls victim to inconsiderate gardeners who dig it up to plant as a garden ornamental, and uneducated walkers who trample the young shoots without even knowing they are there. The interest of foragers is an excellent antidote to such ignorance, disinterest and carelessness, and the good news is sea kale recordings have been increasing steadily in recent years. My advice is to not interfere with sea kale if it is solitary or in small groups, but I see no issue with careful thinning from large colonies.

A traditional practice is to cover emerging sea kale shoots by mounding shingle over them in early spring, forcing them to grow longer, paler, more tender stems, in much the same way as you might force rhubarb. This isn't really necessary as they produce a steady succession of tender shoots without interference when they are naturally, and inevitably, covered with seaweed. You can also rummage among the giant older leaves in summer, where you will usually find some long-stemmed tender babies that are contributing little or nothing to the success of the plant.

In stable locations, individual plants can live for decades but usually take five years to produce flowers. The young flower heads, which look and eat like purple sprouting broccoli, can be thinned by taking one or two from larger plants. As the flowers open, they too can be thinned with very little inconvenience to the plant. If you wish to try a few of the pea-like seed casings while they are still green and tender, please go easy and return to spread a few to likely new locations when they become woody.

Do not dig up the roots. However, should you encounter them uncovered and broken by a storm, the young side roots make the best eating: they have a slightly nutty flavour when roasted on a fire, and they make a nice rösti. Remember that the broken roots are still viable and are an important part of sea kale's survival strategy, so you can replant them in similar habitats to nurture and encourage these incredible plants.

Eating sea kale

Leaf shoots and unopened flower heads (florets) can be used just like kale and purple sprouting broccoli – in salads or coast-slaw (see page 75), as steamed veg (though the lovely purple colour tends to run out of them), in stir-fries, or as a stand-alone snack (raw or lightly cooked) with a nice hollandaise sauce or wild garlic mayonnaise to dip them in. Try adding them whole to gently poach in seaweed dashi broths too (see page 207). Shoots and florets keep well in the fridge in sealed bags for up to a week, though you should re-trim the cut stems before using as they blacken and become a little bitter. Be sure to wash them thoroughly: they trap sand and small snails, and, as the plants are often the only things standing upright on a flat beach, dogs like to pee on them.

The larger flannel-like summer leaves can be cut into thin strips and boiled for 5–10 minutes until tender and eaten like a vegetal tagliatelle. They aren't a patch on younger leaves flavour-wise, but they can grow large enough to wrap fish in prior to cooking, in the manner described for seaweeds on page 158.

The open flowers, which taste of pea and smell of honey, are excellent in salads or as a garnish for savoury or sweet dishes. The green seed casing, during their all-too-short period of succulence, can be used like peas.

Preserving sea kale isn't straightforward. I've tried both blanch-freezing and lacto-fermenting, but the mild kale flavour rapidly becomes sulphurous, cabbagey and quite disgusting. The best way to preserve them is to hot pickle the young shoots (see page 261).

Opposite: Sea kale has many edible parts throughout the year: shoots, florets, flowers and young seed pods.
Overleaf: Thinning my favourite sea kale colony, which I have harvested, tended and defended for over 20 years.

In its first year of growth, a basal rosette appears, but no flowering stem.

Seed capsules (siliques) contain between one and five seeds.

Leaf stems are usually, but not always, red.

In its second year, a thick flowering stem bears many yellow, cross-shaped flowers.

Sea radish

Raphanus maritimus

Sea radish is biennial, occasionally perennial, forming attractive rosettes in its first year that can provide a steady supply of tasty greens throughout the winter. In its second year, clouds of flowers form a hazy yellow fringe along the coast. Its leaves are not fleshy like other salt-tolerant plants but coarse and rough, and don't expect cute little pink radishes – the root is a grey, woody anchor and more of a survival food than a culinary treasure. Where sea radish is established, it usually grows in large numbers and can take plenty of thinning. I was once invited by the residents of a coastal village near me to teach them how to eat it into submission as it was taking over their paths and playpark.

ALSO KNOWN AS *Raphanus raphanistrum* subsp. *maritimus*.

EDIBILITY Leaves, leaf stems, flowers, young flowering stems (peeled) and young seed pods all have a wonderfully radishy flavour.

IDENTIFICATION Leaves grow to 30cm (12in), or twice that in very sheltered locations, with paired toothed lobes growing off a central pinkish-red or green stem. Leaves are roughly textured and grow in a low rosette in their first year; in year two, fibrous flowering stems grow to around 1m (3ft), bearing cross-shaped yellow flowers typical of the cabbage family. Later, green seed pods appear, like a string of up to five pearls with a long tapering point at the end.

DISTRIBUTION Coasts of Europe, especially the west and south-west coasts of the UK, and the east and south-west coasts of Ireland. Less common elsewhere in Europe, except Brittany. On the Atlantic coast of North America, sea radish is replaced by wild radish (*Raphanus raphanistrum*) – see similar species.

HABITAT Shingle foreshore above the high spring tide line, coastal field edges, maritime hedgerow and especially coastal road verges.

WHEN TO HARVEST Leaves all year. Flowers from mid-spring to autumn. Seed pods (known botanically as siliques) from late spring to early autumn.

SIMILAR SPECIES Confusion is only likely with other edible brassicas, especially black mustard (*Rhamphospermum nigra*), which looks very similar but has more angular leaves. It is not specifically coastal, but often thrives near the sea, especially in southern England. Wild radish (*Raphanus raphanistrum*) has pink/white and occasionally yellow flowers and is not specifically coastal. Oilseed rape and charlock are also similar looking edible relations.

Sustainable harvesting

Pulling a few leaf stalks from their first-year rosettes is the natural way to harvest sea radish. Leaves from higher up the flowering stems tend to be too fibrous but the young flowering stems themselves, once peeled, are tender and delicious. The flowers, flower buds and siliques can be nipped off by hand. It's common for the siliques to contain between one and four seeds, but five is quite rare – make a wish if you find a 'fiver'. The siliques quickly swell and the seeds inside become tooth-breakingly hard, but not all at the same time; even a single plant tends to have a rolling harvest lasting a month or more. This can make gathering a decent number of seeds quite time consuming. To tell whether seeds are still tender, squeeze them between thumb and forefinger to see if they give a little. By the time the seed bulges look like small peas, they are invariably too hard.

Eating sea radish

The flavour of sea radish is, as you might expect, radishy. This is due to a class of sulphur-containing compounds common to all mustard greens called glucosinolates, which have evolved to deter grazing animals. All parts of the sea radish have this taste to different degrees. Mildest are the flowers, which make tasty additions to salads and very pretty garnishes. Before they open, the buds can be eaten like small, strongly flavoured heads of broccoli. More pungent – in fact, quite mustardy – are the leaves and leaf stems. These can be torn or chopped into small pieces for spiking salads, or shredded finely and added to slaw, salsa verde (see page 107) or salad dressings. Wash them well, as the rough texture holds on to sand. Peeled young flowering stems, or, once divested of their leaves, the leaf stems, make good crudites for dipping into something mild tasting like hummus; they can also be chopped and mixed through a stir-fry. Best of all, they make an ideal centre to a sushi roll (see page 145), adding crunch and wasabi-like notes. Surplus leaves can be blitzed with a little oil and vinegar to make a passable 'wasabi-light' paste, or mixed into pesto to add some mustardy punch.

Though sea radish is available in good quantities throughout the winter, it is a little too pungent to be used as a regular side vegetable. One way around this is to prepare it using a classic Turkish treatment of charlock (a closely related member of the cabbage family): pan-fry the leaves with onion and garlic in lots of olive oil then eat them with yogurt. Another Mediterranean treatment for pungent wild greens is to simmer the tender stems and leaves in salted water for 10 minutes then strain and drizzle with a generous amount of olive oil and lemon juice.

Sea radish siliques are one of my favourite coastal nibbles. The most mustardy part of the plant, they are reminiscent of wasabi, and just strong enough to give your palate a good hit. Try cold pickling them (see page 261) – they mellow with age.

Coast-slaw

The crunchy leaves and vegetables of the coast are ideal for shredding together slaw-style. This isn't so much a recipe as a reminder of how easy it is to combine whatever the coast offers you into something fresh and delicious.

Ingredients

A few handfuls of your favourite wild leaves and stems: e.g. sea radish basal leaves and stems, sea kale shoots or older leaves, wild cabbage leaves, sea beet, sea aster, sea sandwort, sea plantain, sea lettuce

1 large onion, or a handful of wild garlic (ramps)

1 tablespoon wholegrain mustard

Olive oil

Lemon juice

1 teaspoon salt

Any herbs and spices you fancy – Scots lovage leaves and alexanders 'pepper' are nice additions

Seaweed flakes – especially toasted sea lettuce or laver

Mayonnaise (optional)

Finely shred all the leafy parts then mix them with the other ingredients. Cover and leave to meld and soften a little in the fridge for an hour or more before serving. I like it without the mayonnaise that usually drowns lesser slaws, but it can be a nice foil for more pungent wild flavours.

*Four-petalled flowers
can be purple, lilac, white,
or most often, pink.*

*Fleshy,
rocket-like
leaves.*

*White,
four-petalled
flowers.*

SEA ROCKET

*Heart-shaped (cordate) fleshy
leaves, growing from single
stems arranged in a rosette.*

SCURVY GRASS

Sea rocket & Scurvy grass

These plants are both in the mustard/brassica family and although they are found in slightly different habitats, they share a pungent mustardy flavour. Sea rocket is one of few plants that grows on pure sand, while scurvy grass likes all coastal habitats except pure sand. I have grouped them together here as they share similar (and somewhat challenging) culinary merits. To get the best out of them, try not to be put off by your first nibble and think of them as spices or condiments rather than leafy vegetables.

Sea rocket *Cakile maritima*

ALSO KNOWN AS Beach mustard, European searocket.

EDIBILITY Leaves, flowers and seeds all have a strong mustard flavour with a lingering bitter aftertaste. Roots are milder, with some carbohydrate value.

IDENTIFICATION Pink four-petalled flowers, with leaves like succulent rocket.

DISTRIBUTION Common, often abundant, within its habitat. Native to most coastal regions of Europe and introduced in North America, where it is considered to be a non-native invasive, displacing American sea rocket (*Cakile edentula*), which looks very similar, only with fleshier leaves. It can be used in similar ways.

HABITAT Sandy beaches, just above the high tide line and on the edges of semi-stable dune systems.

WHEN TO HARVEST Spring, summer, autumn.

Scurvy grass *Cochlearia officinalis*

ALSO KNOWN AS Common scurvygrass, spoonwort.

EDIBILITY Leaves, flowers and seeds taste strongly of mustard, with a bitter aftertaste for much of the year.

IDENTIFICATION Small (1–5cm/⅜–2in diameter) glossy, succulent, heart- or kidney-shaped (cordate) leaves with distinct veins grow on individual stalks in low rosettes, with flowering stems reaching up to 50cm (20in) long. Flowers are small, white (occasionally lilac) and have four petals.

DISTRIBUTION Widespread and abundant in northern Europe, less common in North America.

HABITAT From the strandline of shingle and rocky shores to maritime hedgerows, salt marshes, cliffs and occasionally walls, often spreading inland on the edges of gritted roads.

WHEN TO HARVEST Early spring, when it flowers, and in autumn, when there is often a second wave of milder tasting growth, especially further south.

Eating sea rocket

I try to find the culinary joy in all edible plants, but the kindest thing I can say about sea rocket is that it is an acquired taste that most people will have no wish to acquire. Almost every part of it is extremely mustardy, which isn't necessarily a bad thing for grown-up palates. The intense nose-scrunching mustard hit of wasabi, for example, is something to treasure. Alas, sea rocket has all of that intensity but with an unforgiving bitter chemical back note that is hard to love.

The flowers are the mildest part of sea rocket, making them about all that most folk will enjoy, and even those should be used sparingly and judiciously, placed on, say, sushi rolls (see page 145), in a salad or with oily fish like mackerel. Think of them as flavour bombs.

Adventurous eaters might enjoy the leaves as a small part of a salad, and they can be blitzed through pesto and dips to add some mustardy pizzazz, or generously swaddled with cheese in a sandwich. If you really want an intense mustard kick, sea rocket's coastal near relations sea radish/black mustard (see page 73) or scurvy grass do a similar job with a little less violence.

Of more interest to foragers is perennial wall rocket (*Diplotaxis tenuifolia*), which is much closer in form and flavour to cultivated rocket (though still with quite a kick), with the classic yellow cross-shaped flowers of the Brassicaceae family. It is an escapee from cultivation, and although not a committed coastal plant, it does like to be near the sea, often growing out of harbour walls. It has a southern European distribution; it is common in southern England and becomes scarce further north.

Scurvy grass

Scurvy grass is not a grass at all, but a member of the Brassicaceae or mustard family of plants, which includes sea kale, sea radish and wild cabbage (see pages 67, 73 and 117). Historically, scurvy grass has been seen as their poor relation due to its pungent flavour, and only really made it onto foragers' radars because it was harvested by sailors then dried or salted down to help stave off scurvy during long sea voyages. It is no higher in vitamin C than many other wild plants but was favoured because it is abundant, easily identified, coastal and available year-round. Scurvy wasn't restricted to sailors in 17th-century England, and it became fashionable to drink a glassful of scurvy grass water every day, in the same way as we might drink orange juice today. In the early 19th century, it was even used to flavour commercially produced beers, and modern craft brewers have recently revisited it (with mixed results).

The hermaphrodite flowers are pollinated by bees, flies and beetles – they are a good early source of nectar. Scurvy grass often thrives near otter haul-out points – perhaps liking the ground disturbance and fertile spraint. It can also proliferate and grow unusually large on sheltered sea cliffs beneath nesting bird colonies – again, enjoying the extra nutrients. Such growth can look much richer and more lustrous than its usual form, and I have got myself into a few scrapes on paddling trips, clambering up sea cliffs from my kayak and trying to work out what the wall of green is.

Similar species are Danish scurvy grass (*Cochlearia danica*), a smaller annual version, growing to just 20cm (8in) high and with smaller pale lilac flowers, often found predominantly on the sides of gritted roads. English scurvy grass (*Cochlearia anglica*) has slightly toothed leaves. All these species readily hybridize and are usable in similar ways.

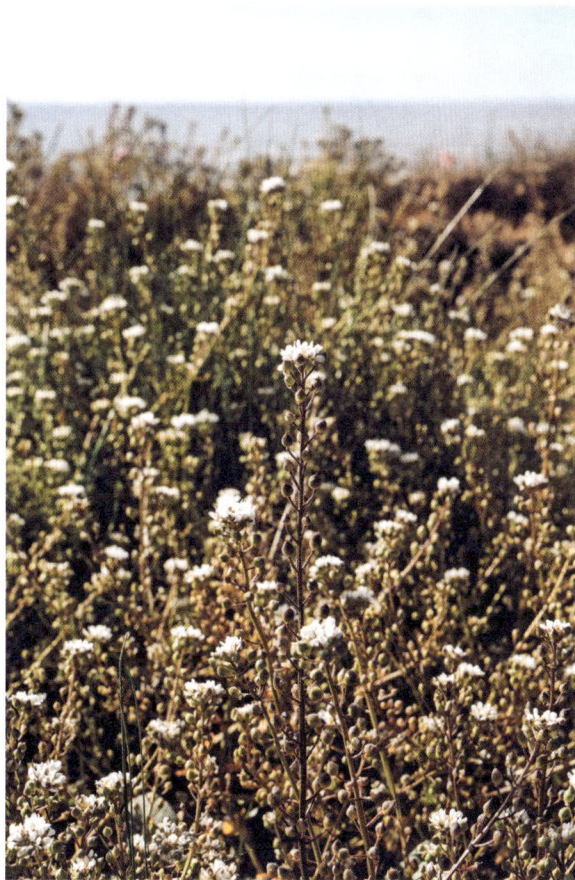

Eating scurvy grass

When scurvy grass is harvested in spring and early summer, the flavour is very mustardy, reminiscent of horseradish and wasabi, but often with unpleasant bitter chemical back notes. In autumn and winter, it can mellow to a more pleasant mustardy-spinach flavour, though this can vary greatly between locations and from plant to plant. In spring, the flowers are a better option, with a milder flavour – good as a garnish or scattered through salads. The globe-shaped seed pods are succulent while still green but very pungent – too much for most tastes. The best ways to enjoy its pungency is to use it as small flavour bombs in salads or pickles; on a piece of coastal sushi (see page 145); with steak; blitzed down into a pesto with nuts, cheese, oil and milder greens like sea aster or sea beet; or simply in a cheese sandwich – dairy is a great way to temper intense flavours.

Tiny green flowers grow in clusters of three on long, slender spikes.

Stems sometimes show purple colouration.

Glossy, succulent leaves can vary considerably in shape and size between individual plants and colonies.

Sea beet

Beta vulgaris subsp. *maritima*

Sea beet is the wild ancestor of familiar crops such as beetroot and Swiss chard, and is the sort of nourishing green that made the coast an attractive place to our hunter-gatherer ancestors. When I'm harvesting it, I think of the delight it must have brought them. I love their contradictory nature, which manage to be unruly in their growth while exhibiting pristine, glossy leaves that squeak as you pick them. They also have a liking for spectacular locations, often with waves breaking and spindrift tumbling across their defiant glossy greenness.

ALSO KNOWN AS *Beta maritima*, sea spinach, wild beet, wild spinach.

EDIBILITY Leaves are similar to its relations spinach and chard, only thicker, with more flavour and a salty tang. In mid- to late spring they develop an unpleasant bitter back note which lasts throughout the summer. Roots are relatively high in sugar, though they can be tough and woody. Leaf stems can be eaten but may become stringy.

IDENTIFICATION Diamond- to oval-shaped glossy green leaves, wavy at the edges, 4–20cm (1½–8in) long, developing initially in straggly rosettes; later, when established, the plant becomes more shrub-like, up to 1m (3ft) tall, though it often grows prostrate. Tiny green flowers are borne on a thick, grooved stem in a leafy spike. Reddish-purple colouration on leaves and stems is not unusual.

DISTRIBUTION Common throughout Europe, becoming sparse further north. Sea beet doesn't appear to be recorded in North America, but beet (*Beta vulgaris*) does grow wild coastally, often as an escapee from cultivation.

HABITAT Upper beach above the high tide line on coarse sand and shingle; also coastal defences, on cliffs, and on rough ground and paths/roadsides close to the coast.

WHEN TO HARVEST All year, but best when not flowering, and can be in poor condition in exposed locations in winter.

SAFETY NOTE Sea beet is, on the whole, exceedingly good for you, but the leaves are relatively high in oxalates. These are not problematic when ingested in moderation as part of a balanced diet by healthy people, but if you have been warned by your doctor against spinach or rhubarb, the same warnings apply here, though sea beet contains approximately half the oxalates of cultivated spinach.

Coastal adaptations

Sea beet is extremely well adapted to the challenges of the coast. I once rescued a load of its roots that had been unearthed, smashed and deposited above the high tide line by a winter storm. Fearing that my local colony might never recover, I planted them in my garden to see if I could save them. To my surprise they grew quite well, but when I tasted the leaves they were thin and flavourless. In the meantime, the storm-smashed colony had fully recovered and was in better health than ever. It has lived there for thousands of years – of course it knows how to cope with storms!

You can occasionally see the purple colouration from which red beetroot was selectivvely bred in the young leaves. This is due to a compound called betaine, that is also found in many sea creatures, including crustaceans and molluscs, which allows cells to survive in rapidly changing concentrations of salt. It is also resistant against drought, heat and many plant pathogens such as viruses, fungi and insects. It's not surprising that, in the face of climate change and rising sea levels, sea beet has become the subject of a lot of research with the aim of transferring its resilience to cultivated crops.

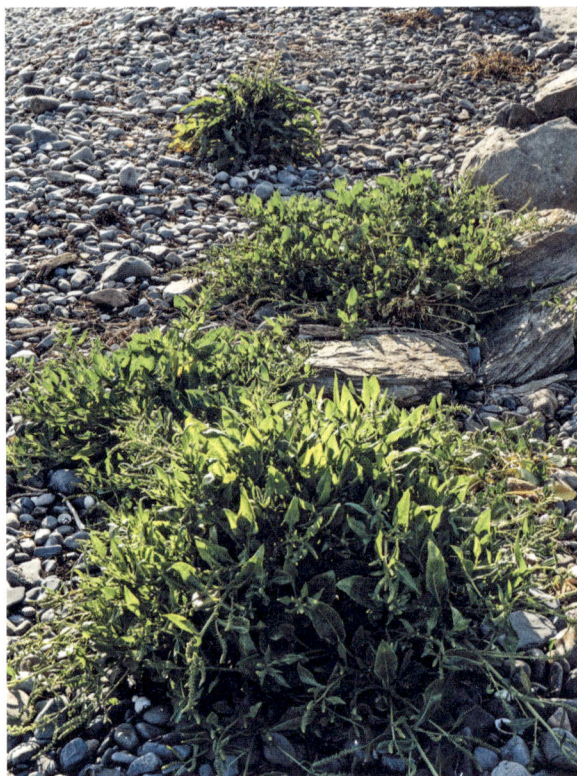

Sustainable harvesting

Sea beet is most often a perennial plant, though in some more marginal locations it can be biennial or even annual. This variability is also evident in its morphology, with plants growing close together often exhibiting quite different growth styles, from sprawling to upright, or with larger or smaller leaves. It's fun getting to know their individual personalities, and you may even find some that are less susceptible to developing a bitter taste in summer. Sea beet makes a windbreak with its thick leaves. In winter, harvest the leaves on the leeward side of the plant, as those on the windward side tend to be in poorer condition and have wind-burned patches. Vibrant new leaf growth will be well underway by the middle of spring and progresses fast, with hand-sized leaves developing. Large and small leaves are equally worthwhile, but I recommend folding bigger leaves in half and pulling out their central vein, which can be a bit stringy.

Towards the end of spring, just as it reaches its most improbably glossy verdancy, flower spikes begin to stretch, and the leaves develop an unpleasantly bitter aftertaste. Foraging is about anticipating peaks and troughs like this, so if you are lucky enough to have access to lots of sea beet, harvest and preserve as much as you reasonably can before mid-spring. Even when the glossy leaves look pristine, I recommend thoroughly washing them, as they are perfect targets for dogs and foxes to pee on (the plants no doubt appreciate the extra nutrients, on top of their already rich bed of dead seaweed).

Above: Sea beet often looks improbably lush in its windswept and exposed home.
Opposite: Sea beet can also thrive on coastal cliffs and crags.

Eating sea beet

Sea beet leaves do everything that spinach or chard does in the kitchen, only better. Their wind- and salt-repelling succulence gives them more body, so while a bag of cultivated spinach cooks down to barely a cupful, the same amount of sea beet leaves will yield two or three times that. They have more flavour and natural seasoning than spinach leaves, but not in an overpowering way, provided you harvest them before summer. The thickness and saltiness of the leaves also helps them to keep better than other leafy greens – up to two weeks in the fridge.

The new leaves in spring make an excellent backbone to any salad – small leaves whole or large leaves de-veined and chopped or torn. Steamed or sautéed in a little butter, sea beet is a fine vegetable accompaniment to fish or meat (especially lamb). Chuck it in stir-fries, soups, omelettes, curries and anything that would benefit from a bit of spinachy goodness – it makes a mean saag aloo.

Tender young roots of sea beet can be cooked and eaten like sweet potatoes, but they quickly become tough as the plant becomes established. If you want to eat sea beet after late spring, you'll need to learn to enjoy its bitter summer back notes, which is unlikely, or preserve it. I recommend blanching and freezing – you will lose some texture but the flavour and many of the nutrients will remain.

Blanching and freezing

This preservation technique works for sea beet leaves as well as other greens. Bring a large pan of lightly salted water to a rolling boil. Drop the leaves into the boiling water in small batches (too many will cool the water below boiling). Boil for 1 minute, then scoop them out and immediately refresh them in iced water to help retain their colour.

Once the leaves are cool, squeeze them firmly in your hands, removing as much water as possible. (Retain this green liquid – it is excellent in smoothies or as a soup base). Freeze in portion-sized tubs or ziplock bags.

Unlike most perennials with an over-wintering taproot, sea beet stores its carbohydrates as sugar rather than starch or inulin, which gives its roots a sweet taste. Selective breeding resulted in sugar beet, with a whopping 20 per cent sucrose content in its roots, which has become the source of most cultivated sugar in temperate regions.

Sea beet and smoked haddock tart

This tart also works well with cubes of goat's cheese or halloumi instead of fish, and you can substitute some (or all) of the cooked sea beet leaves with cooked laver, sea aster, orache or marsh samphire. You'll need a tart tin 30cm (12in) in diameter.

Ingredients

Pastry

125g (4oz) butter, very cold

250g (½lb) plain (all-purpose) white flour, sieved

½ teaspoon salt

Black pepper

Optional: any or all of 1 teaspoon toasted dried laver powder, ¼ teaspoon ground black alexanders seeds, ¼ teaspoon pepper dulse or wrack siphon weed powder

Filling

250g (½lb) smoked haddock, steamed or poached in milk until just cooked, then flaked

500g (1lb) sea beet leaves, blanched, firmly wrung out and roughly chopped

5 large eggs plus 3 large egg yolks

300ml (11 fl oz) double (heavy) cream

½ teaspoon salt

Optional wild embellishments: 1 tablespoon sea lettuce flakes

Make the pastry

Preheat oven to 180°C (350°F). Grate the butter into a bowl containing all the other pastry ingredients. Mix and crumble with light fingers, keeping the mixture cool. When fully mixed, add small amounts of water – just enough that you can form the mixture into a rough ball. Cover in plastic wrap and refrigerate for at least 30 mins (shortcrust pastry freezes well in this form).

On a flour-dusted surface, roll out the pastry to fit your tart tin plus 2cm (¾in). Using your rolling pin, carefully drop the pastry into the tart tin and work it into the corners (a small bit of surplus pastry dusted with flour is an excellent tool for this job), allowing it to drape evenly over the edges (trimming with scissors can be helpful here). Prick the base gently all over with a fork and return to the fridge for 20 minutes.

After chilling, cover the base with baking parchment and add something weighty such as dried beans, rice or pasta for blind baking. Place in the oven for 20 minutes. Remove the base from the oven and take off the weight and parchment. If any holes or cracks have developed, brush them with a little beaten egg, or patch larger cracks with thin bits of surplus pastry. Return it to the oven for a few minutes until it looks toasted and there are no doughy bits.

Assemble the tart

Arrange the cooked, shredded sea beet evenly in the pastry. Flake the cooked smoked haddock and arrange it evenly on the sea beet. Place the eggs, cream and seasonings in a bowl and mix vigorously. Pour the egg and cream mix evenly over the sea beet and smoked haddock. Bake in the oven for 25–30 minutes, or until the tart stops being wobbly in the middle (some wobble is good, though).

There are several similar-looking species of orache. This illustration is of common orache, Atriplex patula.

Tiny drab flowers and later seeds grow at the stem ends.

Blue-green leaves are roughly triangular.

Some species and variants of orache can have red stems.

Tender young shoots emerging from seaweed deposits are delicious; they do not develop the angular goosefoot shape until later.

Orache

Atriplex spp.

Some form of orache (pronounced 'orak') has been eaten throughout human history, and it is nutritious in similar ways to its cultivated relation, spinach (only more so). Unless you are in the far north, you'll never be very far from orache on the coast. It can be fiddly picking if you are moving between a few straggly plants, but with a little exploration you will usually find thick beds of it growing out of decomposing seaweed, especially where it has accumulated for many years.

ALSO KNOWN AS Saltbush, orach, sea orach, sea spinach.

EDIBILITY Leaves are a delicious slightly salty, succulent spinach with nutty overtones when young, usually developing bitterness towards the end of spring that persists through summer as flower spikes form. It is related to quinoa, and the seeds, once properly processed, can be eaten in a similar way.

IDENTIFICATION Easy to identify to genus level, but hard to identify individual species. Look for spearhead (halberd), arrowhead or goose footprint shaped fleshy green (occasionally reddening) leaves, often mealy textured or with a pale bloom. Racemes of tiny drab or greenish-red flowers and seeds appear in summer and autumn. Oraches are annuals, and can grow prostrate or upright up to 1m (3ft), depending on the species, location and exposure.

DISTRIBUTION Common and often abundant around the North Atlantic but sparser farther north.

HABITAT Upper beach above the high tide line on coarse sand and shingle, often growing from the dead seaweed band stranded by high spring tides; also in coastal defences, salt marshes or with grasses and other plants by the beach.

WHEN TO HARVEST Leaves from mid-spring, seeds from midsummer.

SAFETY NOTE The leaves are relatively high in oxalates, which are not problematic when ingested in moderation, but be cautious if you have been warned by your doctor against eating spinach or rhubarb, or suffer from kidney stones. The seeds, and the leaves when they become bitter in summer, contain saponins. These are poisonous compounds, but they are poorly absorbed by the human body and mostly pass through the digestive system without causing any harm. They can be removed by leaching the seeds in water, thorough cooking, and changing the cooking water once. Orache can efficiently absorb contaminants from the soil (especially nitrates), so avoid harvesting from contaminated ground.

Similar species

The very poisonous thorn apple (*Datura stramonium*) has superficially similar leaves, but has large, trumpet-shaped white or violet flowers and large spiky seed capsules. It is not a coastal plant but may conceivably grow there. Other members of the nightshade (Solanaceae) family also have a superficially similar leaf shape, but only woody nightshade (*Solanum dulcamara*) is likely to occur coastally. It has woody stems, very different flowers, juicy fruits and a scrambling growth. It is not one of the troublingly toxic nightshades, but if this makes you nervous, remember that foraging isn't a race. Spend a year observing, and when flowers and fruits appear you'll be able to really tune in and the differences will be striking and memorable.

There are around 250 members of the *Atriplex* genus worldwide, dozens of which grow around the North Atlantic. The most common and abundant coastal species of orache are:

- **Spear-leaved orache** (*A. prostrata*), also known as halberd or hastate orache. The most common and abundant species in most regions.
- **Frosted orache** (*A. laciniata*) is smaller, often prostrate and with a distinct white bloom on all leaves.
- **Babington's orache** (*A. glabriuscula*) tends to grow prostrate, and often with some reddish/purple colouration, especially on the stems.
- **Common orache** (*A. patula*) can grow away from the coast.
- **Grass-leaved orache** (*A. littoralis*) is narrow-leaved, as the name suggests.

Some *Atriplex* species in the Northeastern US are rare and protected, including *A. glabrisciula* (Connecticut, New York and Rhode Island) and *A. subspicata* (New Jersey and New York). If you live in these regions, you should learn to identify and avoid them.

You may also encounter other non-coastal near relations in the goosefoot (*Chenopodium*) genus, variously known as fat hen, lamb's quarters and Good-King-Henry, that look similar (though usually less fleshy) and can be used in similar ways. Their most obvious difference is that the leaf base of orache is usually at right angles to the stem, while on most leafy goosefoots it tapers towards the stem.

Sustainable harvesting

To enjoy orache leaves as a forager, I have two pieces of advice: first, harvest it early in the year – the bitter soapy flavour the leaves develop in summer turns them from gourmet to survival food; and second, seek out the dense colonies that emerge from well-rotted seaweed deposits. By thinning the abundance of spots like these it's easy to pick enough tasty greens in a few spring visits to keep you stocked for the rest of the year by blanching and freezing them (see page 83).

Everything you can do with spinach or sea beet leaves (see page 81), you can do with orache leaves. Orache leaves make even tastier salad (when young), but they are less substantial and don't keep so long in the fridge.

Processing and cooking orache seeds

The seeds of orache can be a good protein source and make a pleasant, if fiddly, grain, akin to quinoa but not as soft. Harvest them on a dry day in late summer or autumn (as they begin to turn from green to red) by drawing your hand up the stems to free the dry seeds in their casings. Dislodge them from their papery wrappings by rubbing them firmly and vigorously between your hands over a tub.

Next, separate the small dark seeds from the papery chaff by winnowing – an ancient practice that will make you feel closer to your foraging ancestors. This is best done on a breezy day by gently pouring the rubbed seeds and casings from one container to another. By allowing a few hand-widths of drop, the lighter chaff will be blown away. Repeat the process until you are happy you have removed most of the chaff. If doing this outdoors isn't practical, you can do it by placing the seed/chaff mix on a tray then gently vibrating it at a shallow angle – the seeds should roll to the corner. They can then be dehydrated for storage or grinding into flour, or they can be cooked fresh.

Before cooking, soak the seeds in fresh cold water for at least 30 minutes. To cook them, simmer for 30 minutes in water until the seeds swell and crack. They are nice mixed with fried coastal greens like sea aster or sea plantain and some wild spices.

Opposite: Thick hedges of tender orache emerge from accumulated seaweed deposits in the more sheltered parts of bays.

Seed casings start off
green and mature to
a deep rusty brown.

Leaf edges
are wavy.

Older leaves
usually develop
rusty blotches.

Young shoots, yet
to unfurl, secrete
a soothing gel.

Curled dock

Rumex crispus

Curled dock is not a coastal specialist (ask any farmer and they will curse it as a 'weed' of the field), but its hardy nature means it can be very common by the shore. The rippling corrugations of its long leaves remind me of the frills on the edges of sugar kelp (see page 203), and I suspect they serve a similar role – in this case, helping the plant ride strong winds, rather than waves and currents.

ALSO KNOWN AS Curly dock, yellow dock, narrow leaf dock.

EDIBILITY Young leaves are sour and juicy, quickly becoming more bitter and astringent as they grow. Seeds have a nutty flavour and some nutritional value but require processing. The roots have been eaten after roasting by some First Nations peoples but tend to be too woody and bitter for most tastes.

IDENTIFICATION Long, thin, pointed (lanceolate) leaves, with rippled edges growing to 15–25cm (6–10in). The plant can grow to 1.2m (4ft). Tiny green flowers form in clusters on branching spires and look more like seeds to the naked eye. Seed casings turn rusty brown in late summer to autumn.

DISTRIBUTION Widespread and abundant.

HABITAT By no means exclusively coastal, but extremely successful on foreshores and exposed coasts. Often the predominant plant on shingle, especially further north.

WHEN TO HARVEST Leaves are best harvested in early spring, seeds in autumn.

SIMILAR SPECIES There are many types of dock, and all can be used in similar ways, but few are so abundant near the coast, and curled dock tends to make the best eating.

SAFETY NOTES The leaves of all dock species are relatively high in oxalic acid, which is not problematic when ingested by healthy people in moderation, but if you have been warned by your doctor against eating spinach or rhubarb; suffer from kidney stones, rheumatism or arthritis; or are breast feeding, proceed with extra caution. Boiling the leaves significantly reduces the amount of oxalic acid.

Healing properties

Rubbing dock leaves on the skin to alleviate nettle stings is one of the most widespread pieces of ethnobotanical knowledge in the Western world. Scientists have struggled to work out why the remedy works, usually attributing it to a combination of simple rubbing action, the placebo effect, and the fact that one is never very far from a dock plant. However, they, and many generations of sting sufferers, may have been looking in the wrong place. The real key to the soothing qualities of dock lies in a cooling gel that appears in negligible quantities in open leaves but positively oozes from young leaves before they unfurl. This gel has many compounds in common with aloe vera, a plant famed for its cooling, soothing and moisturizing properties. These chemicals have pain-killing and anti-inflammatory properties, all wrapped up in a transparent cooling goo that leaves no sticky residue. Our hunter-gatherer ancestors almost certainly knew this, but over many generations the knowledge was slowly abbreviated to 'any old dock leaf'.

These young shoots, along with older, less gloopy stems, also contain pectin, a natural setting agent used in jam making. Just tie them up in muslin when jamming low-pectin fruits.

Eating curled dock

Leaves
Dock leaves are an excellent source of vitamins A and C, iron and potassium. Enjoying them fresh relies upon harvesting the young basal leaves in early spring. At this stage they make a pleasant sour addition to a mixed salad or a sandwich. Remove the stems, as they are tough, and on larger leaves you may also wish to strip out the central vein too. As dock leaves mature, they quickly develop astringency and bitterness. This, and their oxalic acid content, can be reduced by blanching them, perhaps after drying them in the traditional method I outline below. Once blanched, they become a useful multipurpose sour green vegetable.

Seeds
Curled dock produces prolific quantities of seeds which mature to a deep rust brown colour in late summer and autumn, and often persist on the skeletal remains of the plants well into winter. They are reminiscent of buckwheat (a near relation), with a more tart, nutty flavour, and with similar uses. What you harvest is not just seed, but also its papery casing that allows it to catch breezes and stick to animal fur. On many grains this chaff is removed, but it's a difficult job with dock seeds and as it isn't problematic to eat, it can be left on as a bit of extra dietary fibre.

Processing dock seeds
First ensure the seeds are absolutely dry by gently roasting them (in their casings) on a baking tray in a low oven for 10 minutes. This also helps to develop their nutty flavour. After this, if you want to try to remove some chaff, rub them vigorously between your hands and winnow them (as I describe for orache seeds on page 88), or stir them in a basin of water and skim the chaff off the surface, before straining the seeds and drying them again.

The whole seeds (winnowed or not) can be mixed through granola, sprinkled on salads and cooked dishes, used in cracker or biscuit recipes, or blitzed (using a high-speed blender on 'chop' setting) into a flour then used for baking. The flour is gluten free and won't rise on its own. If you want to use it in risen bread, you'll need to combine it with bread flour in a 50/50 mix, but use less dock flour if you want your bread to rise more. Dock flour works better for making crackers: mix it with rye flour and seasonings (seaweed powders work well), moisten with a little honey, water and oil, then spread thinly on baking sheets and bake until crisp.

Aveluk and aveluk soup

In Armenia, curled dock leaves are known as wild sorrel, and braided then dried into fat, rough ropes known as *aveluk*. The process promotes oxidation and fermentation, and when the aveluk is soaked before use, most of the bitterness and oxalic acid is removed. Dried aveluk can be stored for long periods (up to four years) then reconstituted and used as the basis of salads and soups.

Ingredients

Aveluk, about 20cm (8in), roughly chopped

Butter, for sautéing

2 large onions, chopped

2 large potatoes, chopped

1 tin chopped tomatoes or 2 tablespoons rosehip purée (see page 50)

1 tin chickpeas

Spices – your selection from chilli powder, turmeric, coriander, etc.

Chopped herbs – whatever you have or enjoy: e.g. fennel seeds or leaf, dill, ground ivy, (Scots) lovage, etc.

Salt and pepper

Optional: handful of chopped walnuts

Optional: 2 cloves of garlic

To make aveluk

Use long curled dock leaves at least 15cm (6 in) long, harvested with their short stems in spring. You can include other long leaves like wild garlic (ramps) and dandelions, provided they don't have a wiry central vein. Tie the stem end of five or so leaves together with a piece of string, then begin to braid them, adding a new leaf with each turn. Add the leaves stem side up, with the end of the stem sticking out of the main braiding so it can be snipped off later. Make the braid as long as you like, but traditionally the length should be four times the height of the person braiding it!

When finished, tie off the end with another piece of string then snip off all the protruding stems. Dry the braid gently but thoroughly, until crisp. If you can dry it in direct sunlight it will retain some greenness, but this isn't essential. Your beautiful aveluk should be stored in airtight containers – any moisture may cause it to go mouldy.

Making the soup

Place the aveluk in a bowl and cover with boiling water. Leave for 30 minutes, then strain. Repeat this process. Rinse the aveluk in cold water, then chop into bite-sized pieces – the sort of size you'll enjoy eating in soup.

Melt the butter in a large pan and add the onions, sautéing them until translucent. Add the potatoes and cook for a few more minutes. Add all the other ingredients, including the chopped aveluk, and top up with water. Bring to the boil and simmer gently for 15 minutes.

A very brisk blitz with a hand blender breaks up the potato and adds body to the soup, but don't overdo it – the texture should not be smooth. Traditionally, chopped walnuts are added near the end of the cooking process and the garlic cloves grated fresh on top of the soup as it is served.

Other species of interest

Sea holly

Eryngium maritimum

ALSO KNOWN AS Sea eryngo, sea eryngium, sea hulver, sea holme.

DISTRIBUTION Occasional or rare on European coasts, from Scandinavia to the Mediterranean and the shores of the Baltic and Black Seas. Introduced on the eastern seaboard of North America, chiefly in the Carolinas and New Jersey.

Sea holly grows to a height of up to 60cm (2ft), with spiny, waxy grey-green leaves protruding from sturdy, wind-hardy stems and egg-shaped lilac-blue flowers. It's usually visible from late spring to autumn and keeps company in the sand with sea rocket and sea sandwort, or further up the shore in coastal grasses. You will also find it in dune systems and fine shingle, occasionally among short vegetation.

Needing plenty of light, sea holly is easily outcompeted by non-native invasive species such as sea buckthorn and beach rose. It has a large root system, specially adapted to shifting sands – good for storing water and staying anchored, and it responds to burial by rapidly developing new shoots.

Sea holly is a curiosity of the carrot (Apiaceae) family, related to alexanders (see page 29), rock samphire (see page 105) and Scots lovage (see page 109), but you wouldn't guess that by looking at its blueish spiky leaves and sculpturesque, thistle-like flowers. If you try nibbling a bit of a leaf (being careful to avoid the spines), you'll find the taste is reminiscent of rock samphire in its carroty intensity. The flavour of the roots is interesting and historically the most sought-after part. They taste peppery and somewhat citrussy, with perhaps a back note of carrot and pine and were used as a spice rather like galangal or fresh turmeric or candied to make sweet treats that were said to have aphrodisiac properties. Sea holly is generally too rare to forage. In much of its range it is protected and/or under threat due to the erosion of its native habitat and being out-competed by non-native plants. I include it here because it is strikingly beautiful and has an interesting ethnobotanical history, not because I wish to encourage anyone to go and harvest it.

A similar species is field eryngo (*Eryngium campestre*) but it is more erect and has greener leaves. It is not a coastal species and is even rarer than sea holly. The striking foliage and flowers have made *Eryngium* species popular with gardeners and you are more likely to meet hybrids of it in cultivation than in the wild. Wild delicacies rarely taste as good in captivity, but perhaps the interest of foragers might help reintroduce sea holly to the wild.

Oyster plant

Mertensia maritima

ALSO KNOWN AS Oyster leaf, sea bluebells, northern shore-wort, sea lungwort.

DISTRIBUTION In Europe, from the Scottish border northwards; in North America, from New Jersey northwards.

In Scots Gaelic, this little plant is known as *Tiodhllac na mara* – 'gift of the sea', and it is indeed an absolute treasure with its striking leaves, pretty flowers and unkempt growth habit. Blue-green hairless, succulent diamond-shaped leaves can grow to 4cm (1½in) and often have wavy edges, growing prostrate in a straggly, creeping rosette. Flower buds are tinged pink but soon turn forget-me-not blue as they open (see page 14 for a detailed photograph).

Oyster plant is admirably tenacious, with a large, spirally twisted taproot that reaches down through sand or shingle to find fresh water and anchor the plant to its storm-tossed home. You'll find it in stable and semi-stable shingle, small pebble or occasionally coarse sand beaches, just above the high spring tide line.

Colonies can persist for hundreds of years when conditions are right, but plants growing in pure sand are usually short-lived. The flowers are pollinated by insects, and the seeds need a sharp winter in order to germinate. Oyster plant is rare or threatened, and often protected across much of its range, and is becoming less common every year. It should not be harvested from the wild without careful research, consideration and stewardship.

The leaves are succulent with a salty-creamy-umami flavour reminiscent of fresh oysters. Don't take any more than a leaf or two to taste, and even then, only if you find a healthy colony. As is so often the case, it is not the nimble fingers of foragers that have reduced oyster plant populations, but more exploitative practices. For example, commercial shingle extraction severely damaged one of

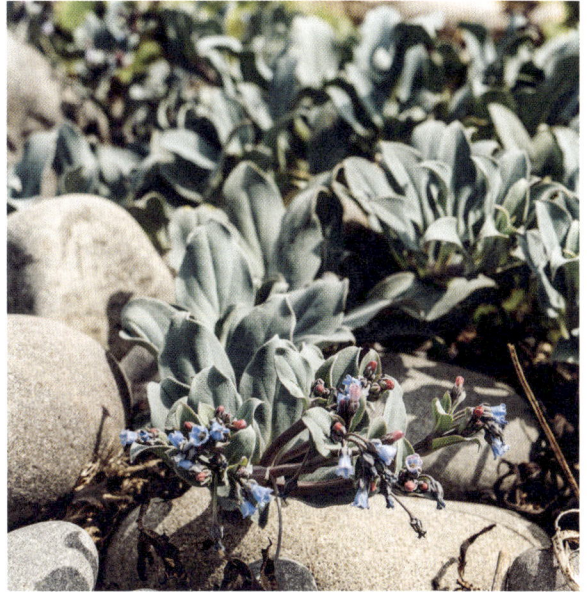

Northern Ireland's populations, and grazing by sheep decimated colonies across Orkney and Shetland. Projects are currently underway to restore them, and the outcomes can be good. When stock fencing was introduced to protect them on Fair Isle, two plants became 2,360 plants 20 years later.

Oyster plant leaf is popular as a garnish in upmarket restaurants, but when you see it on a menu it will almost invariably have been cultivated. Hopefully, careful cultivation can help support future wild populations. It is my hope that by including it here, foragers will notice, advocate for, and help protect these beautiful little plants.

Some people question just how 'oystery' oyster plants actually taste. To my taste (and I've eaten a lot of oysters), the leaves of wild (not cultivated) oyster plant taste more oystery than an oyster! Chemical analysis bears this out – the leaves are high in dimethyl sulphide, a compound that is a major part of the flavour profile of raw oysters.

A similar species, *M. maritima* var. *tenella,* is found in Northern Canada and on the shores of the sub-Arctic North Atlantic. It is similar in looks and edibility.

Cliffs & Crags

Life dangling by a thread

ancient rock seeking
vibrant plants for fun and more
– time wasters welcome

Of all the unlikely-looking places in which plants proliferate, it is perhaps coastal cliffs and crags that seem most surprising. In summer, all but the sheerest, most austere rock faces become implausibly festooned with colourful blossoms hanging from every crack and ledge, bending with the wind, like a dancing, vertical garden.

The upsides for plants that can ply their trade in such vertiginous places are less competition from other plants, and reduced exposure to grazing animals. Adaptations such as salt tolerance, creeping growth, the ability to flex in strong winds, and extensive root networks that both anchor them and access precious water help with this. They are also masters at taking advantage of 'nanoclimates' – just one small outcrop may break enough of the prevailing wind to allow luxuriant growth.

In my sure-footed youth, some of my happiest times were spent botanizing among the flamboyant cascades of cliff-dwelling plants, but it goes without saying that these are potentially dangerous places for foragers with their eye on a prize. The Everyday Life and Fatal Hazard in Sixteenth Century England Project records three instances of 'death by samphire gathering' within 10 years, and it was common enough for Shakespeare to describe the harvesting of rock samphire in *King Lear* as a 'dreadful trade'.

There is no need to be a mountain goat to access the plants I explore in this chapter. To them, a small craggy outcrop is as good as dangling in the void, provided there isn't too much grazing, or competition from other plants. Occasionally they may even treat the stony shore as a sort of horizontal cliff face, making for easy pickings.

The pale pinkish
flowers have four lobes
of almost equal size.

Paired leaves.

Woody creeping
stems.

Wild thyme

Thymus spp.

Wild thyme is magical when its scent drifts on summer zephyrs and its small pink flowers turn rocks into aromatic cushions. No wonder it has long been regarded as a favourite flower of fairies. I find its smell quite intoxicating and carry bunches of it in my pockets on coastal forays, purely for the pleasure of sniffing it. The ancient Greeks believed that the scent of thyme represented activity, valour and courage, and planted it on graves to banish evil spirits. Bees love wild thyme, and on a warm day you can often hear them first. It struggles to compete with larger plants, which is why it favours poor soils and creeps over rocks.

ALSO KNOWN AS Creeping thyme, Breckland thyme, elfin thyme, wild mountain thyme – see notes on similar species.

EDIBILITY Leaves and flowers make a delightful aromatic pot-herb, especially in summer.

IDENTIFICATION A diminutive perennial creeping plant with tiny oval oppositely paired leaves on wiry stems 5–10cm (2–4in) long, densely packed heads of pinky-purple aromatic flowers in the summer.

DISTRIBUTION One or more species of wild thyme can be found in most North Atlantic regions.

HABITAT Creeping over rocky outcrops and edges between rock and turf and in thin soils near the coast. Although it thrives near the sea, wild thyme is not a coastal specialist and is also common on chalk and limestone soils and mountain crags.

WHEN TO HARVEST Mid-spring to mid-autumn. It flowers in summer, when it is at its easiest to spot and most aromatic.

SIMILAR SPECIES *Thymus polytrichus* is the most commonly encountered wild thyme of coastal Western Europe, and is illustrated and described here. *T. serpyllum* is the species most commonly encountered in North America. Several other *Thymus* species, including escapees from herb gardens, grow coastally around the North Atlantic, and all of them may reasonably be referred to as wild thyme. All look similar, with the main variations being the shade of pink in the flowers and the tendency to grow upright or prostrate. All are edible, though the intensity of aromatics can vary.

Harvesting and eating wild thyme

Although it is a perennial plant, wild thyme is so diminutive that it is almost invisible for most of the year, getting lost among grasses and moss. That soon changes when its flowers appear in early summer, and this is the best time to harvest it. Snip the creeping stems or pinch out the flowers, leaving plenty on each plant, and visit different areas each year.

Unless you have stumbled on a garden escapee, or a particularly pungent localized strain, you will find wild thyme less intense than its cultivated relations, especially if you harvest it outside its flowering season. Even when it is flowering, reckon on using about twice the amount of wild thyme as cultivated thyme if you are using it as a direct substitute. What it lacks in oomph it more than makes up for in delicacy and complexity, with hints of lavender and mint underlying a more earthy version of cultivated thyme.

A scattering of fresh flowers on a salad, or as a garnish on a dessert, is nice, but wild thyme is at its best as a pot-herb (an aromatic ingredient in cooked dishes). The stems are tough and wiry, so either strip the flowers and leaves from them before use or tie whole twigs up in a bouquet garni to infuse their flavour during cooking, then remove them before serving. Infuse it both early and late in the cooking process for maximum impact.

Wild thyme works in most savoury dishes and lots of sweet dishes too. Try pushing sprigs under the skin of a chicken along with butter before roasting, or tucking them into the belly cavity of fish before baking. It is a delightful addition to mushroom dishes, a natural partner for most fruits, and is particularly happy alongside lemon. You can also infuse it into carrageen pudding (see page 189).

It can be preserved by drying, though it loses some pungency. A better method is to infuse it into oil, alcohol, honey or vinegar, or add it to herb butter, which can be frozen.

Wild thyme is used by herbalists for its antispasmodic and antiseptic properties, especially for coughs and sore throats, and is often taken as a tea (or, once cooled, as a gargle). It also makes one of the nicest-tasting wild teas – a firm favourite on summer camping trips.

Honey and thyme ice cream

Wild thyme is the smell of summer, so what better way to enjoy it than in an ice cream? If you have already made wild thyme honey, you could use that as the honey and reduce or omit the wild thyme. For a wilder version, add a handful of dried sweet woodruff or dried meadowsweet flowers instead of vanilla.

Ingredients

475ml (17 fl oz) double (heavy) cream

70g (2½ oz) light brown sugar, loosely packed

60ml (2 fl oz) honey (wild thyme-infused if wanted)

A pinch of salt

A generous handful of wild thyme: 20–30 good-sized sprigs, including the flowers

240ml (8fl oz) whole milk

Seeds of 1 vanilla pod, or 1½ teaspoons of vanilla extract

In a medium saucepan, add half of the cream, sugar, honey and thyme sprigs. Cook over medium heat, stirring occasionally, until the sugar is dissolved. Remove the saucepan from the heat as soon as the mixture simmers. Stir in the remaining cream, milk and vanilla, then leave to cool. Place in the fridge to infuse for at least six hours or, better still, overnight.

Strain into an ice-cream maker and churn until thick. Pour into a plastic container and freeze. If you don't have an ice-cream maker, just put it in the freezer, working it thoroughly with a fork several times over the freezing process. It will be ready for eating after an hour or two.

Wild thyme honey

This honey makes an extra-soothing addition to wild thyme tea. Fill a preserving jar with wild thyme flowers, then pour good-quality honey over the top until the flowers are covered. Firmly close the jar, turn it on its head, and leave it for four weeks.

The flower umbel has
8–20 umbelules and
green bracts beneath.

Flowers are
yellowish-green.

Leaves are narrow
and fleshy.

Rock samphire

Crithmum maritimum

Rock samphire is common around the southern coasts of Europe, where it has been used as both food and a medicine since antiquity. This is the original samphire, its common English name being derived from the French *sampier*, which is a corruption of *herbe de Saint Pierre*, after the fisherman apostle St. Peter, whose own name was derived from the Greek *petra*, or rock. Very apt for a coastal cliff dweller.

ALSO KNOWN AS Sea fennel, samphire, crest marine.

EDIBILITY A strongly flavoured succulent herb or vegetable. The leaves are the principal harvest, but the flower buds can also be eaten and the seeds make a good spice.

IDENTIFICATION Leaves are narrow and finger-like but succulent, like pumped-up fennel, arranged in much-divided antler-like fronds that are round or oval in cross-section. It has a sprawling, straggly growth. Small greenish-yellow to white five-petalled flowers grow in umbels. Early in the year, skeletons of the previous season's flower heads usually persist, which aids identification.

DISTRIBUTION Widespread and quite common in its habitat throughout the Mediterranean and maritime Europe as far north as the Scottish Borders. It does not grow on the Atlantic coast of North America.

HABITAT Mostly grows in cracks in cliffs, crags and sea defences, but also on pebbly beaches above the spring high tide line.

WHEN TO HARVEST Spring through autumn.

SIMILAR SPECIES Although a member of the carrot (Apiaceae) family, which includes some poisonous species (see page 22), rock samphire is quite distinctive within its habitat.

Rock samphire vs marsh samphire

Rock samphire's unrelated namesake marsh samphire (a curiosity of the goosefoot family of plants; see page 88), is now a fashionable wild vegetable, recognized even by non-foragers and sold in supermarkets, while rock samphire can't be bought for love or money. This wasn't always the case: there was a roaring trade in pickled rock samphire in England up until the early 20th century. But harvesting it can be a dangerously vertiginous business, and as accessible colonies were depleted it started to be cut with similarly textured but less aromatic and easier to harvest marsh samphire (which until then was known as glasswort). The similarity between the two stops at their succulent, mini cactus-like appearance and crisp texture when trimmed and cooked or preserved. Marsh samphire is mostly salt and crunch (albeit in a delicious way), while rock samphire is salt, crunch and an intensely aromatic carrot/parsley flavour

Below: Rock samphire becomes more abundant the farther south you go – here it is basking on a rock in Northern Spain.

Harvest and eating rock samphire

If foraging conjures up images of bimbling along tranquil hedgerows, gently picking berries with a warm sun on your back, then picking rock samphire may come as a surprise. Though it does occasionally grow on the foreshore, its preferred home is clinging to precipitous coastal cliffs. Take care getting to it, and just thin out the succulent leaves. Where it is abundant, snipping off seed heads is fine too.

Rock samphire has a pungent flavour, like carrots on steroids, with overtones of petrol fumes. Some people taste hints of fennel. It divides opinion, being just too pungent for some and wowing others. I recommend spending some time getting to know it. Like all pungent herbs, it shines when sensitively used.

It can be steamed or stir-fried, but even with its flavour softened with melted butter it is too much for most people to eat as a stand-alone vegetable. It comes into its own when chopped through salads (especially rice salads), blitzed in pesto, included in sushi rolls, used as a garnish for fish, or pickled and eaten with cheese, cured meats or smoked fish (see my general pickling recipe on page 258). When hot pickled, it will lose some of its crunch and intensity. I prefer to embrace its flavour by cold pickling, embellishing the pickling solution with the spices of other members of the carrot family such as alexanders (see page 29) or Scots lovage seeds (see page 109).

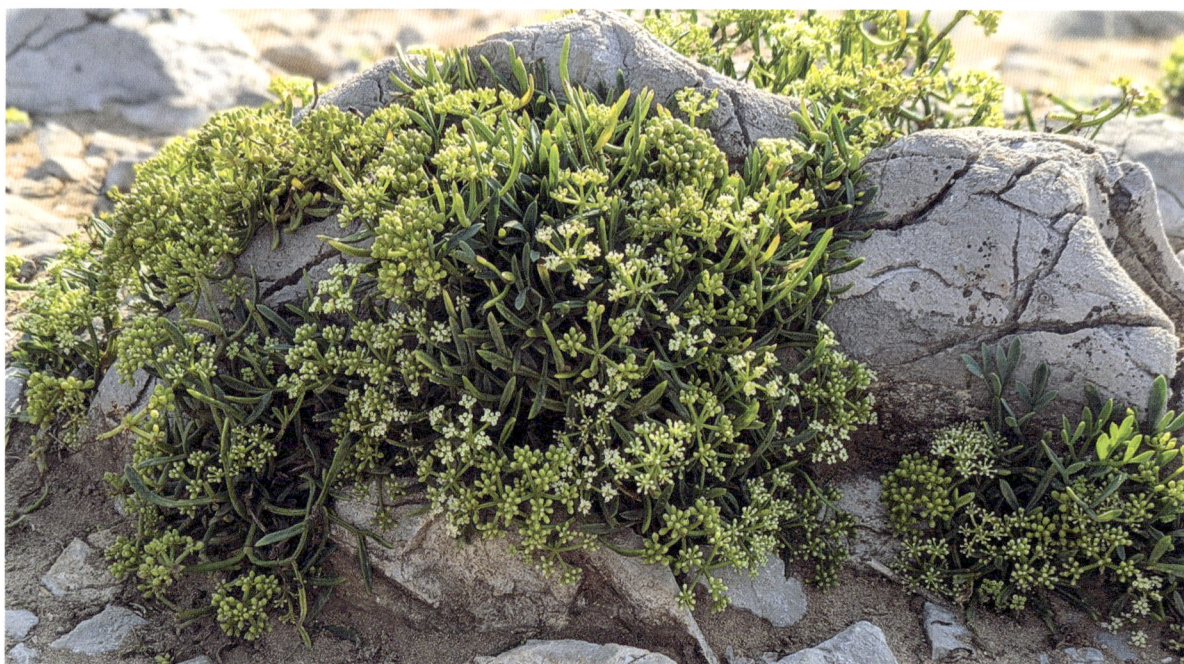

Rock samphire salsa verde

There isn't a country in the world that doesn't have its own version of 'green sauce' – *persillade* or *sauce verte* in France, *chimichurri* in Argentina, greensauce in Britain and North America, or *salsa verde* in Spain and Italy – all verdantly life-affirming mixes of pungent green herbs combined with seasonings and oil. Whatever you call it, it is a great template for foragers, a way to use what is in season and locally abundant to make a quick and versatile sauce for fish, meat or vegetables, or a dressing for salads and shellfish. Try drizzling some on baked oysters or a pizza, or mixing it through freshly cooked (sea) spaghetti. Rock samphire combines the flavours of several herbs commonly used in versions of salsa verde – parsley, sorrel, fennel, watercress – so is ideal for the job, but you can mix, match and dilute it to suit your taste with the optional ingredients I mention.

Ingredients

100g (3½oz) rock samphire fronds, finely chopped

4 spring onions (scallions), or wild garlic (ramps), finely chopped

2 tablespoons capers, or seaweed capers (see page 169), chopped

2 teaspoons apple cider vinegar

2 teaspoons Dijon mustard

50ml (3 tablespoons) olive oil, or more if you want your salsa to be more like a salad dressing

Salt and pepper

Optional additions

1 tablespoon lemon juice

2 anchovies, finely chopped

1 tablespoon fish sauce or clam garum (see page 249)

Alexanders leaf (see page 29)

Scots lovage (see page 109)

Mix all the ingredients together: for a smooth sauce, use a blender; for a more textured sauce, use a mortar and pestle; or just chop and stir for a chunky sauce.

This salsa is intended to be pungent, but if it is too much for you, it can be diluted by simmering the rock samphire in water for a couple of minutes first, or adding more oil and a mild green leaf like spinach, orache (see page 87) or sea beet (see page 81).

*Glossy green leaves
divided into three
toothed leaflets.*

*Seed casings are up to
6mm (¼in) long, with
prominent ridges.*

*Stems usually have red
colouration, especially
where they sheath
the main stem.*

Scots lovage

Ligusticum scoticum

If you are familiar with garden lovage, you will recognize both the leaf structure and flavour of Scots lovage – though it is much squatter in its growth habit and stronger tasting. You may struggle to find it outside its northerly range, but you can console yourself with its cousin rock samphire (see page 105), which occupies a similar niche further south. The aromatic seeds float, enabling them to be distributed along rocky shores during winter high tides. It can't tolerate grazing, which explains why populations tend to stick to cliffs and rocky outcrops, but where deer and sheep are controlled, it can establish itself on beach edges.

ALSO KNOWN AS Scottish licorice-root, Hulten's licorice-root, beach lovage.

EDIBILITY The leaves taste like an intense version of garden lovage – parsley meets celery, with a spicy back note. The seeds have notes of fenugreek, cumin and celery. Despite being known occasionally as licorice-root, the roots do not taste significantly of licorice and are best left undisturbed.

IDENTIFICATION A low-growing (up to 90cm/3ft, but usually less) perennial with ribbed, reddish stems bearing three groups of three oval-toothed or lobed hairless green leaves. Small green-white flowers are arranged on umbels.

DISTRIBUTION North-western Europe as far south as northern England, and in eastern North America as far south as New York. Becomes more abundant further north, though it is often rare or protected on the limit of its range.

HABITAT Cliffs, rocky outcrops and among sea defences, occasionally on stable shingle and sand among other coastal vegetation, just above the shore, provided they are not grazed. Prefers north-facing aspects, especially in the southern part of its range.

WHEN TO HARVEST Leaves in mid-spring and summer. Seeds ripen by mid-autumn.

SIMILAR SPECIES A member of the Apiaceae (carrot) family, so take care to familiarize yourself with the hazards of this family. Hemlock water-dropwort (see page 23) can occasionally grow in sheltered rock crevices where fresh water collects. Most similar though is (feral) garden lovage (*Levisticum officinale*), which grows much taller.

Eating Scots lovage

Scots lovage leaves taste like a combination of celery and parsley, with a hint of anise and curry leaf. Rather like the leaves of its cousins garden lovage and alexanders (see page 29), the flavour of Scots lovage can be a bit intense for some tastes but, used in moderation, they make an excellent salad- or pot-herb for grown-up palates. Blanching it before use diminishes its pungency. Cultivated lovage is extremely popular in Eastern European cuisine, especially in Poland and Romania, where it is used in soups and sauces, as seasoning for meat, and added to the water when boiling potatoes, and you can use its wild cousin in similar ways.

Use the leaves as you would parsley only more sparingly, as part of a bouquet garni during cooking, in sofrito (especially for fishy risottos), or chopped and strewn on finished dishes. It is especially good with fish. The leaves and stems infuse a nice herby perfume through oily fish like mackerel if stuffed into the belly cavity before roasting, barbecuing or cooking sous weed (see page 206).

Traditionally, Inuit have captured the aromatics of the leaves and stems by storing them in seal oil, but olive oil is rather more convenient for home cooks – just blitz with oil then strain. Alternatively, gentle drying retains plenty of their flavour, or they can be made into a very tasty salt. Scots lovage seeds are an excellent addition to your wild spice rack, great in curries and pakora. Harvest them late in the season, ensure they are thoroughly dry and store them whole. They are good infused whole into pickling solutions (see page 258) or toasted and ground then added to spice blends. Try using them with, or instead of, alexanders seeds to make cocktail bitters (see page 33) or in rye bread.

Opposite: Scots lovage clings to sheltered crevices on cliffs – here along with scurvy grass and thrift.

Scots lovage aioli

This is a delicious sauce that goes with almost anything, but is especially good with fish and/or chips. You can up the intensity by adding more Scots lovage, or dilute it by substituting in other herbs like sea arrowgrass, ground ivy or cultivated herbs. Mixed with chopped rock samphire and pickled wrack 'capers' (see page 169), it makes an excellent tartare sauce.

Ingredients

40g (1½oz) fresh Scots lovage leaves and tender stems

1 large egg yolk

3 tablespoons lemon juice

½ teaspoon kosher salt, to taste

1 clove of garlic

2 tablespoons cold water

240ml (8 fl oz) olive oil (not extra virgin)

Blanch the Scots lovage in boiling water for 1 minute, refresh in cold water, squeeze out excess water and roughly chop. Place in a blender with all the other ingredients except the oil and blitz briefly. With the blender still running, pour in the oil gently, in a slow but steady stream. The quantity of oil I have given here should make a sauce the consistency of thick yogurt – if you'd like it thicker, add more oil.

Flowers have five deeply notched petals and are usually borne on a single stalk.

Pale blue-green leaves can be variable in shape, but are usually lanceolate.

Sea campion

Silene uniflora

This hardy yet delicate-looking little plant clings tenaciously to sea cliffs and the upper reaches of shingle beaches, waving its pretty blossoms at passing pollinators and foragers. The flowers provide a delightful wayside nibble, made even more fun if you first pinch the open end of their bladder between your fingers then pop them against your palm.

ALSO KNOWN AS *Silene maritima*.

EDIBILITY Young leaves, once cooked, make a good vegetable. Flowers are a charming garnish or addition to salads.

IDENTIFICATION Unruly, dense cushion-like mops of small, waxy, hairless lance-shaped leaves. The flowers are distinctive with pink- and purple-veined bladders opening into five white petals that are split down the middle, giving the illusion of ten petals. There is usually just one flower per stem.

DISTRIBUTION Common in northern Europe, from Scandinavia south as far as North-West Spain. There are some (unverified) accounts of it being found in the wild on the west coast of North America, but if present at all, it is likely to be too rare to harvest.

HABITAT Coastal cliffs and shingle foreshores, occasionally inland if limestone is present.

WHEN TO HARVEST Mid-spring to late summer.

SIMILAR SPECIES Bladder campion (*Silene vulgaris*) is not coastal and has similar but usually more slender flowers that grow in clusters. It is usable in similar ways.

SAFETY NOTE As summer progresses, the leaves develop saponins, which are toxic but poorly absorbed by humans and so tend to pass through the digestive system without causing harm. Saponins are found in many edible plants, including staples like beans, but it's sensible to go easy with the raw leaves. Saponins are diminished to safe levels by cooking.

Eating sea campion

The tips of the foliage have a unique sweet flavour, though with a somewhat bitter aftertaste that can become almost acrid in summer. Cooking both diminishes the saponins and makes them tastier – try the last 5cm (2in) of the shoots chopped and added to soup, blanched quickly in boiling salted water, or simply sautéed and served in an omelette or as a side vegetable.

The flowers are excellent raw, and contain no saponins. They have a delicious hit of sweet nectar followed by a subtle but unique flavour which I can only describe as pleasingly metallic – two words that seldom go together! They make charming additions to salads or garnishes for cooked dishes and their bladders can be stuffed with other dainty wild treats – perhaps the surprise sourness of a sea buckthorn berry, some sea arrowgrass seeds or a little pepper dulse. If harvesting them in summer, check that they don't contain tiny flies, which find the bladder a good refuge from the wind.

When I introduce Italians to sea campion, they usually get extremely excited and misty-eyed as they recall its Mediterranean relative known as sculpit or stridolo (*Silene inflata*), the leaves of which are used to flavour risotto. Sea campion makes a good substitute – just follow my directions for cockle and sea sandwort risotto (see page 253).

Other species of interest

Buckshorn plantain

Plantago coronopus

ALSO KNOWN AS Stagshorn plantain, star-of-the-earth, star grass.

DISTRIBUTION Widely distributed around the North Atlantic and beyond.

Buckshorn plantain is the daredevil cousin of sea plantain (see page 131), preferring to ply its trade in more vertiginous locations – usually growing from cracks and thin soil on rocky outcrops and occasionally on foreshores. It has antler-shaped hairy leaves, 4cm (1½in) to 20cm (8in), arranged in a distinct and often flattened rosette, with tough-stalked flower spikes above.

Its leaves are usable the same ways as sea plantain – as a salad or cooked as a vegetable, but unless you can find it growing from a sheltered spot, it tends to be smaller and more fiddly to harvest. It has a similar pleasant flavour, but with a little more bitterness and mushroomy back notes. In southern regions it can be harvested year-round.

It has a long history of use in Italy, where it is widely cultivated and known as *minutina* or *erba stella* (star grass), and is a popular component of leafy salads, simply dressed with a little olive oil, vinegar and seasoning.

Crowberry

Empetrum nigrum

ALSO KNOWN AS Black crowberry, mossberry, blackberry (Canada), crawberry.

DISTRIBUTION Widely distributed across North Atlantic coasts, especially in the north.

Crowberry is a tough little ericaceous creeping evergreen shrub that produces dark, pea-sized fruits. While it is by no means a coastal specialist, its seeds are often spread by birds to sea cliffs and crags, where its ability to thrive in thin, exposed soils make it at home.

The berries start to ripen in summer and are often available well into winter. They taste quite tart eaten raw, but improve when dried or cooked. They have a high lipid content, making them a good source of energy, and they are widely used in indigenous North American cultures to make calorie-rich foods such as pemmican, a dried mixture of meat and fruit.

Sweet crowberry vinegar is delicious as a salad dressing, cordial, or to make sticky rice for sushi (see page 145). To make it, mix 250ml (9fl oz) of cider vinegar into 175g (6oz) of crowberries and leave to infuse for 1 week. Strain the fruit out, squishing out their juice as you do then add 175g (6oz) of white sugar per 130ml (4½ fl oz) of strained liquid, bring to a boil then bottle.

Wild cabbage

Brassica oleracea subsp. *oleracea*

ALSO KNOWN AS Sea cabbage.

DISTRIBUTION Scattered and nationally scarce in the UK, being more common in southern and north-west England, largely absent from west Scotland and Ireland. In North America, there are scattered populations between New York and Newfoundland, becoming more common farther north.

This perennial (occasionally biennial) develops a large woody stem up to 4cm (1½in) thick after the first year. The stem shows lateral scars where the previous year's leaves grew. Flowering stems grow up to 2m (6ft) with sprays of four petalled cross-shaped yellow flowers. The leaves are fleshy, dull green with wavy edges and often with hints of purple. You'll find them on coastal cliffs, especially on calcareous soils in full sun. They are intolerant of other plants and grazing.

With their propensity to store their food reserves in fleshy leaves, wild cabbage made an appealing crop for early farmers, and over many generations, they were selectively bred into the large, fleshy brassicas we enjoy today. All of them, from romancsco to kohlrabi to Brussels sprouts, can trace their lineage back to *Brassica oleracea*. There are so many variants nowadays that we add the suffix 'subsp. *oleracea*' to make it clear when we are talking about the original.

Conditioned as we are to its cultivated ancestors, the appearance of wild cabbage can look rather odd, with its long, woody stems, which give them the colloquial name of silver whips on the North Yorkshire coast. Plants can live to a venerable age, which you can estimate by counting the lines on the stem where earlier leaves once grew. The plant grows more slowly in winter, leaving scars that are closer together, so by noting how many areas of close banding are on a stem, you can work out how many winters it has endured. Individuals as old as 20 have been recorded.

The leaves can be eaten as you would cabbage; the flower buds are like a thin, sparse broccoli; and the open flowers make a pleasant addition to a salad. Harvest the leaves in spring and summer; the flower buds and flowers only in summer.

I'm not convinced that wild cabbage makes better eating than its tame descendants. The leaves have a tendency towards bitterness unless you catch them young, and the flowers and florets are fiddly picking, especially considering their often precipitous locations. Don't let me put you off tasting a few leaves if you find a healthy colony, but do keep in mind that while it can be locally abundant, wild cabbage is not a common plant and plays host to a large range of beetles, butterflies, moths, flies and sawflies. More a species that is fun to seek out, admire and learn from than to eat, perhaps.

Salt Marsh & Estuary

Mud, mud, glorious mud

where land melts to sea
mud grows soft as chocolate
oozing sweet life

Salt marshes are liminal landscapes, neither land nor sea, but a blurred merging of the two, characterized by winding brackish channels, cathedral skies, a mosaic of fascinating inhabitants, and a great deal of mud. Specialized plants, known as halophytes, can cope with salt and regular tidal inundation and build salt marshes by stabilizing muddy sediments. They are rich habitats, bustling with specialized worms, bivalves and snails that attract wading and migratory birds. They are also an important carbon sink – British salt marshes alone hold about 2.3 million tons of carbon in their top 10cm (4in).

Historically, salt marshes have migrated in step with sea level changes, but in recent times drainage and enclosure by levees to make space for agriculture and urbanization has drastically reduced them. Those that remain struggle to keep pace with sea level changes associated with global warming: trapped between rising seas and man-made barriers, many are drowning, especially in the Northeastern and Mid-Atlantic regions of North America.

The ability of halophytes to store and shed surplus salt using their fleshy leaves, makes salt marshes abundant foraging grounds. But, as well as being potentially dangerous mazes of steep-sided channels, rapidly moving tides and sucking mud, they are often protected habitats and you should do careful local research before harvesting from them, especially in North America, where the spread of European common reed (*Phragmites australis* subsp. *australis*) is overwhelming native species. With a bit of practice, you will learn to spot accessible mini salt marshes that contain all the same treasure on the fringes of more forager-friendly bays, beaches and estuaries.

In addition to their delicious salty tang, the species I explore here offer the added benefit to foragers of reaching their prime in high summer, just as many other plants (including coastal plants of other habitats) are flowering and turning bitter. Better still, their waxy coatings and succulence make them excellent candidates for cold pickling and crisp summer salads.

Daisy-like flowers with
yellow disc florets surrounded
by mauve ray florets. Some
variants lack the ray florets.

Individual leaves
can redden, and
these tend to taste
more salty.

Lanceolate leaves
can grow as rosettes,
or can appear to
emerge individually
from among
coastal grasses.

Sea aster

Tripolium pannonicum

Sea aster is a tenacious and unkempt-looking perennial plant that manages not only to thrive in salty mud and sand, but to look pretty and charming while doing it. Like other halophytes, it helps to stabilize coastal mud and sand, reducing erosion and forming habitats for less salt-tolerant plants. It flowers well into autumn, providing a valuable source of nectar for late-flying butterflies. The flowers, flowering stems and seeds are unpalatable, but the leaves are richly rewarding and by harvesting from individual plants in well-established colonies, you'll have a reliable supply year after year. It's worth hunting for where they grow longer and fatter – usually in sheltered spots on muddy riverbanks and the edges of brackish channels.

ALSO KNOWN AS *Aster tripolium*, *Aster pannonicus*, seashore aster, blue chamomile, sea daisy.

EDIBILITY Leaves are crunchy and crisp, with a juicy consistency, pleasingly salty/umami with notes of spinach, oyster, seaweed and citrus.

IDENTIFICATION Plants are perennial, growing up to 75cm (2½ft) tall, usually less, especially in windy situations, with succulent, waxy lanceolate dark-green leaves. Flowers appear in the second year, looking like large scruffy daisies, with mauve or pale purple (occasionally white) ray florets surrounding yellow disc florets.

DISTRIBUTION Common and often abundant within its habitat in northern Europe, not recorded in North America.

HABITAT Salt marsh, estuaries, coastal mud and sheltered sandflats, just above the mean high-water mark. Occasionally it will grow from damp cracks in coastal rocks and crags.

WHEN TO HARVEST Appears in mid-spring but best harvested between midsummer and mid-autumn. Dies back in late autumn.

Similar species

Prior to flowering, sea aster can be easily confused with sea lavender (*Limonium vulgare*), which grows in exactly the same habitat and can be distinguished by its slightly wider, less succulent, less waxy leaves and unpleasant, fishy aftertaste (see centre-left photo on page 120). While not recommended for eating, sea lavender is harmless in small amounts, so tasting is a reasonable aid to identification. Once the plants flower, the differences are obvious: sea lavender has sparse, lavender-like mauve flowers, while sea aster has daisy-like flowers. A variant of sea aster, *Aster tripolium* var. *discoideus*, lacks the mauve ray florets but is otherwise the same. If you see similar flowers in gardens, they are probably one of a host of inedible cultivars collectively known as Michaelmas daisies.

Eating sea aster

Although often eclipsed in culinary circles by its near neighbour marsh samphire (see page 127), sea aster is easier to harvest and every bit as delicious, with a more rounded flavour. The leaves remain juicy and pleasant right through summer and into autumn, and don't become bitter like some other coastal plants. Leaves that are prematurely yellow or red are being used by the plant to store surplus salt. Unwashed leaves will keep in the fridge for up to two weeks. Wash them thoroughly in fresh water just before using them, as they often have a fine covering of tide-washed silt. They are a versatile and rewarding green vegetable. Raw, they can be treated a bit like mangetout or sugar snap peas – great in salads and sushi rolls (see page 145), and larger leaves are good for dipping in things. Uncooked leaves can also be finely chopped and mixed through laverbread (see page 184) or blitzed and added to smoked fish and seaweed paté (see page 193) or savoury carrageen pudding (see page 189).

When cooked, sea aster leaves resemble spinach, only with more heft and flavour. Lightly steamed or sautéed in a little butter, they are an excellent accompaniment to fish and meat (especially lamb) and will add crunch and body to stir-fries. They carry a fair bit of natural salt, so leave seasoning until the end. Like many coastal succulents, they pickle well, retaining their texture if cold-pickled (see page 261).

Below: Sea aster often grows prolifically on the upper reaches of salt marshes and becomes unmistakeable when its unruly mauve flowers open.

Sea aster, chorizo and tomato stew

Sea aster stands up to a bit of light stewing and is especially good with tomatoes. This recipe also works with other juicy coastal greens, such as sea beet, sea kale and sea plantain. I serve this as a hearty meal on my kayak foraging trips, using venison 'chorizo' to keep things wild, but traditional pork chorizo works well and adds more fat. If you like a bit of spicy heat, this recipe can take a fair bit of chilli. If you have lots of wild garlic (ramps), you can omit the bulb garlic and add extra shredded leaves just before serving. You could also use beach rose hip tomato sauce (see page 50) instead of the tomatoes.

Ingredients (Serves 4 generously)

Olive oil, for frying

300g (11oz) chorizo sausage (or a similar weight of halloumi for a vegetarian version), cut into 1cm (⅜in) pieces

2 medium onions, chopped, or 300g (11oz) of wild garlic (ramps) leaves and stems, roughly chopped

4 cloves of garlic, chopped

Optional: 4 red chillies, finely chopped, or ½ teaspoon chilli powder

A glug of balsamic vinegar or sweet elderberry vinegar

A large glass of red wine

2 x 400g (14oz) tins chopped tomatoes

2 x 400g (14oz) tins chickpeas

2 teaspoons smoked paprika

500g (1lb)sea aster leaves, roughly chopped into bite-sized pieces

Seasoning: salt, pepper and any ground seaweed seasonings you might have, such as pepper dulse or toasted laver

A handful of parsley or wild aromatic herb such as alexanders or Scots lovage

Heat the oil in a large pan and add the chorizo. Cook on a high heat until it begins to colour and adds its seasoned fat to the pan, then lift out and reserve. Turn the heat down a little then add the onions or wild garlic, sweating them until they become translucent but not brown. (If you are using wild garlic, reserve a handful for garnishing.) Add the garlic and chillies (if using). Add the vinegar and cook for a minute more.

Add the wine and cook for another few minutes, until it has reduced a little. Stir in the tomatoes, chickpeas, paprika and reserved chorizo, and bring back to a simmer. Add the sea aster and seasoning (remembering that the sea aster has some natural saltiness) and gently simmer until the sea aster is cooked but retains some texture.

Serve in bowls and garnish with the chopped herbs. A grating of cheese on top is a nice addition.

There are many subtly different
species of marsh samphire, and
considerable variation within
species. Illustrated here is
Salicornia europea.

Grows sprawling and bushy,
or remains as fine spears,
depending on tidal exposure
and substrate.

Turns yellowish as summer progresses,
then red in the autumn. As it grows, the
fleshy stem becomes more woody.

Minute yellow flowers
are wind-pollinated.

Marsh samphire

Salicornia spp.

Marsh samphire is a curious member of the amaranth family of plants that includes coastal spinaches such as sea beet (see page 81) and orache (see page 87). It is one of very few flowering plants that can grow below the high tide line. Here it stabilizes mud and sand, paving the way for other, less salt-tolerant halophytes such as sea aster (see page 123), sea arrowgrass (see page 135) and sea plantain (see page 131). Its miniscule yellow flowers are wind-pollinated. Its pollen and seeds don't travel far, resulting in in-bred localized colonies that can have distinct characteristics, such as more branching or fatter stems. It's nice to get to know the personalities of different colonies, and with a little muddy exploration, you'll find the spots that offer the easiest harvesting.

ALSO KNOWN AS Glasswort, sea asparagus, picklewort, pickleweed, saltwort, samfur, sea beans, sea/beach asparagus, crow's foot greens (Canada).

EDIBILITY Delicious salty crunch.

IDENTIFICATION Leafless spikes, looking like tiny spineless cacti when they first emerge, soon branch and grow up to 20cm (8in) tall. In the autumn they can turn spectacular yellow and red colours before dying back, leaving their standing skeletons behind.

DISTRIBUTION Common within its habitat across the North Atlantic.

HABITAT Salt marsh, coastal mud and very sheltered sandflats, between the mean high tide line and the splash zone. Salt marshes are often protected habitats, so check the conservation status of areas where you find it.

WHEN TO HARVEST An annual plant, appearing in mid- to late spring and becoming woody by mid-September, so best harvested in June and July.

Similar species

Over 50 species of what we might broadly call marsh samphire have been recorded globally, and there is a good deal of variation within species too, depending on local conditions and in-breeding. Nevertheless, safe identification of the family is relatively straightforward, with no troubling lookalikes.

Common glasswort (*S. europea*) is the most typical of the genus, and this is illustrated and described here. Other species tend to be variations on the theme, with the main differences being morphology (from erect single stems with little branching to more prostrate bushy growth), height (from a finger length to an arm length), substrate (from muds to gravelly sand) and tolerance of wind and wave exposure.

Perennial glasswort (*S. perennis*) is very similar, with creeping woody stems, a bushier growth habit, and tends to grow on the upper, firmer parts of the salt marsh.

A number of other edible coastal succulents resemble marsh samphire in form or name:

- **Annual sea-blite** (see page 139).
- **Salty fingers** (*Disphyma crassifolium*), also known as purple dewplant, has showy purple flowers. It is native to South Africa but is considered a non-native invasive in the North Atlantic.
- **Rock samphire** (see page 105) is an unusual member of the carrot family and the original edible samphire that inhabits rocky shores and cliffs.
- **Golden samphire** (*Limbarda crithmoides*) is in the daisy family and more closely related to sea aster (see page 123). It grows up to 1m (3ft) tall and has dandelion-like flowers.

Sustainable harvesting

Up until the 19th century, marsh samphire beds were commercially harvested and burned to make soda ash for use in making glass and soap. This suggests a certain amount of durability in wild populations, but keep in mind that it performs an important role in stabilizing fragile habitats.

Never uproot marsh samphire, and where it grows densely, move your harvesting around (you will naturally do this as picking is hard on the back). Try to visit different sections of salt marsh each time you go picking, and thin from the middle of colonies, not the edges.

There is a volume-versus-tenderness calculation to make in deciding when to harvest marsh samphire. The first tender spires start to appear in late spring, but they are seldom worth more than a nibble before midsummer. From then on, stems develop fibrous cores that start at the base, slowly becoming more noticeable as they grow. The best harvesting method is to firmly grasp the top third of a stem and trim it off with scissors. If you use a not-too-sharp pair, you will be able, with a little practice, to feel where the fibrous core gives way to nothing but juicy flesh, in much the same way as you might locate where the tender stem of asparagus begins using a knife. Harvesting like this means that, after a good wash, everything you harvest is ready to eat and doesn't require further picking through at home. The plant will continue to grow, albeit rather more densely than it would if left to its own devices. Its little yellow flowers will still appear, and it will set seed as summer progresses.

If you can find some clean seawater to thoroughly rinse the samphire in before taking it home, so much the better. You will save yourself a sinkful of silt and increase the fridge-life of your samphire to a couple of weeks. If you rinse away its salty protection in fresh water, it will degrade much more rapidly, so leave that until you are ready to use it.

Eating marsh samphire

Trudging through thick mud, bent double, can be hard work, but it is well worth the trouble for such a unique and versatile vegetable. Marsh samphire is salty to the point where you can reduce your usual seasonings when cooking with it, yet it still manages to be succulent and refreshing. Wash it thoroughly under a fast-running tap before use; if it has dried-on mud, it may help to soak it for 10 minutes in cold water first. Raw, the tender tips add a delicious saline crunch to sushi, coast-slaw, and potato or rice salad.

Steamed for 2 minutes (or microwaved in a covered bowl with a trickle of water), it makes a delicious finger food with lemon butter or hollandaise sauce for dipping. If you are using older specimens that have developed a woody core, it is practical and pleasurable to drag them between your teeth to remove the flesh. Cooked marsh samphire is often served as an accompaniment to fish, but I think it is at its finest served with lamb – preferably salt marsh lamb, which is quite likely to have nibbled a fair bit of it when it was alive.

If you wish to freeze marsh samphire, first blanch it for a minute, then refresh it in cold water before patting dry and freezing.

A nicer way to preserve marsh samphire is to pickle it. Curiously, its more pungently flavoured namesake rock samphire was the 'original' pickled samphire that became extremely popular in Elizabethan England. Both make exceptionally good, but quite different, pickles. See my guidance for pickling coastal succulents on page 262.

*Flowering stems are
tough and wiry.*

*Tussock-forming
lanceolate leaves often
(but not always) have
a few small points
on the edges.*

*Sea plantain can
grow in most coastal
habitats, but is happiest
in salt marshes.*

Sea plantain

Plantago maritima

Sea plantain is a marvel of evolutionary adaptation. Its narrow leaves offer little resistance to wind and water flow when its marine habitat floods and it can alter its cellular structure in response to increased salinity. A deep taproot anchors it firmly while allowing it to gather precious drops of fresh water. The succulence and waxy coating of the leaves help prevent desiccation. On the salt marsh it can help to stabilize silt and mud, reducing erosion, allowing soil to form and other plants to colonize. Its unshowy flowers are wind-pollinated but still attract insects, bees and butterflies. Grazing animals recognize its rich nourishment and it tends to be tightly cropped where sheep or deer occur in numbers near the coast.

ALSO KNOWN AS Seaside plantain, beach plantain, goose tongue.

EDIBILITY Leaves are crunchy, salty and succulent with some sweetness and mushroomy back notes. Flowers, flower stalks and roots are too fibrous to be worth eating. The seeds are edible, but they are a small and hard-won prize.

IDENTIFICATION Quite a variable plant depending on exposure, substrate and access to fresh water: from small rosettes to large, tussock-like growths reminiscent of candelabras when in full flower. Long, thin, upward-pointing succulent leaves (like fleshy grass), grow up to 30cm (12in) long and up to 1.5cm (½in) wide, V- or U-shaped in cross-section, sometimes (when mature) with sparse, small points on the side of the blades. The flowers are small and greenish-brown with brown stamens, produced in a dense spike on top of a stem that can grow up to 30cm (12in) tall.

DISTRIBUTION Common on most North Atlantic coastlines.

HABITAT Common and prolific in almost all coastal habitats except pure sand/dune systems. Most abundant (and most tasty) in salt marshes and muddy estuaries. It can withstand regular immersion.

WHEN TO HARVEST Year-round in sheltered southerly locations, but generally mid-spring to mid-autumn.

Similar species

There are a few subspecies of sea plantain, all edible and all similar looking to non-botanists: *Plantago maritima* subsp. *maritima* is native to Europe, var. *borealis* grows in Arctic and sub-Arctic regions, and subsp. *juncoides* is native to North America.

Sea arrowgrass (*Triglochin maritima*) often grows right beside sea plantain. It has thinner, rounder leaves that are sheathed at the base, with flowers and seeds more widely dispersed along the stems. (See page 135.)

Buckshorn plantain (*Plantago coronopus*), also known as stagshorn plantain, has flattened rosettes of hairy antler-shaped leaves and usually grows from rocky coastal outcrops, seldom growing as lushly as sea plantain. It is usable in similar ways, but it tends to be more fiddly to harvest and is more bitter. (See page 116.)

Ribwort plantain (*Plantago lanceolata*) is the inland cousin of sea plantain. It is very common in gardens and hedgerows, but often also does well in coastal grasslands, so there is some overlap of habitat. Ribwort plantain can be distinguished by its less succulent broader leaves, with defined longitudinal ribs. If you have tasted ribwort plantain but were put off by its bitterness, you will find sea plantain more rewarding.

Sustainable harvesting

When harvesting sea plantain, thin well-established plants and colonies. Spread your harvesting around, cutting clumps of leaves from bushy growths while taking care to leave the tough flowering stems intact, then moving on to the next clump.

It's a mystery to me why sea plantain rarely gets much more than support-act billing in most foraging guides. Perhaps it is quickly dismissed if sampled from suboptimal locations, where it can become stringy and bitter. But where it grows plump and happy – usually on the salt marsh – I think it is one of the great coastal wild foods. It doesn't quite reach the tenderness of marsh samphire or sea aster, but its rich, crunchy salinity and intriguing back notes of sweet mushroom are delicious and unique. On top of this, it is super-abundant and very easy to harvest in meal-sized quantities for much of the year.

Eating sea plantain

The distinct mushroomy flavour of sea plantain (and other members of the *Plantago* genus) is a gastronomic mystery that I've pondered for many years. *Plantago* species are saturated with endomycorrhizal fungi (fungi that live within the plant), and I hypothesize that these beneficial partners contribute to their mushroomy flavour as well as helping them to grow in challenging locations (though my mycologist friend scoffs at my theory!). Sea plantain also contains sorbitol, a sugar alcohol that offsets the challenges of salinity. It contains one-third fewer calories than sugar and is 60 per cent as sweet. It can have diuretic, laxative and purgative properties in large doses but is generally good for us as part of a balanced diet.

Sea plantain's crunchy succulence makes it great for stir-frying – think of it a bit like string beans – and its long, thin leaves are perfect for rolling in the middle of wild sushi. I like to cook it with mushrooms, where it adds seasoning, spinachy richness and intriguing fungal back notes. It keeps its form well during more extended cooking and is great in risotto – it can be used in place of sea sandwort (see page 59) when it becomes bitter in summer. Its succulence also lends it to pickling, as the leaves don't break down in the acidic pickling solution like thinner inland greens. I particularly like raw sea plantain chopped quite small and added to salads or coast-slaw (see page 75), and it works really well in potato salads.

Coastal potato salad

The first harvests of new potatoes come from sandy coastal soils, which is perhaps why they go so well with pretty much all coastal plants and seaweeds. Treat the following as general guidance rather than a recipe to be slavishly followed – you can make a perfectly delicious bowlful with just the first five ingredients – then embellish it with what you have of the rest.

Basic Ingredients

500g (1lb) new/salad potatoes, washed, boiled in their skins until just cooked, and chopped into 2cm (¾in) pieces

200g (7oz) sea plantain leaves, chopped into 1cm (⅜in) pieces

2 tablespoons grain mustard

Olive oil

Sea salt and pepper to taste

Optional embellishments

6 hard-boiled eggs (or smoked eggs if you can get them), chopped into 2cm (¾in) pieces

Dried seaweed flakes: dulse is best

Dried seaweed powder: pepper dulse is best

Fresh dulse, chopped

Any other crunchy coastal plant, chopped: sea aster, marsh samphire, sea sandwort, sea radish leaf stems and rock samphire all work well

A handful of herbs, finely chopped: fennel, dill, (Scots) lovage, alexanders, etc.

A few spicy leaves, finely chopped: scurvy grass or sea rocket, for example

Pickled wrack 'capers' (see page 169)

Coastal flowers: sea radish, scurvy grass and sea campion are all perfect

Combine the first three ingredients in a bowl, add a good glug of the oil and stir. Season to taste, and add in any of the other ingredients you fancy, scattering the flowers on top just before serving.

Very young flower spikes are tender and delicious.

Leaves sheathe together at the base, which is often tinged with white and purple.

Sea arrowgrass

Triglochin maritima

I stumbled on sea arrowgrass while foraging with a chef on the shores of Loch Etive in north-west Scotland. I thought I was showing him sea plantain and he said 'Wow! Tastes like coriander!' There then followed an exciting half hour as, knowing there were no poisonous grass-like plants on the salt marsh, we learned to distinguish the two by their subtly different flower stalks and flavour. Through subsequent research and personal consumption, I ascertained its safety (with the warning mentioned in the safety note below), and it has become a welcome member of my wild spice rack since.

ALSO KNOWN AS Seaside arrowgrass, common arrowgrass, shore arrowgrass, sea spike-grass.

EDIBILITY The pale base of the leaves, entire young flowering stems, and young seeds all taste of cucumbery coriander/cilantro.

IDENTIFICATION Look for fleshy grass-like leaves up to 60cm (2 ft) that are sheathed together at their pale base, sometimes showing hints of purple around the sheath. A flowering spike has tiny unshowy greenish-purple flowers that look more like seeds to the naked eye. They are very close together when the flower spike first emerges (at which point the whole flower spike can be eaten), growing more distant as it matures (during which time the flower spike stem becomes too tough to eat), and ultimately forming green seeds, which are edible at first but soon harden and turn pale brown. There are no similar-looking poisonous plants in the same habitat, so a small nibble will help to confirm the coriander (cilantro) flavour.

DISTRIBUTION Common around the North Atlantic.

HABITAT Salt marshes, muddy estuaries and low-lying coastal grassland.

WHEN TO HARVEST First leaves appear in early spring, flowering stems in late spring/summer.

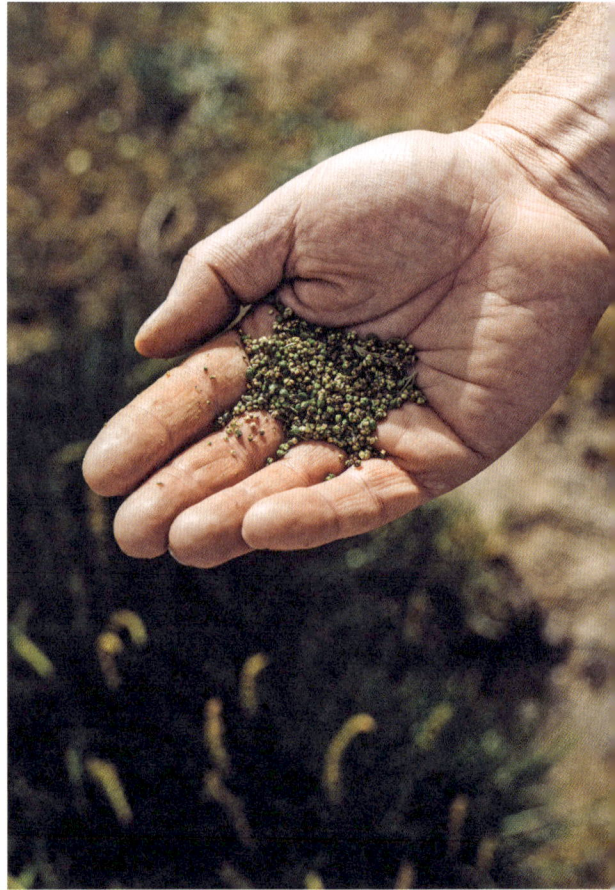

Safety note

Sea arrowgrass in general, and the green parts of the leaves in particular, can contain toxic compounds known as cyanogenic glycosides. These compounds are similar to the precursors to hydrogen cyanide found in apple pips and cherry pits. They develop when the plant is stressed by drought or intensive grazing. They are considerably more problematic to grazing ruminants than humans, and a healthy adult would need to eat over 300g (11oz) of the green or dried parts in one sitting to receive a problematic dose. Given that it is the pale stem base, tender flower shoots and young seeds that are eaten, and that all parts become tasteless and unpalatable when dry, it's highly unlikely that you'd be able to consume a troublesome amount.

Similar species

Sea arrowgrass often grows beside sea plantain (see page 131), and it can be easy to mix them up. The key difference is that sea plantain leaves are distinctly U-shaped in cross-section, while sea arrowgrass leaves are more rounded in cross-section. A non-coastal and similar looking relation is marsh arrowgrass (*Triglochin palustris*), which grows in freshwater marshes. It can be used in similar ways and has the same health warning.

Sustainable harvesting

Sea arrowgrass is tussock-forming, creating a ring of elevated soil with its root mat that does not become water-logged, which other plants can colonize. It can make up to one third of the ground cover of salt marshes and can be thinned easily. In less favourable locations, it may form just the occasional tussock, especially on the edge of water channels. Use a knife to cut leaves and young flower spikes at the base, and strip the green seeds from older flower spikes. As the seeds mature, they harden and lose flavour, so they are not a substitute for the dry coriander seeds widely used as a spice in curries and gins.

Eating sea arrowgrass

I once had someone attend one of my guided walks who had a severe coriander (cilantro) allergy and was curious as to whether they would be able to safely eat sea arrowgrass. Not being aware of any research in that area, I advised against it, but they decided to try some, with their partner poised beside them with an EpiPen in case they went into anaphylaxis! After a nervous wait, they confirmed they were fine and were delighted to have a new herb/spice in their repertoire. I pass this on in the hope that it may help someone else in the same situation, but with the proviso that one person's allergy may not be based on the same chemical mechanisms as another's ... so have the EpiPen ready if you try!

If you catch the flower spikes young, when they are still greenish-purple and tender, they are a delight to eat raw, like tiny aromatic asparagus spears – one of the best gourmet treats of the coast and a fantastic garnish for fish, shellfish and vegetable dishes.

The green seeds and chopped stem bases can be used in place of fresh coriander – scattered on curries, tossed through salads or in sushi. Try adding them to pickles, pestos and ferments too. They lose some of their aromatic flavour and emit an unpleasant smell when cooked, so they are best used fresh and raw. Do not dry them.

*Succulent but
narrow leaves.*

*Stems quickly become
tough and wiry.*

*As sea-blite matures,
it turns red and seed
capsules form.*

Sea-blite

Suaeda spp.

Don't be put off by sea-blite's discouraging sounding name. Blite is an old English word derived from the Latin word for spinach, and sea-blite can be used as a salty, thinner version of just that. Sea-blite occupies similar niches to marsh samphire (see page 127), and novices sometimes confuse the two. This is not a troublesome error, as they can be used in very similar ways. The key difference is that sea-blite has distinct (if needle-like) leaves, while marsh samphire is all (fleshy) stem and tends to be more regularly submerged at high tide.

ALSO KNOWN AS Annual sea-blite, herbaceous seepweed, common sea-blite, white sea-blite, seaspray, sea rosemary, shrubby sea-blite. Various species and subspecies often go by overlapping names; see notes on similar species overleaf.

EDIBILITY The thin but succulent shoots and leaves are pleasant tasting, if somewhat salty. The seeds can also be eaten.

IDENTIFICATION Alternate, hairless, narrow leaves (like soft, fleshy needles) are green or green-blue at first, often turning yellow or red as the summer progresses. Tiny, petalless flowers grow in small whorls at the bases of the leaves in summer.

DISTRIBUTION One or more species of sea-blite is common all around the North Atlantic – see notes on similar species overleaf.

HABITAT Predominantly the upper reaches of salt marshes, occasionally sheltered shingle or sandy beaches.

WHEN TO HARVEST Spring and summer. More red colouration as summer progresses signifies higher salt content.

Similar species

There are three species of sea-blite in the North Atlantic of interest to foragers, all similar enough in appearance and usage to be interchangeable. This is fortunate, as there is a great deal of overlap in their common names and distinguishing them can be tricky, especially early in the year.

Suaeda maritima is a sprawling, low-growing annual known as annual sea-blite in the UK, but as herbaceous sea-blite in North America. *Suaeda linearis* is a perennial of the east coast of North America that grows more upright and is (confusingly) known there as annual sea-blite. *Suaeda vera*, or shrubby sea blite, develops woody stems and grows up to the size of a small shrub in sheltered salt marshes in southern Europe up to southern England.

If this weren't all confusing enough, there are two rare species of sea blite native to the east coast of North America that are protected and should not be picked: *Suaeda calceoliformis* (American sea-blite) and *Suaeda maritima* subsp. *richii* (the native strain of American herbaceous sea-blite). Both look very similar to the more common species. On top of this, all sea-blites exhibit high phenotype plasticity, meaning they will grow slightly differently according to the tidal conditions, substrate, exposure and salinity of their locale.

The upshot of all this is that European foragers can harvest sea-blite freely (though, of course, with their usual sensitivity), while North American foragers should invest some time in learning to distinguish between species if they wish to harvest any at all – see my notes on the sensitivity of salt marshes on page 121.

Harvesting and eating sea-blite

When the first shoots appear, the stem of sea-blite is tender enough to eat along with the leaves. As spring progresses, the stem becomes wiry, and the leaves should be stripped from a few twigs per plant. The best way to do this is to hold the tip of the twig and pull your fingers from top to bottom – the leaves detach much more readily in that direction.

Sea-blite can be used in all the ways I describe for marsh samphire – salads, stir-fries, sushi, pickles, as a side vegetable, etc. – though it tends to be a little less juicy and can become somewhat astringent towards the end of its season. It stores surplus salt in its leaves, which turn an intense red as they become more saturated. In this condition, they make a glamorous seasoning sprinkled on salads and cooked dishes.

Opposite page: Sea-blite in early summer. Right: Sea-blite can turn spectacularly red later in the year. It is still edible at this stage, but saltier.

Thick, oval, blue-green leaves, often with a mealy texture.

Sea purslane

Halimione portulacoides

Halimione, the generic name of European sea purslane, means 'daughter of the sea', and it is certainly well adapted to life by the ocean with its squat growth and small fleshy leaves. These contain micronutrients like zinc, iron, copper and cobalt, and have a silvery appearance due to the tiny papery scales that cover them, trapping air and protecting the plant against the drying effects of salt and sun.

ALSO KNOWN AS *Atriplex portulacoides*.

EDIBILITY Leaves are tasty, if somewhat fiddly to harvest.

IDENTIFICATION Bushy perennial shrub up to 45cm (1½ft), but usually sprawling, with thin woody stems bearing oppositely paired small oval leaves that are blue-green with a silvery sheen. In summer, tiny yellowish flowers grow in small sprays on branch ends.

DISTRIBUTION Common in its habitat throughout Europe as far north as southern Scotland. *Halimione portulacoides* does not grow in North America, but another edible coastal plant, *Sesuvium portulacastrum*, goes by the same common name – see notes on similar species overleaf.

HABITAT Salt marshes and estuaries, favouring the sides of small creeks and channels in more exposed locations. Occasionally found in other coastal habitats such as sheltered shingle.

WHEN TO HARVEST Year-round in most of its range, but best in spring and summer.

Similar species

There are a number of wild plants that have purslane in their names but are unrelated to any of the species mentioned here. I recommend checking the binomial name of any 'purslane' you research online.

Pedunculate sea purslane (*H. pedunculata*) is an extremely rare annual with alternate leaves, found at just a few sites in south-east England. It should not be picked.

Shrubby orache (*Atriplex halimus*) is a larger, shrubbier-looking version of sea purslane that is native to France and the Mediterranean but recently established and spreading in southern England.

Shoreline purslane (*Sesuvium portulacastrum)* is found in the US, from the Carolinas southwards. Although not related to the sea purslane of Europe, it is edible in similar ways. It grows not in salt marshes but on the seaward side of sand dunes and has small five-petaled, showy pink flowers that open for just a few hours each day. Slender purslane (*Sesuvium maritimum*), also grows coastally and is too rare to harvest in most states.

Below: Shoreline purslane is found beside dunes in south-western states of the US but not in Europe.
Below right: European sea purslane (*Hermalione portulacoides*) grows plumpest on the edges of brackish channels.

Harvesting and eating sea purslane

Sea purslane can't tolerate deer or sheep grazing, but copes fine with some considered human thinning by plucking individual leaves, or carefully pruning off the tips and picking out the tough stems at home. The largest leaves and most efficient harvesting is usually from the plants growing furthest from the sea, but even then picking is fiddly work. Try not to disturb the flowering tips as the seeds are good winter foods for sea birds.

The dainty size, elegant colour and salty tang of sea purslane leaves make them an excellent raw garnish for fish or lamb dishes. Try scattering them on roast potatoes or pizza for the last 5 minutes in the oven, or mixing with new potatoes just before serving. They work well with tomatoes and are good in potato salad (see page 133).

Light cooking by boiling, steaming or stir-frying will reduce the saltiness of the leaves, but don't overdo it or they will also lose all their charm. If you have the patience to gather enough, they pickle very well – see my directions for cold pickling on page 261. Their texture and salty tang also make them an excellent ingredient in green oil-bound sauces like chimichurri or salsa verde – see page 107 for a recipe.

Wild Coastal Sushi Rolls

My favourite way to taste the vibrant flavours and textures of wild coastal plants is to roll them into sushi. The long, thin leaves of salt marsh plants such as sea plantain, sea aster and marsh samphire lend themselves particularly well to this, as do seaweeds like sea spaghetti or Dumont's tubular weed and the stems of sea radish and sea kale. The pungent mustardy kick of sea rocket, scurvy grass and sea radish siliques make good wasabi substitutes and sweet crowberry vinegar (see page 116) mixed through the rice make it extra sticky (and pink!). A garnish of umeboshi sloes (see page 37) completes the wild sushi experience.

You could even have a go at making the nori sheets from laver seaweed, but it is a tricky process. Producing sheets thin and pliable enough to roll requires specialist equipment like screens and clamps, and they don't keep at all well. After some moderate but time-consuming success making tasty cardboard, I have admitted defeat and buy pre-made nori sheets when I want to roll sushi.

The Intertidal Zone: Seaweeds

Forests of the sea

tormented by air
we wait for our fierce mother
to quench and caress

Seaweed has historically had a bit of an image problem around the North Atlantic. Disliked as a stinky, slip-hazard on the beach, or for its slithery groping of swimmers, even its name – sea-weed – dismisses it as a nuisance.

Part of the problem is that most casual coast users only experience seaweed when it is either washed up dead, or lying asleep waiting for the sea's return. We probably wouldn't feel so fond of our meadows and forests if they laid prostrate and impenetrable every time we visited them. The best way to fully appreciate seaweed is to meet it in its own world, underwater. Through a snorkelling mask, those sorry strandings that hold their breath on the beach at low tide, grow vibrant and vivacious, beckoning sunlight, rejoicing in currents, and every bit as animated as a forest in full leaf on a breezy day.

Marine forests are just as complex and diverse as those made by their plant descendants on dry land. From tiny moss-like growths on rocks through a complex understory to a broad tree-like canopy, seaweeds are food, home and nursery to a wealth of aquatic animals. They are also good at sucking up carbon dioxide (though perhaps not so good at sequestering it for long periods), and help dissipate the destructive action of waves.

Foraging is a wonderful and rewarding way of entering into a wider appreciation of this world. In terms of both flavour and nutrition, no other area of foraging brings so many surprising rewards with so few worries. The very act of searching for seaweeds nourishes our souls as much as our bodies by leading us to one of the last accessible truly wide places – the intertidal zone, where beauty and treasure cling to every rock.

Understanding seaweeds

Seaweeds are as diverse as their descendants on dry land: a large kelp and a small encrusting algae are as different from one another as a tree is from a blade of grass, and even more distantly related. Nevertheless, the challenges of living in turbulent seas have resulted in some shared characteristics.

Seaweed anatomy

In scientific circles seaweeds are known as macroscopic marine algae and are divided into three groups according to their pigmentation: green, red and brown. This variation in colours comes from light-harvesting pigments that have evolved to maximize photosynthesis in different depths of water and levels of light. These labels can be misleading though, as some scientifically red seaweeds can look decidedly brown, and many brown seaweeds can look green(ish). Most scientifically green seaweeds, however, are a definite vibrant green colour.

Almost all seaweeds have a strong holdfast to anchor them to rocks, and slippery coatings to allow them to move freely through potentially destructive waves. These coatings are high in alginates and glutamates – important compounds in the food, medicinal and cosmetic uses of seaweeds. Some use gas-filled bladders to lift them towards daylight when underwater. Some also form gel-filled bladders (known as receptacles) that release reproductive eggs and sperm into the water, often during spring tides.

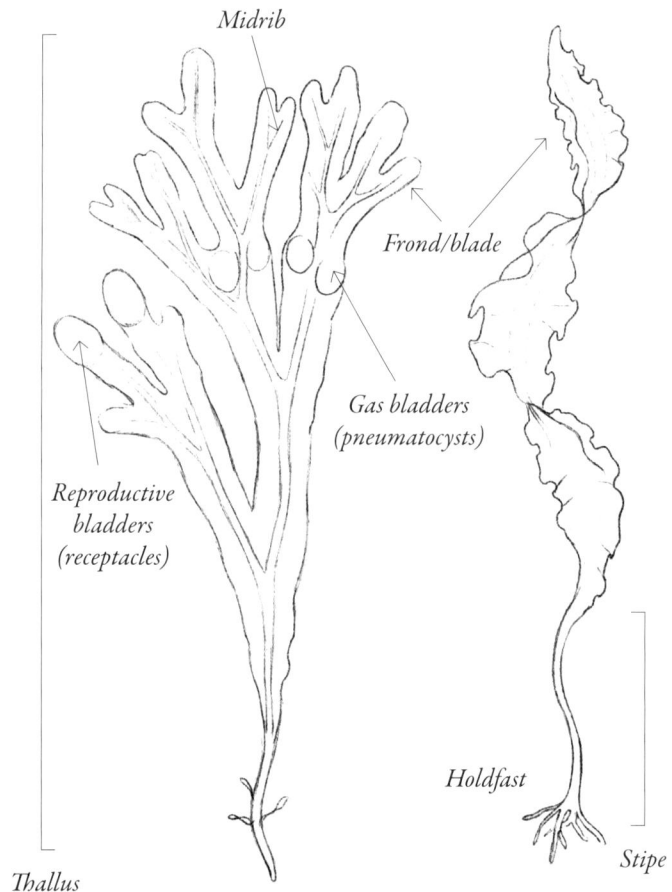

Midrib

Frond/blade

Gas bladders (pneumatocysts)

Reproductive bladders (receptacles)

Holdfast

Thallus

Stipe

Medicinal and nutritional benefits of seaweeds

Seaweeds are the most highly mineralized vegetables on earth, accumulating and concentrating minerals directly from the ocean. Research is ongoing into just how bio-available these nutrients are when eaten by humans, but there is little doubt that regular consumption of seaweed is, in general, very good for us. Below are some of the key scientifically validated benefits of seaweeds. These apply to some degree to all the seaweeds I mention in this book so I won't repeat them for each species. There is of course some variation between species, and I have noted any significant differences in the individual species pages.

High iodine content supporting healthy thyroid function: The thyroid is a gland in your neck that helps produce and regulate hormones. An underactive thyroid can result in a wide range of symptoms such as fatigue, muscle weakness, high cholesterol, depression, a higher susceptibility to diseases and difficulty losing weight. It is possible to consume too much iodine so don't gorge on seaweeds, and anyone diagnosed with an overactive thyroid should consult their doctor if they intend to eat a lot.

High levels of vitamins A and C, and a great source of calcium: Red seaweeds in particular can be useful in the treatment of osteoarthritis.

Potent source of antioxidants: Helps prevent inflammation, and can help the body fight a host of ailments that include arthritis, cancer, coeliac disease, asthma, depression and obesity.

Helps regulate oestrogen and estradiol levels: These are hormones responsible for proper development and function of sexual organs, potentially reducing the risk of breast cancer.

High protein content: Some seaweeds are almost as high in protein as legumes.

High in vitamin B_{12}: Vitamin B_{12} is important for DNA synthesis, red blood cell formation, nerve function, and converting food into energy. It is most often encountered in animal products, especially fish, meat, poultry, eggs and dairy products so seaweed is an excellent natural source for anyone following a plant-based diet.

High levels of soluble fibre, supporting healthy digestion: Seaweed fibre forms a gel in the gut, slowing down the digestive process and inhibiting the absorption of sugars and cholesterol. Eating a small amount of seaweed can leave you feeling full for some time afterwards.

Where to find seaweeds

All but a handful of seaweeds need to anchor themselves to rock, so in general, you'll encounter a greater variety on a steeply shelving rocky coast as opposed to, say, gently shelving sandy beaches.

Different species of seaweed are highly specialized to a particular tidal range. Some can survive with only a splattering of spindrift at high tide, while others need to be fully immersed for almost all their lives, only being exposed to foragers on the very lowest tides. Strong currents and exposed locations can result in bigger, tastier seaweeds due to the higher flow of nutrients in the water. The ability to cope with the destructive force of crashing waves is a significant factor in where different species grow, and how big they grow. Different levels of wave exposure can result in varied growth forms within species too.

Seaweeds feed by absorbing nutrients from the sea and by photosynthesis. Silty water can reduce the maximum size a seaweed will grow to, though there are some specialists of murky estuaries. Some species can tolerate variable levels of salinity, and these tend to proliferate in estuaries. The species I cover here prefer the cooler waters of the North Atlantic, but there are regional variations, and on a local scale, some may prefer the quick-warming waters of shallow coasts, while others may do better in cooler ocean swells.

With a little practice, you will start to notice patterns and learn to predict where and when different seaweeds will be in good condition. The best general guidance I can give is that the optimum time and place to forage for seaweed is on a rocky outcrop on a relatively exposed bit of coast on a super-low tide in spring.

DISTRIBUTION OF CHOICE SEAWEEDS BY TIDAL RANGE

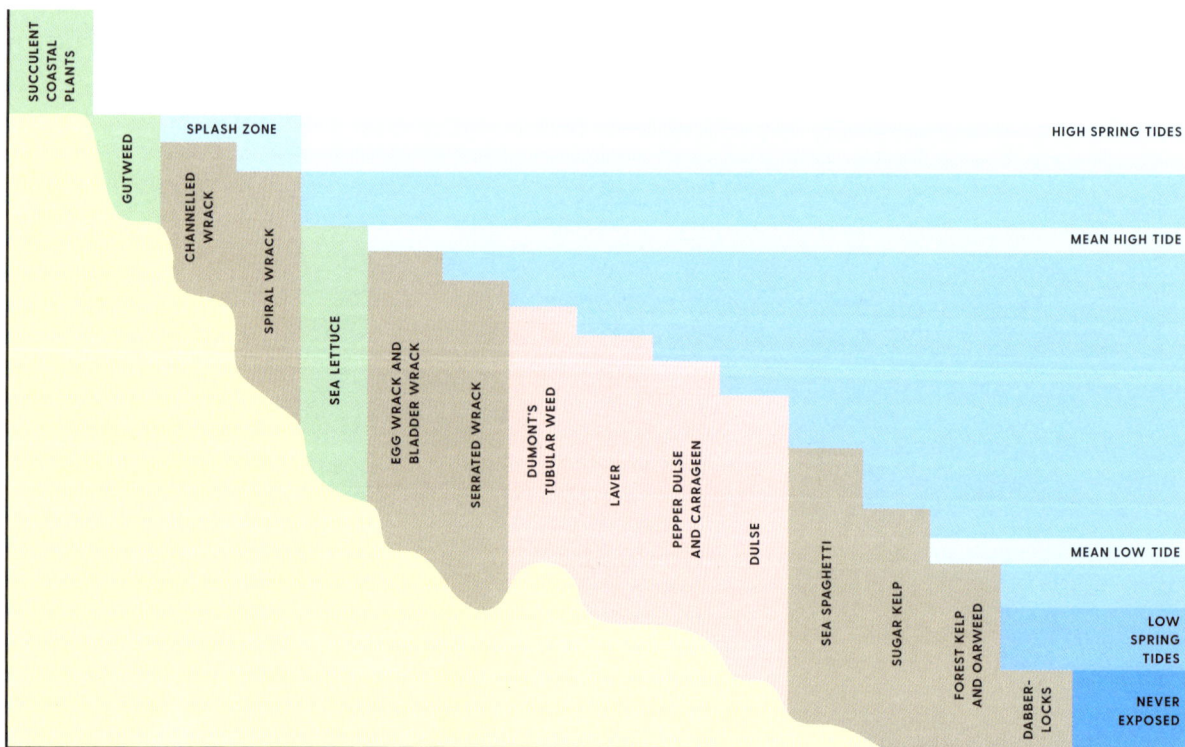

When to find seaweeds

Like plants, seaweeds have distinct life cycles. Some are annual, growing and drying back completely each year, while others are perennial – kelps over 50 years old have been recorded. Most have periods of strong growth (characterized by more vibrant flavours and higher nutrient content), reproduction (where they are likely to be weaker and out of condition, but may offer swollen 'fruits'), and dormancy. Different species follow different rhythms but, in general, April to June are the best times to harvest most seaweeds for the pot in the North Atlantic. Most spawning occurs during May to September.

SEAWEEDS BY SEASON

	SPRING	SUMMER	AUTUMN	WINTER
WRACKS				
SEA LETTUCE				
GUTWEED				
DUMONT'S TUBULAR WEED				
LAVER				
CARRAGEEN				
PEPPER DULSE				
DULSE				
SEA SPAGHETTI				
MERMAID'S TRESSES				
KELPS				
WIREWEED				
DABBERLOCKS				
VELVET HORN				

BEST TIME TO HARVEST	OK TO HARVEST	UNAVAILABLE/NOT WORTHWHILE

Harvesting seaweeds

Although there are vast amounts of seaweeds around our coasts, complex ecosystems are intricately entwined around that abundance. Though they may look like slimy piles of goo when the tide is out, try to treat them with the same respect you would the plants and trees of a forest or hedgerow, taking no more than you need, and appreciating them as food and home for a great many other fascinating and ecologically important species. Be prepared to adapt your harvesting techniques and strategies to different species and different locations.

Look for living seaweeds
Harvest only living, healthy seaweeds that are still attached to rocks in clean water. Free-floating or stranded seaweeds are dead and decomposing (see pages 220 and 265 for how to evaluate water quality). With experience it is safe to selectively harvest freshly storm-tossed seaweeds, but I don't recommend this for beginners.

Don't pull seaweeds from the rocks
This is equivalent to uprooting plants – and you don't get any root! Using a sharp knife or scissors, cut only up to the top one-third of any individual plant (or see my species-specific variations). This will allow it to regrow and/or spawn. I favour scissors over a knife for harvesting most seaweeds, especially the small fiddly ones that you are trimming from rocks – like giving a rock a haircut!

Try to keep trampling to a minimum
This should come naturally, as seaweeds tend to be very slippery!

Spread your picking around
It may be a rock pool to you, but it's a universe to a shrimp. Pick a little here and there, rather than stripping a whole rock of its jungle. Try to rotate harvesting areas from year to year, leaving two to three years between visits.

Handle with care
Don't crush seaweeds – the small red seaweeds like pepper dulse and Dumont's tubular weed will go off very quickly if crushed.

Take multiple containers
Unless you are focused on just one species of seaweed, I recommend taking multiple containers on a low-tide foray. Some seaweeds are small and fiddly while others are large and heavy, and it saves a lot of time and effort if you separate them as you harvest. Lidded plastic tubs work for small species like pepper dulse and carrageen, a good-sized bucket or mesh bag for large blades of kelp, and ziplock bags for everything in between. Seawater can quickly degrade baskets made with natural fibres, but mesh bags, of the type used to transport shellfish, or the reusable ones you get in the vegetable aisle of supermarkets, work well and allow for easy rinsing.

Rinse as you pick
You will usually need to rinse seaweeds again in clean water at home, but the more sand and passengers you can remove at the coast, the better. Seaweed washed only in seawater will taste more salty.

Use as soon as possible
Keep unprocessed seaweeds in the fridge in sealed tubs or plastic bags. Do not store them in fresh water. Do not rinse seaweeds with fresh water until you are ready to use/process them – their sea saltiness helps keep them fresher.

Beware of contaminants

Sadly our oceans, and especially our coastal waters, are becoming increasingly polluted, so you should consider the water quality anywhere you intend to harvest seaweed. I cover how to assess seawater quality in depth in the chapter on shellfish (see page 220). Seaweeds come with much fewer safety concerns than shellfish, but seaweed foragers should certainly pay close attention to the sections on bacteria and water quality, algae and algal blooms, and chemicals.

Later in their growing season, and especially in more sheltered locations, some species of seaweed can become home to Bryozoa – minute colony-forming creatures that form a crust on the thallus or blade. Sea mat (*Membranipora membranacea*) is the most common of these, appearing as a pale hard coating on the blades. Bryozoa are harmless, but unpleasantly crunchy. They can be scraped off with the back of your nail, but this becomes laborious if you are harvesting any quantity, so it's best to avoid settled specimens if possible.

However well you rinse wild harvested seaweeds in the sea, they are still likely to arrive in your kitchen with tiny crustaceans clinging tightly to them. Regardless of how thorough you are with your rinsing, a few of these will hang on and only become noticeable when they turn shellfish orange during dehydration or cooking. These are quite benign, texturally much less troublesome than sand, and can even add a nice bit of seafood flavouring, but they do mean that most foraged seaweeds, especially the finer textured ones, are unsuitable for anyone with a severe crustacean allergy.

Rinsing

When you are ready to use them, rinse your seaweeds thoroughly in multiple changes of clean water – some species trap more sand than others. By washing then straining into a white or clear bowl, you can monitor how much sand is still coming out on each rinse, continuing until the water runs clear. Once rinsed, get rid of excess moisture in a salad spinner, or by gently patting dry with a clean tea towel.

Inedible seaweeds

Seaweed foraging is less fraught with anxiety for novices than plant or mushroom foraging as there are no poisonous species of seaweed in the North Atlantic – provided the seaweed you plan to eat is alive and growing in clean water, and you are harvesting it on foot. But don't confuse this with the common myth that 'all seaweeds are edible' – they are not.

Acid weed (*Desmarestia* spp.)
Four species of this brown seaweed grow in the North Atlantic, usually below the low tide line, though you may find them lurking in deep, non-draining rock pools. They exude an acid with a pH of around 2, which, though not so acidic as stomach acid, would be decidedly unpleasant to eat. This acidity has evolved to deter grazing marine molluscs, so acid weed is usually surrounded by a lot of water. It does not fare well on dry land, dissolving both itself and any other seaweed it gets mixed up with into a gloopy mush rather quickly. It is fine-fronded and doesn't resemble any of the species in this book. You would have to try really hard to poison yourself with acid weed!

Red harpoon weed (*Asparagopsis armata*)
Like acid weed, this small red seaweed and its near relations in the family Bonnemaisoniaceae, which ply their trade below the high spring tide, produce noxious compounds that inhibit grazers and other seaweeds, and, though there is little research on them, would likely make for an uncomfortable gastronomic experience. You are even less likely to come across these than acid weed.

Coral weed (*Corallina officinalis*)
You are much more likely to encounter the group of small red seaweeds known as coral weed. They grow in dense tufts of beautiful fine red fronds with pale tips and are heavily calcified, which makes for an unappetizing crunchy texture. Not on the menu, but they do make decent scourers and exfoliants.

Eating & cooking with seaweeds

I have not found a single savoury dish that can't be improved by adding the right type of seaweed, but if you expect to fill a pan with seaweed, boil it up and eat it like cabbage, you will be disappointed. To help you get the right seaweed for the right job I have summarized the best species for each role below.

Seasoning: *Gutweed, pepper dulse, wrack siphon weed, Dumont's tubular weed, laver, dulse, velvet horn, sea lettuce.* Just as land plants form chemical compounds to deter grazing animals, so do seaweeds, which has resulted in some surprising and delicious flavours. Seaweeds can be used fresh as seasoning but tend to deteriorate quickly, so they are most often dehydrated and ground into flakes or powder, then added to recipes or sprinkled directly on food. They also bring a natural salinity, so you can use less salt.

Vegetable substitute: *Wrack (young tips and reproductive bladders), laver, sea lettuce, dulse, velvet horn, dabberlocks, kelp (young blades).* Not many seaweeds work as direct replacements for vegetables, but with careful handling and an open mind, some species work as 'sea vegetables'.

Pasta substitute: *Dumont's tubular weed, sea spaghetti, mermaid's tresses, kelp (blades, cut like lasagne or tagliatelle).* The texture of a few seaweeds resembles some forms of pasta and can be used in its place or mixed through it. Seaweed is much lower in carbohydrates than pasta, but (with the exception of Dumont's tubular weed) these seaweeds are similarly bulky, filling and neutral tasting.

Flavour enhancer: *Wrack (tips/thallus), laver, carrageen, grape pip weed, sea lettuce, dulse, kelp (blades), dabberlocks.* Seaweeds have a long history of use in Eastern cuisine for their flavour-enhancing properties. Naturally occurring compounds, called glutamates, provide umami, a taste sensation that adds richness and bass notes to anything it accompanies. These properties allow seaweed to make 'meaty' tasting dishes using little or no meat. If added whole, the seaweed is usually removed from the dish before eating, rather like bones or bay leaves from a stock pot, or it may be incorporated by adding dried flakes or powder. All the seaweeds that work as flavour enhancers also add vitamins and minerals.

Thickening or setting agent: *Carrageen, grape pip weed.* Seaweeds produce compounds that help them slip through rough seas. In the kitchen, these substances can be harnessed to thicken soups, sauces and stews, and set desserts such as jelly and blancmange. All seaweeds exude some form of thickener when heated, adding body, minerals and flavour, but carrageen and grape pip weed are used almost exclusively for this purpose as they are high in setting agents but have very little flavour.

Wrapping for food: *Wrack (especially good for hangi and clam bakes, not so good for making parcels), sea lettuce, laver, dulse, kelp, dabberlocks.* As an alternative to the very plastic-reliant, sous vide ('under vacuum') technique, I've coined the term 'sous weed' for swaddling things in seaweed to retain moisture and add natural seasoning during cooking (see page 206). The seaweed wrapping may become a crisp, roasted seasoning to eat with its contents, though how tempting this is depends on which species, degree of heat, length of cooking, etc. You can use any of the larger seaweed species for this, and larger individuals within species that may not be so appealing for other food uses.

Seaweed oil: *Medium to large seaweeds are best for this, e.g. sea lettuce, wracks, kelp.* Seaweed can be infused into oil to release umami seasoning and minerals. Use dried seaweed, as it doesn't introduce water to the oil, reducing the chance of spoilage. To make seaweed oil, first dehydrate your chosen seaweed or seaweed blend. A couple of tablespoons, or the unground equivalent (e.g. four finger-sized pieces of kelp) will do for a standard jam jar. Put the seaweed in the jar and top it up with your preferred choice of oil (a neutrally flavoured olive oil works well) and leave for one month, shaking occasionally. To accelerate the infusion, pop the whole jar, with lid firmly screwed on, in the dishwasher for one regular hot cycle (about two hours). This works like a low-temperature water bath.

Preserving seaweeds

If you aren't going to use your seaweed in a recipe right away, you'll want to preserve it. There are three main ways of going about this: freezing, pickling and dehydrating.

Freezing

Although seaweeds are resistant to natural freezing in the wild because of their relatively high salt content, they can be frozen at home. I recommend cooking them prior to freezing, but if you do want to freeze them from fresh, medium-sized seaweeds such as laver, dulse and sea lettuce are the best candidates. Deeper-water species such as sea spaghetti and kelps have a higher water content, making them prone to cell rupturing when they are defrosted, resulting in slimy, unappealing seaweeds. Small seaweeds such as pepper dulse and Dumont's tubular weed also tend to break down and become unappetizing when frozen and defrosted.

Cooking seaweed prior to freezing is a better way to go, and especially good for those with long cooking times, such as laver. Freeze portion-sized tubs of ready-to-use seaweeds and they will quickly become kitchen staples – there are very few soups and stews that aren't improved by lobbing in some cooked laver, in the same way as you might toss in a lump of frozen cooked spinach.

Pickling

The crisp texture and umami flavour of some seaweeds make them great candidates for cold pickling (see page 261). The best species for this are sea lettuce, sea spaghetti, mermaid's tresses, wrack (tips and receptacles) dabberlocks and kelp.

Seaweeds also make excellent embellishments to other pickles, adding salt, umami and spice – see page 261 for ideas. As unattached seaweeds naturally decompose in the sea, they tend not to do well in brine and hence do not ferment very well. They can be added in small amounts to other more willing ferments, however – for example, try adding a teaspoon of dulse flakes to a jar of sauerkraut.

Dehydrating

Dehydration is the most effective way to preserve seaweeds. By drying them out completely you will shrink them to about a quarter of their original weight and volume, and they will keep in an airtight container for a year or more, losing very little of their flavour and other culinary qualities. Dried seaweeds are quick to rehydrate and easy to grind into flakes or powders.

Once rinsed and superficially dried, there are several ways to dehydrate seaweeds. Naturally drying them in a warm, airy space is usually the most energy-efficient: large seaweeds such as the kelps can be hung on washing lines, while smaller seaweeds are best laid out on wire racks.

Solar dehydrators, glass-lidded cabinets designed to heat up in sunlight and maximize airflow, can accelerate drying, but in most maritime regions it's unlikely that you will be able to fully dehydrate them unless you have a very sunny window ledge or an excellent summer drying day.

For anyone who regularly forages for seaweeds, a dehydrator is well worth the investment. I recommend getting something bigger than the smallest models – their racks won't fit more than a blade or two of kelp on each shelf. To preserve as much flavour and nutrition as possible, try to use the minimum amount of heat practicable when using a dehydrator, though it's fine to nudge it up a little to initially get rid of the bulk of the moisture.

Partially dehydrated seaweeds will lose flavour and may become mouldy, so don't take short cuts. I often get asked how long seaweed should be dehydrated for, but there are too many variables to give an exact answer, including species of seaweed, temperature and air flow. A fully dehydrated seaweed should feel bone-dry and brittle rather than bendy, though some – notably dulse, laver and kelp – can remain pliable when fully dehydrated. The drying process can be finished in a very low oven with the fan running, but watch it like a hawk – you don't want to cook your seaweed, and dried seaweed burns quickly!

Storing and grinding dehydrated seaweeds

Once seaweeds are fully dehydrated, there are a number of ways to store and use them. If you expect to keep them for a while, it is better to store them in larger pieces, then grind them in small batches as and when you need them, a little like storing and using whole spices. Keep the pieces in sealed jars or ziplock bags and label them clearly, as they can all look quite similar once dried. Keep them out of direct sunlight.

Lightly toasting dried seaweed in a low oven or dry frying pan before grinding enhances umami and adds a delightful toasted flavour (especially to laver and sea lettuce) and ensures it is fully dry, which helps with grinding.

Some dried seaweeds can be flaked and crumbled by hand, others may require a mortar and pestle, and some are best done in a spice or coffee grinder. How finely you grind your seaweed will depend on the species and what you plan to use it for – flakes are nice for sprinkling on things, while powders are better for general seasoning.

Cooking with dehydrated seaweeds

For making stock and background flavours in soups, sauces, etc, whole dried blades, fronds or pieces can be added straight to the pan during cooking. For example, try adding some kelp blades to rice or couscous as it cooks. Flakes and powders can be used just like bouillon powders – added directly while cooking or mixed into hot water first to make stock.

Where you intend to use dried seaweed in a salad or as a vegetable, it can be rehydrated by leaving it in cold water for 10 minutes or until it regains its fresh texture.

I have provided quantities for fresh and dried seaweeds in the recipes in this book, but if you are ever looking to convert between the two, reckon on dried seaweed being 25–30 per cent of its fresh weight.

Below: Dried seaweed spices and seasonings. Clockwise from top: carrageen, whole, for thickening/nutrients; pepper dulse powder, a potent spice; gutweed salt; powdered sea lettuce, a delightful seasoning; toasted laver powder for instant umami; sugar kelp flakes for adding salt/umami to stews. Centre: dulse flakes, great for sprinkling on salads.

Channel wrack

Tooth wrack

Bladder wrack

Spiral wrack

Egg wrack

Wracks

Wrack is the general term for a group of medium-sized branched brown seaweeds that dominate the upper and middle intertidal zone, especially in sheltered areas, providing dense cover for crustaceans, anemones and small fish, and grazing for marine gastropods such as winkles and limpets. Many species have air-filled bladders to help them float, and gel-filled reproductive bladders known as receptacles. Different species of wrack occupy subtly different niches according to their tolerance of exposure to air, wave action and salinity. Although classed as brown seaweeds, they look browny-green, becoming more vibrant as their growth season progresses, then duller again in their dormant season. They darken in colour as they dry, so can look almost black between tides, especially on a dry, breezy day. The following wrack species comprise 95 per cent of all the wracks you are ever likely to meet in the North Atlantic, listed according to their place in the tidal range, from top to bottom.

EDIBILITY Not the most glamorous of seaweeds in the kitchen, but useful and abundant so well worth getting to know. The principal edible parts are the growing tips and the receptacles. Stems and float bladders tend to be too tough for general use, but can be dried and ground to make a mineral-rich umami thickener.

DISTRIBUTION Widespread and abundant all around the North Atlantic.

HABITAT Attached to bedrock and boulders from the splash zone to the subtidal.

WHEN TO HARVEST Year-round, but different species and different parts are in season at different times – see individual species notes.

The word wrack comes from the Old English word wræc, *meaning 'persecution' or 'misery'. This evolved into meaning something wrecked or destroyed, and from there it was just a short jump to referring to storm-cast seaweeds as wrack. Because of limited understanding of what constitutes a healthy seaweed, it became the general term for this family.*

Channel wrack

Pelvetia canaliculata

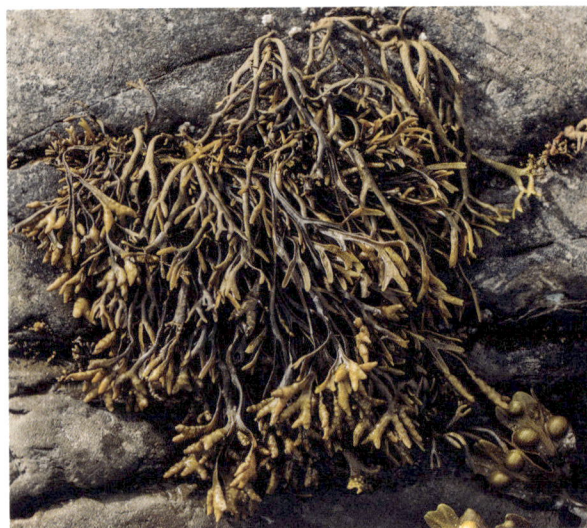

ALSO KNOWN AS Channelled wrack, cow tang.

SIZE Grows up to 15cm (6in) long with fronds 5mm (¼in) wide.

BEST USES Add tender fronds and young tips to soups and stir-fries, or simmer in water for 5 minutes to tenderize, refresh in cold water and add to salads. Pickles well.

Smaller than other wracks and hyper-abundant around the high tide line/splash zone, channel wrack can be harvested on all but the highest tides. Look for tufts of olive-brown fronds, made of branching narrow blades that are curved to form distinct channels along their undersides, which trap water to keep them hydrated between tides. They turn more yellowish-brown throughout the summer, developing small, elongated receptacles at their tips. They can survive for long periods between tides, becoming dark, crunchy and unappetizing as they dry out but quickly rehydrating. Lift the dry outer fronds and you'll often find wet tender ones beneath. Crofters in the west of Scotland and Ireland once held channel wrack in high esteem as a reliable and accessible food source in times of hardship. Compounds extracted from it are widely used in the beauty and skin industries for their regenerative, moisturizing and anti-ageing properties.

Spiral wrack

Fucus spiralis

ALSO KNOWN AS Twisted wrack.

SIZE Grows up to 30cm (12in) long with fronds 2cm (¾in) wide.

BEST USES As for bladder wrack, plus they grow juicy plump fruits in summer, which are good in soups, salads, pickles or dirty martinis.

Usually forming a narrow but distinct band below channel wrack, spiral wrack is superficially similar to bladder wrack. However, close observation reveals that its stems do not lie flat but twist and spiral. This is most obvious where fronds are dangling down. It has no float bladders, and its large, warty reproductive bladders often form heart shapes. It occasionally hybridizes with bladder wrack.

Egg wrack

Ascophyllum nodosum

ALSO KNOWN AS Knotted wrack, asco, rock weed (US), bottle kelp (Canada), sea whistle, sailor's whistle, yellow tang, Norwegian kelp, knobbed wrack.

SIZE Grows up to 2m (6½ft) long, occasionally longer in sheltered fjords, with fronds up to 1cm (⅜in) wide.

BEST USES Gel-filled reproductive bladders are juicy and succulent but smaller than those of spiral wrack. Except for the tips, fronds are generally too tough for anything but grinding to powder.

Very common in sea lochs and sheltered water. Look for the egg-shaped float bladders, developing within stems. By counting the number of air bladders in the central thallus, you can estimate the age of the seaweed – one per year, plus its first year or two when it might not produce them. Twenty-year-old specimens with float bladders as big as a hand are not unusual in sheltered sea lochs and fjords. The float bladders are generally too tough to eat, but larger ones, once dried, make good whistles if you make a small hole in them and blow across it. Egg wrack often hosts wrack siphon weed (see opposite). In the very sheltered sea lochs of west Scotland, a free-floating form of egg wrack known as wig wrack (*Ascophyllum nodosum ecad mackaii*) has evolved, which is a little tough to eat but great fun to wear as a wig!

Wrack siphon weed

Vertebrata lanosa

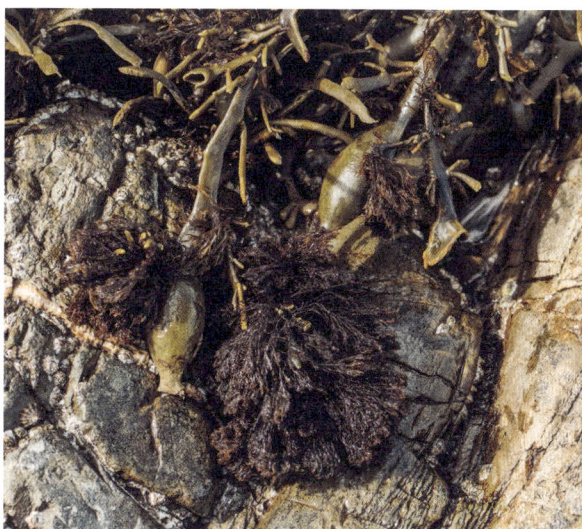

ALSO KNOWN AS *Polysiphonia lanosa*, *Polysiphonia fastigiata*, woolly siphon weed, ocean truffle, Icelandic truffle weed, truffleweed, truffle of the sea.

SIZE Finely branching fronds up to 8cm (3in) in length.

BEST USES Dry and grind it to a powder for a salty, mushroomy seasoning with a hint of curry. Sprinkle on soft- or hard-boiled eggs, fried mushrooms, rice or meat, or infuse into fats like butter, oil and cheese. Mix through mayonnaise for an excellent dip.

Wrack siphon weed is not a wrack, but is included here because it is an opportunistic little hemiparasite that anchors itself to damaged fronds of egg wrack, particularly in more exposed locations. Harvest it by snipping off pompoms. Its common name isn't terribly memorable so I've nicknamed it 'mermaid's pubes', which is a reminder of its looks and unpleasant texture if you eat a mouthful of it raw! The name seems to have caught on, which probably isn't doing much for its culinary reputation, but it really is a delicious seaweed spice if rinsed in clean seawater (rather than fresh water) then dried and powdered (which gets rid of its hairy texture) and used as a salty, truffly seasoning.

Bladder wrack

Fucus vesiculosis

ALSO KNOWN AS Pop weed, lady wrack, button seaweed, kelpware, pigweed.

SIZE Grows up to 1m (3ft) long, with fronds up to 3cm (1¼in) wide.

BEST USES Add tender young growing tips to soups and stews or mix raw through salads. Particularly good for making nutrient-rich stock powder.

Bladder wrack is recognizable by its forking, flattened blades with an obvious midrib and (usually) paired air-filled float bladders, which are tough and unappetizing but fun to pop like bubble wrap. This is the most morphologically diverse of the wracks, with individuals varying greatly in size and shape according to salinity and wave action. For example, plants can reach up to 1m (3ft) on sheltered shores with many pairs of bladders, while on exposed shores plants seldom exceed 20cm (8in) and may have no air bladders. In sheltered estuaries with low salinity, a near relation called horned wrack or estuary wrack (*Fucus ceranoides*) occurs. It lacks true float bladders but inflates the edges of its blades to look like horns. It is a tough eat, and not recommended.

Tooth wrack

Fucus serratus

ALSO KNOWN AS Serrated wrack, saw wrack, flat wrack, notched wrack.

SIZE Grows up to 40cm (16in) long, with fronds up to 3cm (1¼in) wide.

BEST USES Tender young tips are good for sandwiches, salads, steaming, soups, stir-fries, stews and pickling.

Farthest down the tidal range of wracks and tolerant of greater wave exposure, tooth wrack does not form bladders and is distinguished by the toothed edges of its flattened fronds, which have a subtle midrib. In summer its usually smooth thallus starts to look textured at the tips as it enters its reproductive phase. In the more sheltered part of its growth range, tooth wrack can be colonized by tiny coiled tubeworms, which are harmless but unpleasantly crunchy.

Beach wrack

When wracks break from their holdfast (see page 150) and accumulate on the high tide line, they become known as 'beach wrack'. These deposits can get quite ripe and smelly by summer's end, but they are still a great habitat for invertebrates and the predators that eat them.

Abundant and accessible, beach wrack has a long history of human use as fertilizer, spread onto fields in autumn, where it slowly releases nitrogen and minerals into the soil. Unfortunately, ocean plastic pollution contaminates beach wrack to such an extent that it is becoming less desirable as fertilizer.

In the 1600s it was discovered that the ash of burnt seaweed could be used to make soda (sodium carbonate) and potash, which were used in glass, soap, linen and gunpowder making. Wracks were predominantly used for this, and their burnt ash was referred to as kelp – a term that is now used only for the larger brown seaweeds found at and below the low tide line (see page 203).

Sustainable harvesting

The growing tips of the thallus and the gel-filled reproductive bladders are of most interest to foragers. The tips should be harvested by cutting up to one third off the end of the thallus, but I don't recommend taking that much from the larger plants: snip the last few inches with scissors, gauging tenderness by touch and taste, and moving your harvesting around between plants and colonies.

Eating and cooking with wracks

For foragers, the different wrack species are broadly interchangeable in the kitchen. It's fair to say that gastronomically they are not the star players of team seaweed – 'chewy' is the most common adjective used to describe their texture, and they tend to lack the deep umami or spicy tang of some of their neighbours. However, their accessibility, abundance and nutritional density make them well worth getting to know, and with a little care, selective harvesting and kitchen know-how they can become a rewarding cornerstone of the coastal forager's pantry.

Wracks are nutritional powerhouses, providing a good source of vitamins A, C, E and K, phosphorus, calcium, iron, copper, manganese, sodium and iodine. The species that grow higher up the tidal range (channel wrack and spiral wrack) contain about half the iodine of the other wracks. All wracks are high in alginates and dietary fibre that help with digestion.

The fronds of wracks can be quite tough. Larger pieces can be used to add body and umami to a stockpot in the same way as meat bones or kelp. Depending on how tender they are, wrack tips can be added to sandwiches, tossed in salads, steamed as a vegetable, popped in soups and stews, or blitzed into smoothies. Tougher pieces are good chopped and added to slow-cooked dishes. If they aren't tender enough for any of those uses, they can be dehydrated and ground to a powder which makes an excellent food supplement-cum-stock powder that adds nutrition, body and umami to soups, stews and sauces; it can also be added to the boiling water for rice or pasta. Wracks don't taste of much in themselves, but they will improve the flavour of any savoury dish.

Several species of wrack form reproductive bladders that are usually somewhat warty on the outside and always juicy on the inside – don't mix them up with air-filled float bladders, which are smooth and tough. These receptacles (to give them their proper name) grow in extraordinary abundance in the run-up to spawning, and there are plenty to spare for foragers. Some people are squeamish about eating them, but they are salty, juicy and pop in the mouth like a small grape and those who try them usually become converts.

They can be tossed raw into salads like capers; added to soups, stews or pizzas; and are particularly delicious cold pickled (see page 169). I also use them – fresh or pickled – as a garnish on a (dirty) martini. They do not dry well.

Wrack and carrot salad

This is a nice accompaniment to steamed or fried fish, or can be bulked up with rice or noodles. Remember to use the tender tips. This recipe also works well made with sea lettuce or wireweed.

Ingredients (Serves 4)

4 large handfuls of fresh (or rehydrated) wrack tips: channel, serrated or bladder wrack are best

1 medium-large carrot, peeled and grated

2 cloves of garlic, finely chopped

1 thumb-sized piece of ginger, finely chopped

3 tablespoons soy sauce

2 tablespoons rice wine vinegar

2 tablespoons toasted sesame oil

1 tablespoon honey

First, rinse the seaweed in fresh water. Strain off the cold water then pour boiling water over it – it will turn vibrant green. Leave to sit for 5 minutes. Check the seaweed for tenderness – it should be supple with just a little bite. If it feels tough, simmer it in the water for a few minutes. Strain out the boiled water and refresh immediately with cold water and strain once more. Toss the seaweed in a bowl with all the other ingredients.

Pickled wrack 'capers'

'Reproductive bladders' is not a pretty term, so I try to rebrand them to sceptics as 'sea capers' – it's more appealing, and by pickling them you can follow through on the notion.

Rinse the fresh bladders thoroughly then follow my general guidance for 3-2-1 pickling on page 258, using the cold-pickling method. The seaweed will exude alginates in the pickling solution, thickening it slightly, but any unappealing gloop can be quickly rinsed off before serving. Provided the pH is below 4, they will keep for up to six months in the fridge, but use within two weeks of opening. Use wrack capers the same way you might use traditional capers – in salads, on pizzas and in sauces for fish, especially tartare sauce.

SEA LETTUCE

*Forms
bright green
translucent
sheets.*

*Tubes trap oxygen
to help them float.*

*Forms straggly
green tubes
in rock pools.*

GUTWEED

Sea lettuce & gutweeds

Ulva spp.

There are dozens of *Ulva* species worldwide and at least 15 in the North Atlantic. They are all bright green: those that form flattish sheets are broadly known as sea lettuce (*U. lactuca* is the most common), while those that form tube-like strands can be loosely referred to as gutweeds (such as *U. intestinalis*, often found in rock pools at the top of the tidal range). Ribbon weeds are more tape-like (*U. compressa* and *U. flexuosa* are the most common). *Monostroma* and *Ulvaria* species are also green, sheet-like seaweeds, but they are thinner and more translucent. All these species are abundant and edible, with delicious cucumbery-umami flavours and pleasant textures, and can be used interchangeably. The main difference for foragers is how easy they are to harvest and divest of sand.

EDIBILITY Excellent fresh, even better dried.

DISTRIBUTION Common and widely distributed worldwide.

HABITAT Attached to rocks and in rock pools throughout the tidal range on moderately to well-sheltered coasts. Occasionally free-floating colonies form in calm waters.

WHEN TO HARVEST Available year-round, but best harvested in spring to early summer for optimal size, flavour and nutrition.

Sustainable harvesting

Although gutweed is very common and easy to access, even at high tide, it has a major drawback. Its tubular growth, which is cleverly designed to trap water (to avoid dehydration at low tide) and oxygen (which it generates through photosynthesis to help it to float at high tide), tends to also trap significant amounts of sand and grit. Lots of rinsing is part of being a seaweed forager, but in the case of gutweed it can be almost impossible to remove the crunchy passengers from inside the tubes. As the ribbon weeds also tend to hold onto lots of sand, and are fiddly to harvest, my go-to *Ulva* species is sea lettuce. It is abundant, easy to harvest, relatively easy to wash and versatile in the kitchen.

Most *Ulva* species die back in winter to small buds that regrow the following season. They provide valuable ecosystem services, such as sheltering invertebrates, recycling nutrients, and providing food or habitat for a range of animals from otters to sea slugs. They can grow very quickly in areas with lots of nutrients, and enormous blooms sometimes overwhelm bays, estuaries and beaches. These 'green tides' usually indicate nitrogen and phosphorous pollution from agricultural activities or human waste. The stranding and subsequent decomposition of such enormous volumes of seaweed can be extremely smelly – there have been several incidents of beachgoers being overwhelmed by the fumes, and they can suffocate other marine organisms. Avoid harvesting from unusually prolific growth.

Cut well-developed fronds leaving two-thirds behind, or thin whole sheets from among large growths, and spread your harvesting around so individuals and colonies have time to regrow. I happily harvest sea lettuce from the strandline immediately after storms, provided it still looks vibrant green and smells fresh.

Eating and cooking with ulva

All *Ulva* species are very good for you, containing more calcium than whole milk, as well as protein, fibre, amino acids, vitamins and minerals. They can be used fresh, as dried flakes, or reconstituted from dried. Rinse it just before you are ready to use or preserve it. Use several changes of fresh water before patting dry or spinning in a salad spinner.

Eaten fresh, the tender young fronds have a gentle umami-meets-cucumber-skin taste and a pleasant texture. Try adding them to leafy salads or stir-fries, or blitzing them through pesto. Older specimens may become chewy and are best dried and powdered or fried into seaweed crisps. If you want to eat them raw, first marinade them in a little vinegar and oil. They can also be used in the same ways as laver (see page 183), though you may need to adjust cooking times, and in place of wrack in the recipe on page 169.

Once fully dehydrated, sea lettuce's umami qualities come to the fore. It keeps well for many months in a sealed jar. It also makes a delicious condiment by following the recipe for pickled dulse paste on page 197.

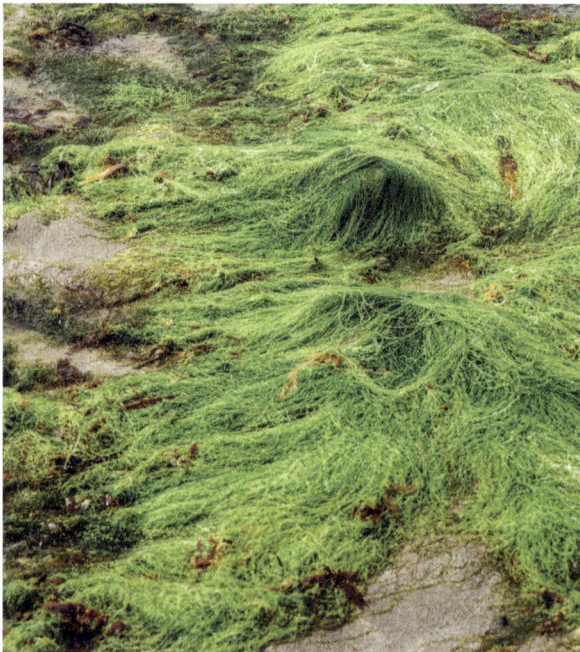

Left: Fine hair-like ribbon weeds are tasty, but can be troublesome to rinse off sand.
Below: Sea lettuce is the easiest to harvest and rinse.

Salt-baked celeriac with sea lettuce

I was taught this recipe by a Danish chef and it cleverly uses sea lettuce in several ways – to impart salty umami to the earthy sweetness of the celeriac; acting as a barrier to stop it from getting too salty from the salt crust; and as a flavourful flourish at the end.

Ingredients (Serves 4)

1 medium celeriac (around 550g/1lb 3oz), scrubbed clean and large roots trimmed

Sea lettuce – enough large fresh or rehydrated pieces to cover your celeriac twice plus a handful for the garnish

200g (7oz) fine salt

300g (11oz) plain flour, plus extra to dust

2 tablespoons finely chopped rosemary

150ml (5 fl oz) warm water

50g (2oz) unsalted butter

2 tablespoons capers or egg/bladder wrack 'capers' (see page 169)

Toasted dried sea lettuce flakes

A squeeze of lemon juice

Heat the oven to 180°C (350°F)/160°C (320°F) fan / Gas 4. Place the celeriac in a small baking dish and roughly wrap the sea lettuce around it. Ideally you want the celeriac to be completely covered, but a few gaps won't matter. Don't worry if it doesn't stick – it will be held in place by the salt dough.

To make the salt dough, add the salt, flour and chopped rosemary to a bowl. Mix, then pour in the warm water while stirring to create a dough. Roll out on a floured surface into a large circle, about 1cm (⅜in) thick. Carefully wrap the dough around the celeriac, trapping the sea lettuce between. If the dough rips a little, you can tear bits off and plug the holes.

Put the wrapped celeriac back in the baking dish, seam-side down, then bake in the oven for 1 hour. You can check if it's done by pushing in a skewer; once it's passed through the salt crust there should be no resistance as it goes into the celeriac. Leave to cool slightly, then use a serrated knife to break open and remove the salt dough. Scrape off the seaweed and the celeriac skin – it should peel away easily. Slice the celeriac into wedges.

Add the butter to a large frying pan over a medium heat. Once the butter is foaming, add the celeriac wedges and cook, turning occasionally and basting them until golden. When they are nearly done, roughly chop the remaining sea lettuce and add along with the capers to the pan for 30 seconds. Finish with a squeeze of lemon.

Arrange the wedges on a serving platter and spoon over the crispy capers and seaweed. Drizzle any butter left in the pan over the wedges, then sprinkle with the toasted dried sea lettuce flakes.

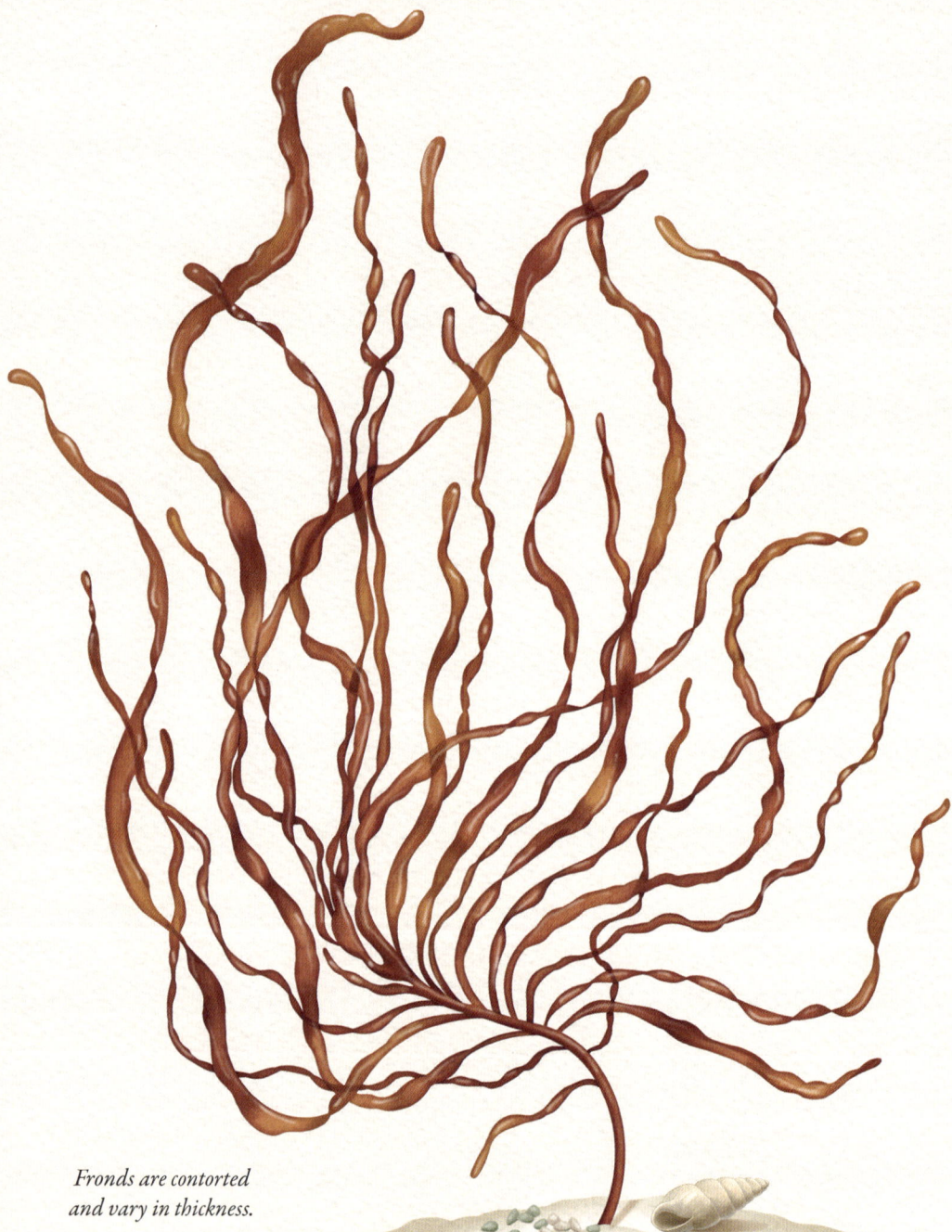

Fronds are contorted and vary in thickness.

Dumont's tubular weed

Dumontia contorta

This wonderful gourmet seaweed is quite easy to find in the right habitat and fun to eat straight from the sea. Its delicious flavour is created by compounds it makes to deter grazing gastropods – a bit of an own goal when it comes to grazing humans! Along with pepper dulse, this is the seaweed most likely to make you say 'Wow!' when you first taste it.

ALSO KNOWN AS *Dumontia incrassata*, sea noodles, Dumont's weed.

EDIBILITY Delicious salty, truffly umami 'sea noodles'. Eat them fresh, fried or lightly poached, or dry them as seasoning.

IDENTIFICATION Diminuitive straggly rosettes of dark-brownish branching noodle- or shoelace-like tubular fronds, hollow and somewhat contorted, up to 50cm (20in) long, but usually less.

DISTRIBUTION Widespread around the North Atlantic.

HABITAT Attached to bedrock, rocks and pebbles in the mid-tidal range in sheltered channels and rock pools, especially those that gently flow between tides, and areas not exposed to full tidal action.

WHEN TO HARVEST Starts to grow in winter but best harvested in spring; dies back in summer.

SIMILAR SPECIES A couple of other small noodle-like brownish seaweeds can look similar. The best way to tell if you have Dumont's tubular weed is by taste – it should be tender like cooked noodles and have a truffly umami flavour. If you don't think 'Yum!' you probably have something else. It is much browner, smaller and more fragile than the other string-like seaweeds on page 199.

Sustainable harvesting

To harvest, gather the floating rosettes gently in your hand. If they are more than 12cm (5in) long, cut off the top third. For smaller fronds, thin the full strands from the rosette, leaving at least two-thirds of them. They come out of the water naturally clean and do not usually require much further rinsing at home. They are delicate, so take care not to crush them.

Eating Dumont's tubular weed

The fresh fronds do not keep well; they will begin to exude purplish liquid and go off after 24 hours in the fridge. They are great rolled in sushi or as a garnish on sashimi or cooked fish. They can be used in salads (perhaps mixed with regular noodles) or dropped into seaweed dashi broth (see page 207) just as it is served.

If you aren't going to use it right away, dry it by placing it in small piles the size of your palm on dehydrator racks. After a few hours on the gentlest heat setting, the nests will collapse into fragile mesh-like discs. These can be eaten as they are, as a salty beer snack, or crumbled over dishes as seasoning (they are particularly good with mushrooms and poached eggs), or used as instant noodles. Alternatively, they can be ground to a powder and added to your wild spice rack. Fresh or dried, Dumont's tubular weed quickly turns to mush when cooked – so drop it into broths and soups at the very last minute.

Crispy fried sea noodles

These salty snacks are perfect with a cold beer, perhaps dipped in some pepper dulse mayonnaise, or laid on top of laver bread with a pickled cockle or two. I'm grateful to my friend and fellow foraging teacher Mo Wilde for introducing me to Dumont's tubular weed and passing on this great way of cooking it.

Ingredients (Serves 4)

Fresh Dumont's tubular weed, rinsed and patted dry

Plain flour

Vegetable oil for shallow frying

Heat enough oil to just cover the base of a shallow frying pan. Ensure the seaweed is patted dry – it should be moist but not wet. Place it in a bowl and sprinkle with a little flour. Lightly work it with your fingertips (or better still, chopsticks) until it is evenly coated in flour, adding more flour if necessary. It should be beginning to stick together in clumps, but not a big doughy mess. Form the floured seaweed into rough nests.

Drop the nests into the hot fat and fry until crispy – this will take less than 30 seconds – then flip and fry for a few seconds on the other side. They will turn greenish as they fry. Lift out of the oil onto some kitchen roll or a paper towel to absorb any excess oil, then serve and eat while still warm.

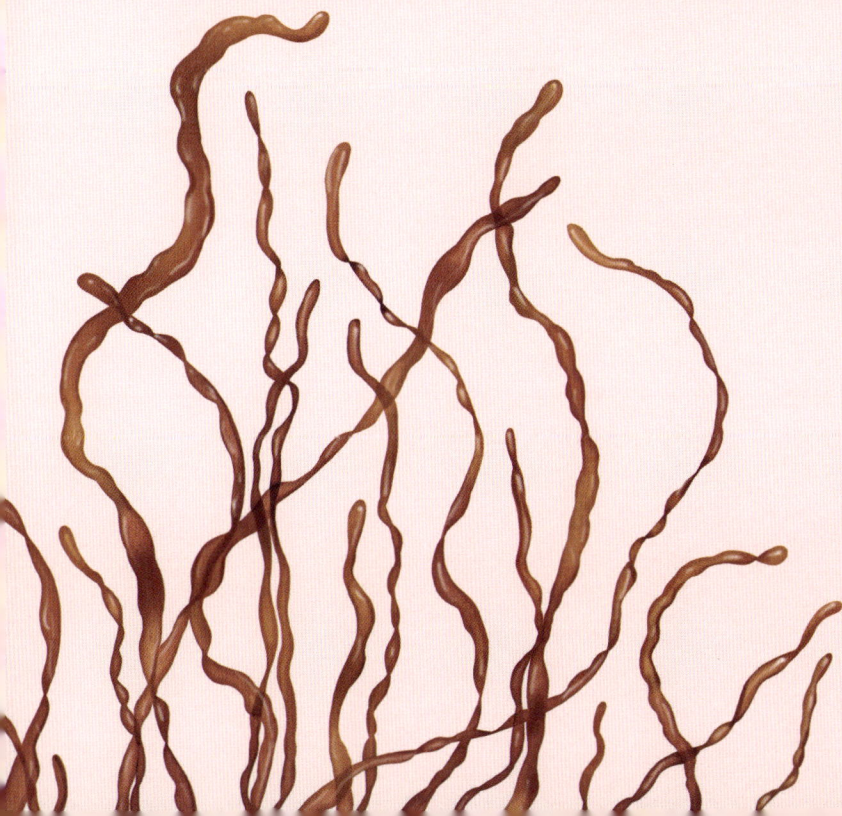

Laver

Porphyra spp., *Neopyropia* spp.

Laver is the wild food with the largest discrepancy between how it looks (melted bin bags) and how it tastes (rich, satisfying umami). Unlocking its delights takes a bit of work, but once you get to know it, you'll come to appreciate its silky flowing movement in the sea, the oil slick-like rainbow translucency of its blades, and its versatility in the kitchen. Although it is technically a red seaweed, it usually looks blackish-purple to blackish-green on the shore, depending on the species and stage of growth. Processing brings more colours – deep purple hues when dehydrated, and rich greens when cooked. Most people will have encountered laver under its Japanese name, nori, wrapped around rice and seafood. Pacific species of laver (*P. yezoensis* and *P. tenera*) are cultivated in vast quantities on floating trellises for this trade.

ALSO KNOWN AS Nori, wild nori, purple laver, slake, sloke, sleabhac.

EDIBILITY A fantastic kitchen all-rounder, though it takes a bit of processing.

IDENTIFICATION Blackish to deep brown/green/purple overlapping translucent sheets, looking like melted black bin bags when the tide is out.

DISTRIBUTION Throughout the North Atlantic.

HABITAT Clinging to rocks on open beaches, in approximately the middle third of the tidal range. Also grows on groins, piers and harbour walls, and occasionally epiphytically on wracks. Tolerance to exposure varies between species.

WHEN TO HARVEST One species or another is available throughout the year, though condition may vary.

Similar species

Of the thirty or so species of *Porphyra* and its very near relations that are native to the North Atlantic, about seven are abundant enough to be of interest to foragers. Even marine biologists struggle to tell laver species apart without resorting to microscopy, so precise identification is often a 'best guess' based on habitat and general appearance. Misidentification isn't problematic in the benign world of seaweeds, and all laver species have similar culinary merits. You are most likely to encounter the following species:

Purple laver (*Porphyra pupurea*) has large, silky textured blades with ruffled edges, up to 1m (3ft) long and 20cm (8in) wide. It grows on rocks in the mid-tidal range in exposed locations, often covering them. This is the most efficient species to harvest due to its size.

Tough laver (*Porphyra umbilicalis*) is smaller, forming rosettes 13cm (5in) long by 10cm (4in) wide, with a slightly tougher texture. It is generally found higher up the tidal range, occasionally attached to mussels and limpets.

Winter laver (*Porphyra linearis*) has narrower blades, appearing more like uneven ribbons. It is at its best in winter and early spring.

Pale patch laver (*Neopyropia leucosticta*) can be found clinging as an epiphyte to grape pip weed and serrated wrack.

Laver might conceivably be confused with sea lettuce (see page 173), though sea lettuce is bright green, never blackish-green. They can be used in much the same way, but sea lettuce tends to be a little tougher.

Harvesting and rinsing laver

Laver avoids drying out by growing in multiple overlapping sheets. The outer sheet dries, forming a wind- and sun-proof barrier for the layers below until the sea returns. This can look like an unappealing 'crust' when you first come across it, but it rehydrates very happily. Considering each sheet is just one cell thick, they are remarkably resilient, coping with crashing waves and shifting, scouring sands and often form large colonies on exposed beaches where few other seaweeds can survive.

The swirling fronds of laver provide shelter for crustaceans, and you will find a few still clinging to it as you process it. Often they are so small and well camouflaged that they are nearly invisible until you cook or dry the laver. They are perfectly harmless unless you have a shellfish allergy (see page 221).

The usual seaweed-harvesting strategy of cutting up to one-third of the blades can be applied to laver, but where it is generously draped over rocks it is fine to thin it by teasing out handfuls, provided you leave plenty on each rock and spread your harvesting over a wide area.

Gather laver on a receding tide so that sand has less chance to dry onto it, and you have easy access to the sea for rinsing handfuls before wringing them out. The more sand you can remove during harvesting, the less work you will have to do at home. Once sea-rinsed, wrung out and covered, laver keeps in the fridge for up to a week.

When you are ready to dry or cook your laver, you will need to thoroughly rinse it in fresh water. Don't take shortcuts with this – it only takes one grain of sand to turn food from delicious to unpleasant! I'm not going to lie: rinsing a decent quantity of laver is a lot of wet, splashy work. That is the price of eating one of the most nourishing and delicious foods known to humanity, and it is absolutely worth it. I know some foragers who wash their laver in the bath. (This is one of many potentially relationship-challenging foraging practices, up there with drying wild mushrooms in the airing cupboard!) However you go about it, I recommend finishing the rinsing process by straining the laver over a white bowl so you can check it is running clear of sand. Once you are content the laver meets your standards, give it a thorough wringing out and it's ready for the next step.

Cooking, preserving and eating laver

If you eat it raw, laver has no great flavour and a surprisingly tough texture for something so thin. It must be dried and/ or cooked to unlock its magic.

To dehydrate it, follow my directions on page 160. Once fully dried, it can be kept in airtight tubs for years. I strongly recommend toasting dried laver in a dry frying pan or low oven before use. This turns its colour from a blackish-purple to deep green, adds a delicious toasted flavour, and accentuates its umami qualities.

Once toasted, it can be ground into flakes for sprinkling on virtually anything – from cheese to vegetables, grains (especially rice) or popcorn. Or powder it for seasoning

pastry, bread, eggs, paté (especially mushroom paté) or almost anything else. On its own, or better still, combined with dehydrated mushroom powder, laver powder will turbo charge anything savoury, especially seaweed broths (see page 209). My chef friend, Craig Grozier, calls this laver-mushroom powder combination 'instant dashi' and it improves everything it touches. It is even good in sweet things – laver meringues are quite delicious (just add a couple of teaspoons to the egg-sugar mix).

Laverbread

Laverbread is the Welsh name for the thick paste made by cooking laver. In Wales it is traditionally eaten cold rather like a spread or paté on toast, or (perhaps mixed with oatmeal), spooned into a hot frying pan and fried into patties. Its alternate names 'black gold' and 'Welshman's caviar' reflect the esteem in which this food was once held. For the avoidance of confusion, I call the paste laverbread and the patties laverburgers.

Ingredients

Laver, fresh or dried

Water

Salt, to taste

Apple cider vinegar or lemon juice (optional)

Place the laver in a pan. If you are using dried laver, it will soon rehydrate and requires half the suggested cooking time. Add a little water – the exact amount isn't particularly important. If you use more, you will get an excellent stock, but don't use more than half the volume of the seaweed. Bring to a simmer and cook, covered, for at least four hours, checking periodically to ensure it isn't sticking. Add more water if you think it's drying out. Don't rush the cooking process – the flavours develop over time. Overnight in a slow cooker works well, but if you need to accelerate the process, one hour in a pressure cooker will do. You can also reduce the cooking time, and improve the keeping qualities of the cooked laver, by adding a generous glug of apple cider vinegar or lemon juice to the pan.

As it cooks, the laver will collapse into a swampy-looking black-green goo. It is ready when it is very soft and the individual sheets are barely discernible. Ladle it into a fine sieve over an empty pan and press out as much liquid as possible. Retain the liquid as it makes a brilliant 'meaty' stock for soups and stews. The contents of your sieve can now, officially, be called laverbread! The seaweed should have disintegrated somewhat, but if there are still noticeable pieces, blitz into a smoother paste with a hand blender or food processor. Laver is surprisingly unsalty for a seaweed, so you may wish to season it a little.

It will keep for about four days in the fridge, or longer if you included some acidity in the cooking process. You can store it in small tubs or ziplock bags in the freezer. Laverbread can be used a bit like frozen spinach to add savoury richness and body to stews and soups, as a filling for tarts and pies, in mushroomy vegetarian or vegan patés, as a layer in pies, or as a umami-rich sauce base, perhaps mixed with passata or rose hip purée (see page 50) and smeared on pizza bases.

Laverburgers

These look and taste like slices of (vegan) black pudding – meaty, savoury, filling and deeply nutritious. They can be eaten cold or reheated later, but they taste best straight from the pan.

Ingredients

2 parts cooked laverbread (see opposite)

2 parts medium oatmeal: you can experiment with finer or coarser oatmeal, or rolled oats; they all give slightly different, but delicious, results

Salt and pepper

Oil for frying: bacon fat is best, but any oil will do

Optional extras

Add any of these you like, chopped finely if necessary, up to half the volume of the laver.

Soy sauce (highly recommended)

Miso paste (highly recommended)

Spicy seaweed powders: e.g. pepper dulse or wrack siphon weed

Fresh seaweeds: e.g. pepper dulse or dulse

Wild garlic (ramps), fresh or fermented

Coastal greens: e.g. sea beet, rock or marsh samphire, sea aster, sea plantain

Onion

Fish sauce/clam garum (see page 249)

Wild mushrooms

Chillis

Sesame seeds, to coat the burgers

Lemon juice or sorrel

This is a very forgiving recipe. You can play around with the proportions of laver and oatmeal, and they joyfully embrace pretty much any kind of embellishment – I've noted some of my favourites. You could also make this with sea lettuce, or a mix of laver and sea lettuce.

Blitz the cooked, strained laverbread with a stick blender or in a food processor until there are no large pieces. Scrape it into a bowl and add the oatmeal, salt and pepper to taste, and any other embellishments you are using. Mix with a spoon until it becomes thick enough to roughly mould into patties. Don't worry if it still feels a bit wet at this stage. Cover and leave to rest for at least one hour, or ideally in the fridge overnight. The oatmeal will soak up any excess liquid and the mixture should feel quite stiff and malleable. If it is still a bit wet for forming into patties, add more oatmeal by increments.

Heat enough oil to just cover the bottom of a thick-bottomed frying pan. Use your hands to form the mixture into small patties roughly 7cm (3in) in diameter and 2.5cm (1in) thick. Wet your hands a little to make it easier. Carefully drop the patties into the oil, which should be hot but not smoking. Fry for a couple of minutes, pressing them with the back of a spatula to a thickness you like as they cook. Flip and repeat. Cook them until the oatmeal starts to bronze and form a nice crust – the best laverburgers are crunchy on the outside and gooey on the inside. Place them in a dish lined with kitchen roll or a paper towel to absorb excess fat.

Serve as part of a cooked breakfast, as an accompaniment to fish and shellfish, with pickled cockles, with meat, like falafel (especially if you've added extra spices), as burgers or cold in picnics, or with pickled sea vegetables like sea sandwort (see page 59). Given the complex prep required, I recommend making large batches then, once they have cooled, freezing them individually and storing them frozen in tubs or bags so you can reheat as you need them.

*Smooth and glossy,
with squarish ends.*

CARRAGEEN

*Small protrusions
like grape pips.*

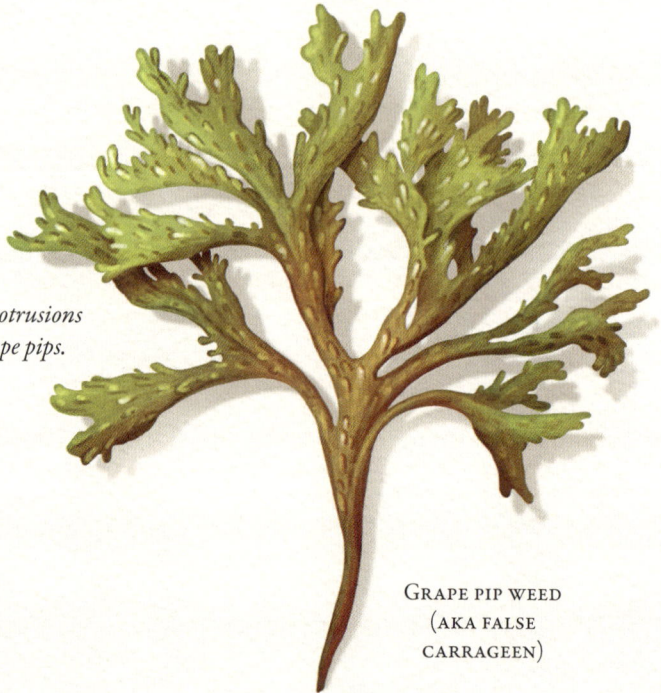

*This illustration shows the extremes
of the colour range for both species,
which span from deep browny-red
in winter/spring to bright greenish-
yellow in summer/autumn.*

GRAPE PIP WEED
(AKA FALSE
CARRAGEEN)

Carrageen

Chrondus crispus

Tough and flavourless, carrageen is not an edible seaweed in the conventional sense, but once heated in liquid it exudes copious amounts of carrageenan – a gelatinous flavourless substance that can be used to thicken soups and stews, or in higher concentrations, to set jellies, blancmanges or panna cottas.

ALSO KNOWN AS Irish moss, carragheen, curly moss, gristle moss, pearly gristle moss, Dorset weed, jelly moss, rock moss, sea moss, sea pearl moss, white wrack.

EDIBILITY Tough and tasteless, but useful as a thickener (like vegan gelatine) and for its nutritional benefits.

IDENTIFICATION Small, bushy, fan-shaped seaweed with flat fronds of 7–15cm (3–6in) with two rounded tips at the end of every branch. Scientifically a red seaweed, but colour can vary to the naked eye depending on its condition. In prime condition, it will be deep brown with an underlying ruddiness, but it can look pink and dark purple with lime-green tips, or pale and creamy later in the summer. The flat tips become crinkly as summer progresses.

DISTRIBUTION Widely distributed and abundant on both sides of the North Atlantic, as far south as New Jersey and Portugal.

HABITAT Attached to rock in the mid- to subtidal range.

WHEN TO HARVEST Year-round, but best in late spring and summer, when it has better setting properties.

SIMILAR SPECIES Grape pip weed (*Mastocarpus stellatus*, also known as false carrageen, false Irish moss, cat's puff or starweed) is very similar to carrageen and often found growing alongside it. It is distinguished by its rounded stipe and channelled fronds that develop a warty surface texture as it matures. It can be used in all the same ways as carrageen.

Sustainable harvesting

Carrageen and grape pip weed are tough little perennial seaweeds that can live up to five years, so harvest only the top third of the fronds with a sharp knife or scissors. Both are very common but are often hidden beneath larger algae. They can form large beds which are heavily grazed by limpets and offer food and refuge to a host of small crustaceans and worms, along with juveniles of larger animals such as sea urchins, mussels, crabs, and starfish. Later in the summer they are often colonized by sea mat (see page 157).

Using carrageen

Once you get them home, carrageen and grape pip weed will keep well in the fridge for up to a week, but as dehydration has no impact on their setting properties, there is no reason not to dry them sooner rather than later.

Carrageen has historically been held in very high regard in crofting communities on the west coasts of Scotland and Ireland, where it is used to make a set jelly or creamy pudding, usually flavoured with fruits, herbs or spices. It was often served as a special treat for Sunday dinner, and used as a nurturing medicine for colds, stomach upsets and hangovers. I suspect part of the pleasure was the sugar and flavourings used to embellish it, but there is no denying that carrageen is a nutritional powerhouse, surpassing even the general health benefits of most seaweeds.

All this goodness as well as the thickening properties can be incorporated into soups and broths by adding a handful of fresh or dried carrageen tied up in muslin during cooking, and squeezing it out before removing.

Carrageen also makes a rich, nourishing addition to herbal teas – just add a pinch to the teapot or your mug. In combination with, for example, spruce tips, sea buckthorn leaves or nettle tops, it makes for a healthy, restorative cuppa that will help keep colds at bay and soothe sore throats.

Basic carrageen gel

This method will yield about 350ml (12 fl oz) of gel; 45ml (3 tbsp) of that gel will firmly set about 300ml (½ pint) of liquid when mixed through and left to cool. It can also be used as a moisturizing hand cream.

Ingredients (Serves 4)

30g (1oz) dried carrageen or 100g (3½oz) of fresh/rehydrated carrageen (rehydrated in cold water for 20 minutes)

500ml (18 fl oz) water

Place the carrageen in a pan and add the water. Bring to the boil and simmer gently without a lid for about 25 minutes. The carrageen will go very gloopy. While it is still hot, strain through a fine sieve, using a spatula or ladle to press all the gel out of the seaweed.

Alternatively, you can tie the carrageen up in muslin, then wear thick rubber gloves to squeeze all the gel out after boiling. (I have half-fond, half-painful memories of squeezing hot gel through a T-shirt with my bare hands to make a carrageen pudding on a wilderness expedition.)

The gel will keep for a week or so in the fridge, and you can freeze what you don't use in ice cube trays for future use as a thickener for sweet or savoury dishes or as a nourishing stock cube for thickening soups and sauces.

Note that there may be some variation in the setting properties of the gel, depending on the condition of the seaweed when it was harvested – spring and summer harvests are higher in carrageenan.

Carrageen jelly or pudding

Make this with water for a set jelly or with milk to make a blancmange-like pudding. You can substitute some of the milk with cream or use coconut milk to make it more decadent, but vegan milk substitutes don't set as firmly.

Add 15ml (1 tbsp) of carrageen gel per 75ml (5 tbsp) of water or milk, then heat it gently, stirring in any embellishments you fancy – cinnamon, nutmeg, chocolate, coffee, elderberry, sea buckthorn juice, beach rose petals and rose hip syrup are all good. You can also make savoury

set mousses by adding crab meat, cheese or blanched, blitzed greens – sea aster (see page 123) makes a spectacular green pudding that tastes surprisingly good.

Simmer gently for 20 minutes then pour the mix into cups, bowls, ice cube trays or jelly moulds and leave to set. To release the jelly or pudding from a mould, sit the mould in boiling water for 20 seconds and it should slip out easily. Set puddings can be decorated with flowers, herbs and thick syrups.

Colour ranges from deep chocolatey brown in prime condition, to pale olive when out of condition.

Pepper dulse

Osmundea pinnatifida and near relations

The flavour of pepper dulse is unique and rather hard to describe – pepper, garlic, truffle and shellfish are often mentioned but don't do it justice. Despite being scientifically classed as a red seaweed, its visual colour varies considerably according to where and when it is growing: its happy colour is deep chocolatey brown (with perhaps a subtle underlying ruddiness), but it becomes paler and ultimately a yellowish green, especially on the edge of its tidal range and as spring turns into summer. Although it is widely dispersed and abundant, it is easily overlooked by novice seaweed foragers, perhaps because of its wide variation in colour and tendency to hide beneath bigger seaweeds.

ALSO KNOWN AS Truffle of the sea, flat fern weed.

EDIBILITY A gastronomic gem: surprising, intense, mineral, aromatic, peppery and garlicky, with powerful umami. The flavour can vary in intensity according to which Osmundea species you have, as well as its condition and stage of growth.

IDENTIFICATION Tufted carpets consisting of small, flattened fronds, 1–6cm (⅜–2½in) long, that are irregularly branched though usually roughly pyramidal in outline, growing in layers. Although technically a red seaweed, it is a deep chocolaty brown when in prime condition, turning paler as the summer progresses.

DISTRIBUTION Widely distributed and common around the North Atlantic, as far south as Portugal.

HABITAT Clinging to semi-exposed rock from the mid-tidal range downwards. In more exposed locations, it will be smaller in size and will grow in the cracks and groins between rocks. It can often be hidden by larger seaweeds.

WHEN TO HARVEST Year-round in more exposed locations, and colder waters, but at its best December – May. The darker its colour, the better it tastes. It is often in poor condition in summer/early autumn.

Similar species

These near relations can be used in similar ways:

Royal fern weed (*O. osmunda*) grows up to 20cm (8in) and likes a more exposed position in the lower tidal range, with a preference for non-draining rock pools. It is much less fiddly to harvest than pepper dulse.

Brittle fern weed (*O. oederi*) grows up to 8cm (3in). It is epiphytic and usually grows on wracks in the lower tidal range.

Iridescent fern weed (*O. truncata*) is very similar to brittle fern weed but grows on subtidal rocks.

All the flat fern weeds often grow intermingled with superficially similar-looking carrageen and false carrageen (see page 187), both of which are tasteless – a quick nibble is all you need to tell them apart.

Sustainable harvesting

Prime spots for harvesting pepper dulse are towards the lower end of its tidal range, and shadier aspects, where it lives in close and complex mutualism with barnacles and other small creatures. It clings tightly to its rocky home with a tangled creeping holdfast. Harvest it by trimming with scissors – rather like giving a rock a haircut. If you inadvertently pull it, it will bring with it some of the rock and barnacle to which it clings and become impossible to clean and unpleasant to eat. Take care of your precious harvest as pepper dulse deteriorates rapidly if crushed.

Eating pepper dulse

Your first taste of pepper dulse should be fresh and raw, and ideally with waves crashing at your feet. It is a delightful nibble, and the flavour lingers well after it is swallowed. I like to lay the fronds on wild sushi and sashimi (especially raw razor clams), or on pieces of smoked egg. The texture is pleasingly cartilaginous and crisp, but not unpleasantly crunchy like wrack siphon weed.

Much of the flavour is due to the presence of compounds called terpenoids and phenols. These are also found in many aromatic plants, where they are used to deter insects, but in pepper dulse they ward off molluscs and fish.

Fresh or dried, pepper dulse makes a great embellishment and seasoning for meat, fish, shellfish, mushrooms, eggs, rice or pasta, and a lovely addition to a white bechamel sauce for serving with fish. It is generally best to add it towards the end of any cooking process.

Once dehydrated, some of the aromatics become muted, but it develops a pepperiness that makes it a rich, spicy, aromatic seasoning. It's best to grind it quite finely as larger pieces can be crunchy. Try adding it to spice mixes for curries and pakora.

Pepper dulse can be cold pickled (see page 261). Never hot pickle it, as this immediately unleashes its volatile compounds. A gin distiller I was working with was keen to use pepper dulse aromatics. As part of his research, he poured boiling water over a bowlful of pepper dulse. He described the vapour that came off it as 'somewhere between raw onions and pepper spray!' He was ultimately fine, but he was crying and struggling to breathe for a few minutes. Worse still, his hard-won pepper dulse turned into an unappetizing, sludgy mess. Even cold-pickled pepper dulse will break down and become sludgy in a week or two – though it is the best-tasting sludge ever, like a truffly Marmite.

Pepper dulse has a short fridge life, developing less pleasant fishy odours after a couple of days. If you must store it fresh for any length of time, don't wash it until you are ready to use it, and store it in shallow layers on a double piece of kitchen roll in lidded tubs.

Pepper dulse salted caramel

This is great served on vanilla ice cream, sticky toffee pudding, or (ideally) both at once. It can be made up to four days in advance and chilled, then gently reheated before serving.

Ingredients

175g (6oz) light soft brown sugar

300ml (½ pint) double (heavy) cream

50g (2oz) butter

½ teaspoon sea salt

2 teaspoons ground, dried pepper dulse

Combine all the ingredients except the pepper dulse in a saucepan set over a low heat, and stir until the sugar has dissolved. Turn the heat up and bubble the sauce for 2–3 minutes until golden and syrupy. Leave to cool for 10 minutes, then stir the pepper dulse through before serving.

Smoked mackerel and pepper dulse paté

Smoked mackerel and pepper are classic bedfellows, so it's an obvious step to substitute black pepper with pepper dulse, which adds extra savoury and aromatic notes.

Ingredients

220g (8oz) hot smoked mackerel, skinned and checked for pin bones

220g (8oz) cream cheese

3 tablespoons dried pepper dulse

Juice of 1 lemon

Optional: herbs such as fennel and dill are excellent additions, and you can add any other seaweed powders you fancy

Place all the ingredients in a food processor and whizz until you have a smooth paté. It is great served on thick oatcakes. It freezes well.

*Slick, translucent
reddish blades.*

Dulse

Palmaria palmata

Dulse has the longest recorded history of consumption of all North Atlantic seaweeds. The monks of St. Columba wrote fondly of it in the 7th century, and it is still widely sold on the west coast of Ireland today. It is a folk food par excellence, traditionally eaten to cure all sorts of ailments from worms to poor eyesight. I suspect it owes its ongoing popularity to its ability to dry quickly and easily into a tasty, nourishing and sustaining snack that can be carried for a week in one's pocket without deteriorating. I was once delighted on a trek to find a clump of it in a rucksack I hadn't used for months – the perfect snack on a windy hillside, chewed like jerky or biltong.

ALSO KNOWN AS Shelldulse, waterleaf, dillisk, duileasc, sheep's weed, handed fucus, red kale.

EDIBILITY A salty, meaty, nourishing sea vegetable, good raw, cooked, dried as jerky, or dried and ground for seasoning.

IDENTIFICATION Smooth reddish-brown flat blades up to 50cm (20in), palmately divided into fingers. Flesh is thin to the point of being translucent when young, though it can become thicker and leathery with age. When exposed, fronds tend to lie on top of one another, giving the appearance of a thicker seaweed.

DISTRIBUTION Widely distributed and common throughout the North Atlantic.

HABITAT Attached to rocks or epiphytic on other seaweeds (especially kelps and tooth wrack) in the lower third of the tidal range, and subtidal.

WHEN TO HARVEST Available for most of the year, though often in poor condition or absent during winter. Best in spring and early summer.

SIMILAR SPECIES There are a number of red blade-like seaweeds, most of which are subtidal and can be disappointing if eaten by mistake. Red rags (*Dilsea carnosa*) is the most likely mix-up, distinguished by its thicker flesh and deeper red colour – it's a little tough for most tastes.

Sustainable harvesting

Dulse inhabits the densest part of the seaweed jungle, from around the mean low tide line down well into the subtidal range. Red seaweeds are adapted to the shades below large kelps, just like the understory of a forest, so you may need to rummage a little. It can be thin and scanty on the margins of its tidal range, so time your forays for a good low tide if you want easy pickings. As usual with seaweeds, cutting the last third of it with scissors or a sharp knife is the best way to harvest, but where it is established it grows so prolifically that teasing handfuls from the stems of kelp is perfectly acceptable.

Eating dulse

The flavour of dulse will vary according to when and where it is harvested and can be hard to predict. In general, it will have more salinity and flavour if harvested from its lower tidal range and/or in spring/summer. Tasting it fresh while you are harvesting and again once it is dried will help you develop a feel for when and where it is at its tastiest in your region.

Dulse is often described as 'vegan bacon', and while bacon aficionados will rightly question its lack of fat (surely a defining feature of bacon?), it is both salty and meaty in flavour and is high in vitamin B_{12} and protein (up to 40 per cent of its dried weight). A word of warning: the meaty flavour can be addictive to those who aren't encountering it in their everyday diet. A vegetarian guest on one of my sea kayak trips once gorged on it so much she felt unwell for an hour or two. Dulse is particularly high in iodine, which is generally good for us, but shouldn't be overdone (see page 151).

Fried

Fresh dulse can be shallow fried in butter or oil for 3–4 minutes to make tasty crisps, and is also good steamed or boiled for a few minutes as a vegetable. It can be added raw to salads, stir-fries and the top of pizzas.

It does not keep well unprocessed. Unwashed in the fridge it will soon begin to exude purple liquid and go unpleasantly smelly. When you are ready to use it, give it a quick rinse under a tap and a whizz in a salad spinner or pat it dry in a tea towel.

Smoked

Dulse has some of the highest levels of umami of any North Atlantic seaweed, so I usually include it in Atlantic dashi broths (see page 207). It's even better for this (or any use) if it's smoked first. If you don't own a smoker, try placing it on rack near a smouldering wood fire. If you are on good terms with a local smokehouse, it's worth asking if you can borrow or rent a shelf during their next cold-smoking session. A couple of hours of gentle smoking can be the first stage of dehydrating it.

Dried

To dry dulse, follow my instructions on page 160. If you are using a dehydrator, it's fine to pack it in a bit if space is tight. It will dry into rough sheets which keep well in ziplock bags or tubs with lids. Occasionally, dried dulse will develop a white bloom: this is not mould (which is highly unlikely provided you have dried it thoroughly) but salt crystals – perfectly fine.

Dried dulse can be dry-fried to bring out its bacony flavour. Heat it in a dry frying pan until it is thoroughly crisp and starting to turn a little green at the edges. Take care not to burn it. Dulse fried in this way can be used to make a DLT – a veggie version of the BLT sandwich.

Dried dulse is tough, pliable and hard to grind. Instead, toast it briefly in a low oven or dry frying pan until it starts to feel brittle, then use the chopping blade of your spice grinder.

Dulse has a natural affinity for potatoes, and it is excellent ground and sprinkled on them, whether mashed, roasted, boiled or served cold in a potato salad. A classic frugal Scottish soup can be made by boiling a generous handful of fresh or dried dulse with chopped potatoes until everything goes gloopy. Add fish, shellfish, some sweated leeks and cream, and before you know it you have a dulse chowder.

Pickled dulse paste

This is an umami-packed condiment that is great in sandwiches, smeared on laver burgers, or as an accompaniment to meat, fish or vegetables. The same treatment also works for sea lettuce (see page 173).

Ingredients

Dried dulse, finely chopped

3-2-1 pickle mix (see page 258)

Pack a clean jar with roughly chopped dried dulse. Top up the jar with 3-2-1 pickle mix and leave for a week in the fridge. The dulse will rehydrate into a delicious paste that will keep for months in the fridge.

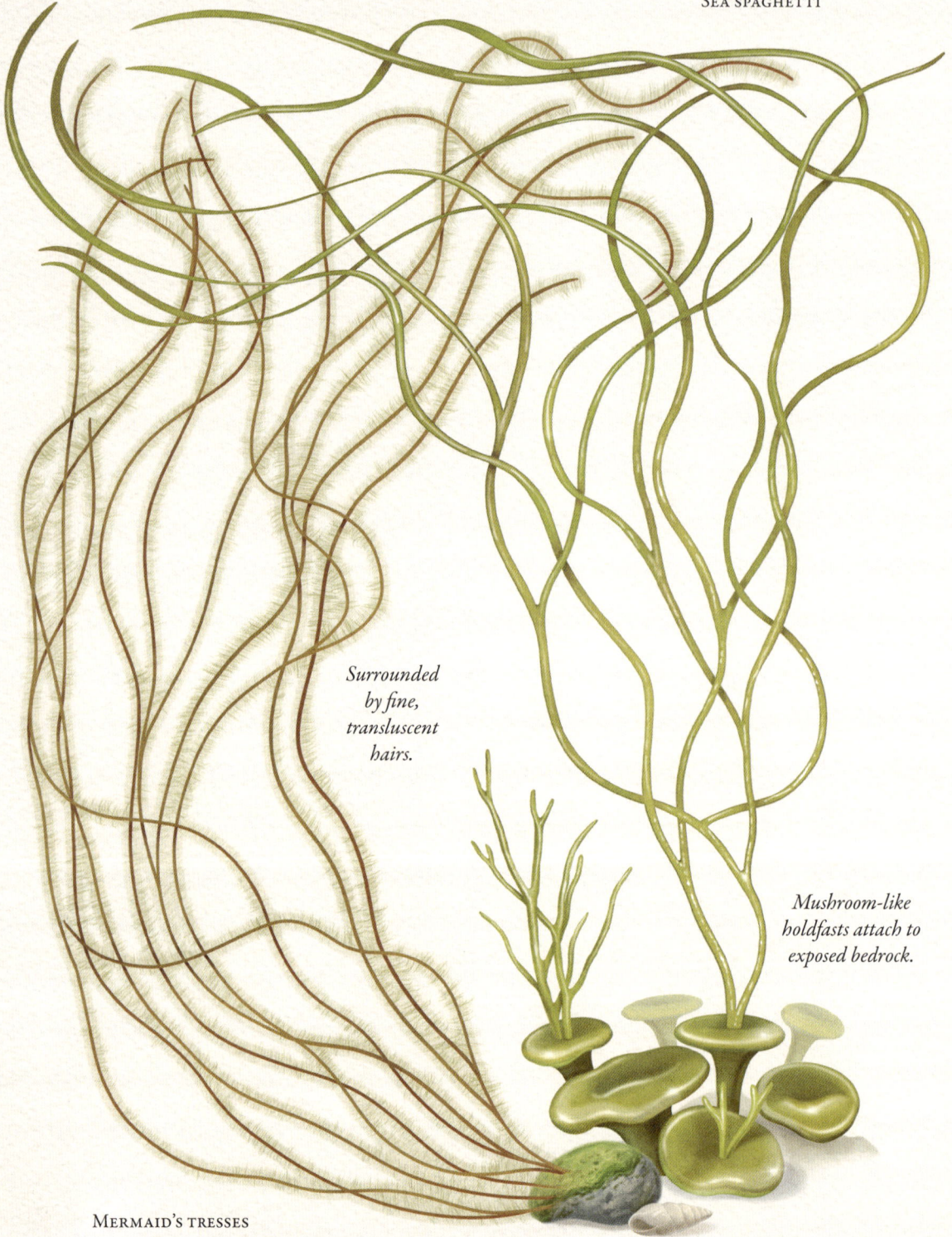

SEA SPAGHETTI

*Surrounded
by fine,
transluscent
hairs.*

*Mushroom-like
holdfasts attach to
exposed bedrock.*

MERMAID'S TRESSES

*Attaches
to pebbles.*

Sea spaghetti & Mermaid's tresses

These long thin seaweeds often confuse foragers, so I have grouped them together to help with comparison. They can be used in similar ways – primarily as a pasta substitute – but young sea spaghetti is best for this purpose. Mermaid's tresses have a crunchier, less pasta-like texture, even after cooking.

Sea spaghetti *Himanthalia elongata*

ALSO KNOWN AS Thongweed, sea thong, buttonweed, sea haricots.

EDIBILITY Mild tasting, filling and tender when young. Can be used as the name suggests, or as a vegetable. Older specimens are less appealing and can develop a strong iodine flavour.

IDENTIFICATION Long flattened spaghetti-like fronds growing from the middle of a green mushroom-shaped holdfast. Fronds are up to 2m (6ft) long, smooth and olive-brown at first, becoming textured and yellowish-brown as they develop. Usually two fronds per holdfast, but can be three or even four. They divide several times along the length.

DISTRIBUTION Widespread and abundant within its habitat in the eastern North Atlantic as far south as Portugal, and in the North and Baltic Seas. Absent from North America.

HABITAT Attached to gently sloping bedrock and large boulders between low mean and low spring tide lines, in semi-exposed and more sheltered locations with a strong tidal current, provided the water is clear.

WHEN TO HARVEST Spring to autumn, though at its best in spring and early summer.

Mermaid's tresses *Chorda phylum*

ALSO KNOWN AS Dead man's rope, sea lace, cat's gut or sea-catgut, bootlace weed, sea-twine and mermaid's fishing line.

EDIBILITY Mild tasting with a crisp texture – good in salads, or cooked in soups and stews.

IDENTIFICATION Grows in long strands up to 8m (26ft) long and is superficially similar to sea spaghetti. However, its fronds are unbranched, darker, thinner and hollow. In summer, the fronds are covered in fine translucent hairs – these are best observed in the water as they flatten against the frond when lifted out.

DISTRIBUTION Common and abundant on both sides of the North Atlantic.

HABITAT Well-sheltered subtidal locations, attached to stones and small pebbles, but its fronds grow so long it is easily harvested when paddling or bathing.

WHEN TO HARVEST Late spring and summer.

Harvesting sea spaghetti and mermaid's tresses

The best things in life may be free, but they usually involve a little effort, and you will have to put in a bit of work and planning to gather sea spaghetti at its best. It grows below the mean low tide line in clear water with plenty of current, so you'll need to plan your foraging around spring tides. This is treacherous terrain – slippery, unforgiving and not somewhere to rush. Take a friend and keep to the non-stick barnacles as much as possible.

The cute little green mushroom-like holdfasts (known rather delightfully as murkles in Scotland) can live for up to three years, but they only produce one lot of fronds during this time. Don't be tempted to harvest the holdfasts – they are tough and chewy, and you'll be impairing future growth. The fronds can be harvested by trimming a third off their length. You can also remove one entire frond from a holdfast: snip the frond off at the holdfast, leaving the second one or two in place.

Although mermaid's tresses grow subtidally, their enormous length and liking for sheltered waters make them easier to harvest. When you see them floating on the surface, a gentle pull on an individual strand should detach it from its holdfast, or, if its pebble anchor is small, it may lift it too – in which case, snip it off.

Eating sea spaghetti

Sea spaghetti fronds start to grow slowly in the winter, accelerating through spring and summer. The stage at which you harvest it will dictate its use in the kitchen. The sweet spot is in spring and early summer, when it is between 30 and 60cm (1–2ft) long. At this stage, it is slick, tender and a good direct substitute for spaghetti. As summer progresses, it enters its reproductive phase when the fronds swell, roughen, toughen and develop more of an iodine flavour. They are still fine for using as pasta at this stage, but not quite as good. By autumn, when its sinuous locks drape over large expanses of rock, it becomes more like tough tagliatelle than soft spaghetti and should be cooked in smaller pieces and for longer.

Sea spaghetti will keep (unwashed) in the fridge for up to a week and is one of few seaweeds that barely needs any washing – just a brief blast under the cold tap to reduce its slippery coating. Once dried, it keeps well for a year or more.

While sea spaghetti can be cooked and eaten like its wheat-based namesake, it is more filling, and a plateful might be a bit much for the uninitiated. If you are unsure, try mixing it half and half with regular spaghetti – this also makes for a nice colour contrast. Boiling time depends on the stage at which you harvested it. Young, thin, tender fronds need just a few minutes to reach al dente, up to the standard 9 or so minutes recommended for regular dried wheat spaghetti. The later, thicker growth may need 15 minutes or more to render it as tender as cooked pasta. At this stage, I cut it into small pieces and treat it more like macaroni or conchiglie and add it to soups and stews as a filler, rather than using it purely as a vehicle for sauce. Cooked sea spaghetti can be cooled and used in salads, especially with other vegetables prepared in long, thin ribbons, such as carrots and courgettes. See the recipe for (sea) spaghetti alle vongole on page 257. It is also excellent cold pickled (from fresh or dried) with lots of ginger, garlic, star anise and soy sauce – see page 261 for instructions.

Above: Young mermaid's tresses in spring. Note how the translucent hairs make it look blurry in the water. Opposite: Sea spaghetti is best harvested when it is about 30–60cm (1–2ft) long.

Eating mermaid's tresses

Mermaid's tresses can be used in similar ways to sea spaghetti, but it has a crunchier texture that is less pasta-like and doesn't readily soften when cooked. My favourite way to use it is to simmer it for 10 minutes, strain, refresh in cold water, then marinade it in soy sauce and sesame oil overnight, before using it in salads. Dextrous and creative cooks looking to impress may like to plait or knot it before serving. Its crisper texture also works well cold pickled (see page 261), but it will exude plenty of alginates that thicken the pickling solution. It does not dry and reconstitute well as food, but you can make an attractive coastal ornament by wrapping or plaiting it around a pebble then drying it – the laces will tighten around the stone.

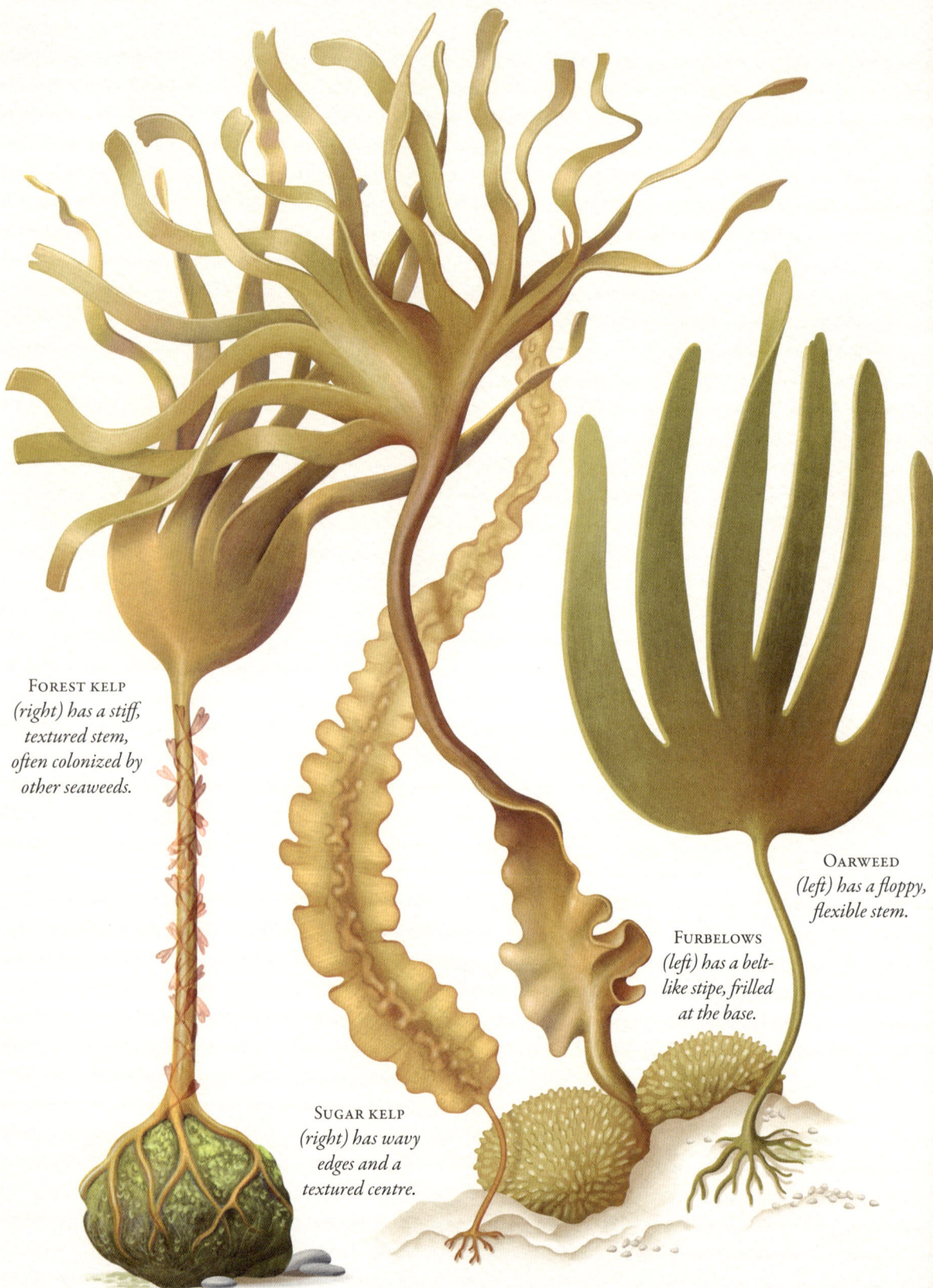

FOREST KELP
(right) has a stiff, textured stem, often colonized by other seaweeds.

SUGAR KELP
(right) has wavy edges and a textured centre.

FURBELOWS
(left) has a belt-like stipe, frilled at the base.

OARWEED
(left) has a floppy, flexible stem.

Kelp

Kelp is the general term for the large brown seaweeds that grow below the low tide line. Kelps of the North Atlantic are characterized by three features: a claw-like holdfast, a flexible stem, and a large, flat blade, which may split into belt-like straps. They grow bigger than other seaweeds, and their rapid growth rate helps them replenish colonies that are regularly damaged by storms. Although they are categorized as brown seaweeds, they can range in colour from olive-brown through golden-brown to yellowish-brown, depending on their stage of growth and condition. There are dozens of species worldwide, but five dominate the North Atlantic. Four of these – sugar kelp oarweed, forest kelp and furbelows – are similar enough that I have grouped them together. Dabberlocks is also a kelp, but is different enough to treat it separately (see page 214).

EDIBILITY A source of umami flavouring. Can be used as 'pasta', and younger specimens as a vegetable. Also makes a good biodegradable wrapping that can protect and season food during cooking.

DISTRIBUTION Widespread and abundant all around the North Atlantic.

HABITAT Attached to bedrock and large boulders below the mean low tide line. Unless you time your foray for the lowest part of a low spring tide, it's likely that you will have to get at least your feet wet to harvest kelps in any quantity.

WHEN TO HARVEST Year-round, but generally best in the spring and summer.

Kelps form the forests of the sea; complex ecosystems supporting a vast diversity of other species, including other seaweeds, which cling to their stems in a similar way as ivy might cover a tree. Others are adapted to the shady understory below the kelp canopy. This jungle of algae is home and larder to countless other organisms, from sea sponges to shellfish, fish to sea otters. Well-developed kelp forests can harbour more than 100,000 invertebrates per square metre, and store around 20 times as much carbon per acre as forests on land.

Sugar kelp
Saccharina latissima

ALSO KNOWN AS Poor man's weatherglass, sea belt, sweet kombu, sweet kelp, sweet tang, sugar tang, devil's apron.

SIZE Up to 4m (13ft) long (usually less), with a short stem and a long blade up to 25cm (10in) wide that has wavy edges and an embossed pattern. The blade does not have a midrib and does not divide.

BEST USES Use blades like kombu, fry into crisps or chips, or cut into tagliatelle or noodles, which are also good pickled.

Sugar kelp prefers sheltered and regularly disturbed locations, and it grows quickly from winter through early spring, reaching maturity at between two and five years. New blade growth happens just above the stipe, so instead of harvesting only the final third of a blade (which is older, tougher growth), cut just above the stipe and spread out your harvesting even more than usual. Once thoroughly dried, larger pieces of sugar kelp may form a white powder on their surface. This is the sweet substance that gives it its name – a natural sugar called mannitol, mixed with mineral salts. Sugar kelp is the closest Atlantic seaweed to *Saccharina japonica* and makes a slightly sweeter dashi than the other kelps.

Oarweed
Laminaria digitata

ALSO KNOWN AS Tangle, red ware, sea girdle, horsetail kelp.

SIZE Up to 2m (6½ft) long, with a large blade that usually divides into up to 10 strap-like fingers, growing from a floppy stipe that is oval in cross-section.

BEST USES Use blades like kombu or pasta. Slice stems thinly and use as a (chewy) vegetable.

The more exposed the location, the more the blades of oarweed will divide. In very sheltered water it may divide only once, or not at all. It lives to between four and six years, and is usually just above forest kelp in the tidal range. See page 146 for an image of oarweed exposed at low tide.

Forest kelp

Laminaria hyperborea

ALSO KNOWN AS Tangle, cuvie, sea rod.

SIZE Up to 3m (10ft) long, with a thick, round, bullwhip-like stem ending in a large tough blade that divides into 5–20 strap-like fingers, depending on local conditions and phenotypes.

BEST USE Use blades like kombu.

The best way to distinguish forest kelp from the superficially similar oarweed is by its thick, round stem, which holds its blades proud of the water like marine palm trees on extreme low tides (see image on page 146). The stems of mature specimens are almost always colonized by a host of smaller algae, including dulse. Individual plants can live up to 15 years, and you'll find large numbers of their stems washed up on exposed beaches. These are too tough to eat but have attracted interest in their possible use as biopolymers. In 2018 a commercial proposal to dredge 30,000 tons per year from inshore Scottish waters met with strong resistance.

Furbelows

Saccorhiza polyschides

ALSO KNOWN AS Sea hedgehog (due to the spiny holdfasts).

SIZE Up to 4m (13ft) long, with a strap-like stipe that has elegant, spring-like pleats near its base and a distinctive warty, scrotum-like holdfast. The blade divides into many long straps.

BEST USE Use blades like kombu.

The largest kelp of the North Atlantic, furbelows looks like an ancient creature of the deep but is in fact a fast-growing opportunist, an annual colonizer of disturbed seabeds that can grow up to four metres (13ft) over a single summer and has been observed to grow over two metres (6½ft) in one month. Its name comes from an old word for the pleats and frills found on dresses. The beautiful sprung pleats allow it to bend with powerful waves. The rather less glamorous warty holdfasts often detach from the stipe and cause much curiosity on the strandline.

Eating and cooking with kelp

Humans have used kelps for food and health for a long time. The giant kelp *Macrocystis* was identified as one of several seaweed species found in hearth remains at Monte Verde, a 14,000-year-old archaeological site in Chile. Another large kelp, *Ecklonia kurome*, was used in China over a thousand years ago to treat thyroid problems, and *Saccharina japonica* has been a food staple in Japan for at least 1,500 years.

The principal use of kelp in the kitchen is as a flavouring, with the blades used a little like bones in bone broth – to impart savoury richness and nutrients. Kombu is the name for the dried, aged kelp blades that are a cornerstone of Japanese cuisine, used, often along with smoked fermented tuna (katsuobushi or bonito), to infuse umami into a light savoury broth known as dashi. Many Eastern cuisines share a similar tradition. Kombu is made from a few species of kelp native to the Pacific, especially *Saccharina japonica*, which is particularly prized for the depth of flavour it imparts. Although North Atlantic kelps do not generally grow as large or contain as much flavour, their blades can be used in similar ways. Thick blades are best for kombu. Cut off up to one-third of the blade(s) with a sharp knife, leaving the stipe and holdfast intact. The blades can be used fresh, but drying and then aging them improves their flavour.

Thicker blades of kelp can also be used like sheets of lasagne. If using dried sheets, soften them a little in hot water for 5 minutes first. Thinner blades are good for cutting into thin strips and used like tagliatelle or noodles. Simmering time will depend on how thick they are.

Kelp blades can also be fried to make tasty crisps (or chips if you are American), but I don't recommend using old, leathery specimens. Moderately thick pieces, or the frill from the edge of a large piece of sugar kelp, can be deep fried, or brushed with oil and baked. Thinner blades can be dehydrated and briefly toasted to make finer-textured crisps. Sprinkling them with other ground seaweeds that have a spicy flavour (such as pepper dulse or wrack siphon weed) before drying will make them even more tasty.

If you aren't averse to a bit of chewing, the floppy stipes of sugar kelp and oarweed can be sliced into discs, boiled and eaten as a rather tough vegetable. Using a pressure cooker will help to soften them. They can also be thinly sliced and hot pickled (see page 261): leave them in the pickle to soften for one month before eating. Don't try this with forest kelp or furbelows stipes – they are too tough.

Sous weed cooking

As an alternative to the delicious but very plastic-intensive cookery technique called sous vide (under vacuum), I've coined the term, sous weed, for swaddling things in seaweed to retain moisture and add natural seasoning during cooking. Large pieces of fresh (or reconstituted) kelp are ideal for this, and there are a few ways to do it:

- Wrap large pieces of kelp around fish and meat joints, or whole vegetables, before roasting or barbecuing them.
- Layer vegetables or fish between pieces of kelp in a steamer to impart seasoning and umami as they cook.
- Lay thinly sliced raw fish, shellfish and vegetables on a mat of kelp, sprinkle with sugar, rice wine vinegar, and any herbs and seasonings you fancy, then place another sheet of kelp on top. Place something flat and heavy on top of that, and then leave to cure in the fridge overnight.

Atlantic dashi

Based on traditional Japanese recipes and my own experiments, I have developed a version of dashi that uses North Atlantic kelp and doesn't require bonito flakes.

Ingredients

5 thick blades of kelp (Fresh blades work, but dried blades, aged for up to one year, will impart a more complex flavour. If your blades are thin, use more.)

5L (8¾ pints) water

Optional but recommended embellishments

Skin of 4 naturally smoked white fish fillets, such as smoked cod or coley/pollock (If you can only get skinless fillets, use the meat.)

1 handful of dried penny bun mushrooms (aka cep, porcini, king bolete)

1 handful of dried shitake mushrooms

1 handful of dulse (see page 195), dried or fresh (Dulse contains more umami than Atlantic kelps: you could make this recipe with only dulse, but it won't be as subtle.)

2 teaspoons powdered laver (see page 181)

Please treat this as guidance rather than a prescriptive recipe: everything but the kelp and water is optional, but the more embellishments you use, the more flavour the broth will have.

Slowly heat all the ingredients in a pan. Remove the kelp (which will have turned green) with a slotted spoon or tongs just before it comes to the boil. Don't be tempted to boil it with the kelp in it as this can cause bitterness. Leave simmering for 20 minutes for the other ingredients to infuse. Strain the liquid completely, or eat it with all but the fish skins still in.

Wild coastal broth

This is a great way to combine the shellfish and succulent plants of the coast in a flavoursome seaweed broth based on the Atlantic dashi recipe on the previous page.

Ingredients

Atlantic dashi (see page 205)

Miso paste

Soy sauce

Optional ingredients

Razor clam garum (see page 249)

Clam juice

Shredded wild garlic (ramps)

Fermented wild garlic (ramps)

Midrib and wings of young dabberlocks

Razor clam meat, raw

Mussels, cockles or winkles, lightly steamed or boiled and removed from their shells

Any of the coastal vegetables in this book, shredded or broken up into bite-sized pieces

Smoked haddock (left over from making dashi), flaked

Pepper dulse, fresh and dried

Hard-boiled eggs, cut into pieces

Dried sea lettuce flakes

Heat the dashi in a pan, stirring in miso paste and soy sauce a tablespoon at a time, until you like the taste.

Divide the embellishments you are using between serving bowls. Pour over the broth while it is boiling hot, and sprinkle on sea lettuce flakes and pepper dulse (if using). If you're using razor clams, the broth will poach them without toughening them.

To ramp up the umami even further, try adding laver stock (see page 181), and for more body, add a little carrageen gel (see page 187).

Pea-sized float bladders.

Small, elongated receptacles.

Wiry stem.

Wireweed

Sargassum muticum

This large and rather beautiful seaweed is a relatively new arrival in the North Atlantic, brought from the Pacific as packaging for oysters and in the ballast tanks of ships. Although it has not been welcomed by marine conservationists, pragmatic foragers can take advantage of its rapid growth.

ALSO KNOWN AS Japanese wireweed, Japweed, strangleweed.

EDIBILITY The main stem tends to be tough and wiry; fine fronds and receptacles are more tender.

IDENTIFICATION Golden brown finely branching 1–4m (3–13ft) long, occasionally longer, pea-sized float bladders and small elongated receptacles. When lifted out of the water, it resembles a washing line with lots of pieces of dirty brown, torn washing.

HABITAT Attached to rocks and pebbles and in rock pools in the mid- to lower tidal range on moderately to well sheltered coast.

DISTRIBUTION Widely distributed on the Atlantic coast of Europe.

WHEN TO HARVEST Summer/autumn. Best in late spring and early summer, after which it can become too wiry. Dies back to its holdfast in autumn.

SIMILAR SPECIES Egg wrack (see page 165).

Sustainable harvesting

Wireweed is a problematic non-native invasive species in some parts of the North Atlantic. Aided by its ability to float freely for months on end, and rapid annual growth, it finds new locations, grabs gaps in the seaweed canopy and outcompetes native species. Over time, it learns some manners and more politely integrates with its neighbours, but you can, on the whole, feel good about harvesting as much wireweed as you like.

Two related *Sargassum* species form free-floating mats in the Sargasso Sea that grow so huge they regularly become a navigation hazard. They are also known for their propensity to bio-accumulate heavy metals such as lead and arsenic. Although wireweed appears to be less likely to do so, take extra care to collect it away from both current and historic industrial areas.

Eating wireweed

Avoid the main stem which is tough and wiry, and focus on the more tender side branches and receptacles, rather like the wracks (see page 163).

Young growth and tender tips are not especially flavoursome but are excellent marinaded in soy sauce and finely chopped ginger, or can be added as an interesting texture/bulker to salads, stews and broths.

Dried and ground, it develops a slightly fishy flavour that is good stirred through créme fraîche with a squeeze of lemon juice to make a dip and also makes a flavoursome seasoning or nutrient-rich stock powder. You'll need to ensure it is fully dehydrated and use a good grinder.

Opposite: Wireweed looks elegant and beautiful in the water but can form dense canopies that dominate other seaweeds.

Other species of interest

Dabberlocks

Alaria esculenta

ALSO KNOWN AS Atlantic wakame, alaria, winged kelp, badderlocks, henware, honeyware, murlins.

DISTRIBUTION Common within its habitat on both sides of the North Atlantic, as far south as Cape Cod and Brittany.

Dabberlocks has a root-like holdfast anchoring a short cylindrical stipe that continues as a distinct midrib throughout the length of the narrow, ribbon-like, crenulated blade up to 1.5m (5ft) long, occasionally longer, with the blade growing up to 7cm (4in) either side of the midrib, tapering inwards towards the tip. The blade is supple to the touch and very flexible. It does not branch, but several short belt-like wings splay from the stipe below the main blade. You'll find it attached to baserock and large boulders at and below the low spring tide line, on exposed coast.

It's the closest native seaweed we have in the North Atlantic to the wakame (*Undaria pinnatifida*) so beloved in Japanese cuisine. Unlike its Pacific cousin, it likes rough, cold waters, and mature plants can't survive long in warmer water. As a result, dabberlocks colonies are currently being explored as a means of tracking rising ocean temperatures. When it grows on the upper extreme of its tidal range – where foragers are most likely to encounter it – its glossy silken blades tear, discolour and almost dissolve as the water warms during summer, often leaving just the midrib behind by autumn. It is best harvested during spring and early summer to avoid this deterioration. It has a shorter harvesting window towards the south of its range, and on the upper fringe of its tidal zone.

Dabberlocks can be used in all the ways I have described for other kelps on pages 204–205, plus a few more that suit its more pliant texture and gentle nutty flavour. It can be used as a substitute for wakame in miso soup, or any soup for that matter. It is rich in sugars, protein, vitamins and minerals, and iodine. The succulent midrib of young to middle-aged specimens make excellent 'noodles'. In Ireland, the midrib of older specimens are traditionally chewed after drying.

For a delicious dabberlocks salad, snip tender fronds across their length into 1cm (⅜in)-wide ribbons that each contain some of the midrib and some of the thin-fleshed blade, then dress with a little oil, vinegar, soy sauce, ginger and perhaps a sprinkling of toasted sesame seeds.

Older, tougher specimens can be steamed or simmered in water until the midrib feels tender – a few minutes is usually ample for all but the largest specimens. It will turn a vibrant green colour, which you can retain by quickly refreshing it in cold water, then using as above, or stir-fried and served as a vegetable.

Velvet horn

Codium spp.

ALSO KNOW AS Sponge tang, spongeweed, green sponge fingers, green sea fingers, dead man's fingers, green fleece, oyster thief, felty fingers, sea staghorn, forked felt-alga.

DISTRIBUTION Widespread, but can be locally rare.

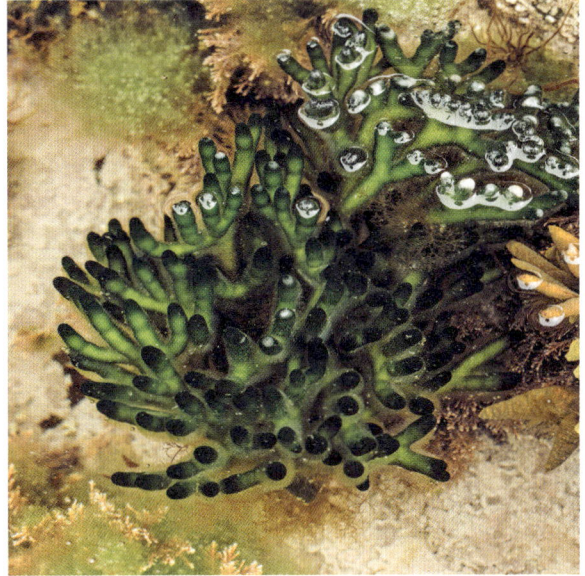

It's always a pleasure to stumble on velvet horn's vibrant green dreadlocks, in deeper rock pools on the upper and mid-shore. The branching 5mm (¼in)-wide, 50cm (20in)-long fronds arise from a small basal disc. They have a velvety sheen, a spongy texture and are round in cross-section. It is easy to identify the genus *Codium*, but tricky to distinguish between individual species. Around the UK and much of northern Europe, the most common species, *C. fragile* subsp. *fragile*, is a non-native that is gradually displacing the native *C. fragile* subsp. *atlanticum*. *C. tomentosum* is also present on both sides of the North Atlantic. *C. decorticatum* is common along the North American coast.

All the different species are similarly edible and good for you. They have a pleasing hint of (salty) French beans, but the spongy texture is not for everyone. A wide body of research points to immunostimulatory, anticancer, anti-inflammatory, antioxidant, antiviral, antibacterial and antifungal properties.

Harvest velvet horn in spring/summer where you see a large, well established colony, thinning it by trimming up to a third from a few fronds per plant. As you do so, look out for a rather splendid little green sea slug with iridescent spots called the sap-sucking slug (*Elysia viridis*), which feeds on it and steals intact photosynthesizing cells that it uses as an energy source. Clever wee thing.

Localized species of *Codium* are very popular as food in Japan, China, Korea and the Philippines, where they are widely cultivated. In the West, we may need to do a bit

of palate retraining to get used to its saltiness and spongy texture. Soaking it in fresh water for half an hour before lightly steaming and dressing with butter is a nice way to start. Frying it in tempura batter allows its softness and saltiness to shine from within a crispy coating.

Fully dehydrated and ground or crumbled, it makes an excellent seasoning, or for a glamorous garnish-cum-seasoning, partially dehydrate whole fronds then quickly crisp them up in hot fat before laying them over dishes. Their attractive silhouettes break up into salty crumbs of umami-rich seasoning as the food is eaten.

Fresh or reconstituted velvet horn works well chopped into salads with juicy fresh fruits and vegetables – think of it like salty capers or soy sauce-dipped noodles. Mixing with chopped tomatoes, finely diced onion, ginger and pepper is the go-to way of eating it in the Philippines, where it is sometimes further embellished with green mangoes.

The Intertidal Zone:
Shellfish

All that burrows & squirts

great battles are waged
empires rise and fall and rise
within a rock pool

The rewards of shellfish foraging are much like other areas of foraging (only with more protein), but the challenges are quite different: less to do with accurate identification than ascertaining that your quarry is healthy, and having the know-how, confidence and time to keep it that way, all the way to your mouth. Mixing up a surf clam with a cockle is a minor foraging faux pas rather than a medical emergency, but eating any shellfish harvested from an algal bloom site may be. Please read my safe harvesting advice on the following pages carefully.

It is also necessary to kill shellfish before (or possibly as) you eat them, something that shouldn't be taken lightly. If you are squeamish or have ethical issues with this, perhaps shellfish foraging isn't for you. Personally, I view thinning a shellfish colony much like thinning a plant or seaweed colony: inconvenient rather than destructive to the larger entity, and with less impact on nature than flying other proteins – animal or plant-based – around the world.

Another challenge around gathering wild shellfish is that you may be seeking something that has significant commercial value. The term 'fishery' describes the commercial exploitation of shellfish as well as fish, including the location at which it takes place, and there may be regulations associated with it. These are seldom aimed at hobby foragers, but should be respected nevertheless.

There are enough things to consider when shellfish foraging to turn careful foragers into nervous foragers. I encourage you to proceed slowly and thoughtfully, researching your coast with the aid of tide tables, chats with experienced locals and the resources section on pages 264–5. The process of looking will open your senses to the incredible diversity of extraordinary creatures that live in the intertidal zone, and perhaps one day your fridge too will echo with squelching noises.

Harvesting & handling shellfish safely

Most experienced wild shellfish enthusiasts have a stoic humour about the risks involved, usually involving quips about staying close to a toilet. However, although the risks should not be underestimated, they are easy to mitigate with a little knowledge and care.

Bivalves carry the most risk because they are filter feeders, sieving large amounts of seawater, collecting and concentrating any problematic compounds it may contain. This chapter covers mussels, cockles, oysters, clams and razor clams, with detailed information on how to handle each species. Less troublesome are the gastropods, such as limpets and winkles. They graze on algae and have a much lower throughput of seawater, though they can still bioaccumulate toxic organisms and compounds.

Key safety concerns

Bacteria and water quality

Not all bacteria are problematic (in fact, we couldn't live without them), but some can cause diarrhoea and vomiting when they occur in sufficient quantities in our food. Chief among these troublesome bacteria for shellfish foragers is *Escherichia coli* (widely known as *E.coli*) which reaches problematic quantities where sewage, agricultural run-off, or animal and bird faeces accumulate in the sea, and is used as an indicator of general bacterial contamination.

Seawater quality is often monitored at popular bathing beaches and where commercial fisheries exist, though to different standards. 'High quality' bathing spots permit around 50 times more *E. coli* than 'high quality' shellfish-harvesting waters. Bathing water ratings are widely publicized (see page 265), but shellfish water-monitoring reports tend to be complex and full of jargon. The challenge is further compounded by the nature of the marine environment: what is safe one week may not be the next.

E. coli and other problematic bacteria are killed by cooking, so they only become a major problem if you eat shellfish raw or undercooked. Only eat raw wild shellfish that you are certain have come from pristine waters, and see my notes on depuration on page 223.

Viruses

Shellfish exposed to human sewage can harbour viruses such as norovirus, which cause gastroenteritis. Like bacteria, they are destroyed by cooking, and should only be an issue if the shellfish is eaten raw.

Algae and algal blooms

Algae are the microscopic cousins of seaweeds that live in aquatic environments and use photosynthesis to produce energy from sunlight. A few types of algae naturally produce compounds that can be toxic. These only become problematic when they grow excessively into large-scale 'blooms', which can be harmful to people, animals, fish, seaweeds and other parts of the ecosystem.

A complex array of factors contribute to algal blooms, but chief among them are warm temperatures and excessive nutrients from fertilizers or sewage entering the water as run-off. Algal blooms are categorized as green, blue-green, red or brown, depending on the type of algae. Some are easy to spot but others are not, and you can't always tell if a body of water has a harmful bloom just by looking at it. Shellfish and seaweeds exposed to toxic algal blooms can harbour a nasty range of illnesses, with symptoms ranging from gastrointestinal distress to neurological impairment and paralysis. *Importantly, cooking shellfish contaminated by algal blooms does not destroy all the toxins.*

Local authorities and environmental agencies monitor for algal blooms and post warning notices along the coast where they occur, but remote locations may be missed. As always, speaking to locals is a good way to gather information, as are local environmental and fishing websites. Most algal blooms occur in the summer, so (in the Northern Hemisphere) not gathering shellfish in months without an 'R' is a good rule of thumb and should minimize risk, but stay vigilant in the autumn too.

Chemicals
Fish, shellfish and seaweeds can accumulate chemical contaminants in their tissues. Some contaminants can be naturally occurring, such as heavy metals and hydrocarbons; others are a result of human pollutants, such as pesticides, coolants, flame retardants and mining operations. Follow water-quality advice and steer well clear of busy ports, harbours, mines (both current and historic) and urban centres to minimize the risks.

Microplastics
Approximately eight million metric tons of plastics enter our oceans annually, breaking down into tiny pieces, resulting in micro- and nanoplastics measuring between 5mm (³⁄₁₆in) and 1 micron (one-thousandth of a millimetre). Conservative estimates suggest 5.25 trillion plastic particles are circulating in ocean surface waters, with 10 times that amount on the seafloor and in sediments.

Inevitably, all shellfish, and filter-feeders in particular, absorb microplastics, which may be ingested as you eat them. The physical effects of accumulated microplastics on humans are not yet fully understood but have been linked to enhanced inflammatory responses and disrupted gut microbiomes. Depuration (see page 223) is an effective way to minimize microplastics in wild harvested shellfish, but it isn't guaranteed to get rid of them all.

Parasites
Over 40 species of parasites associated with seafood, including protozoa, worms and flukes, have been reported in humans. Harvesting in clean water and cooking minimizes any risks.

Radiation
We are exposed to naturally occurring background radiation all the time and it isn't harmful. When non-naturally-occurring radioactive particles enter the sea they can contaminate shellfish and seaweed and, in sufficient concentrations, pose a health threat to anyone eating them by increasing the likelihood of cancer. Where present, radioactive particles are most likely to accumulate in sediment, making cockles and other clams most susceptible. I harvest a good deal of the shellfish I eat from the enormous Solway Firth Estuary, which

is also home (over 80km/50 miles away) to Sellafield nuclear power plant, so this is a topic I've paid particular attention to. After testing, measuring and comparing radiation levels in shellfish along the coast immediately around the nuclear facility, Public Health England concluded that 'the overall health risk from the consumption of radioactive particles within molluscs and crustaceans is estimated to be very low, with the chance of an adult dying from cancer as a result of 1 year's potential exposure being less than 1 in 15 billion'. This is seven times higher than someone who ate no shellfish from the area, but still 10,000 times smaller than the level of risk that the UK Health and Safety Executive considers to be the upper limit for an acceptable level of risk.

Similar work done on Canada's west coast following the Fukushima nuclear disaster noted 'no observed anthropogenic radioactivity in either shells or meat of shellfish' and found that 'radioactive content [was] dominated by naturally occurring radionuclides and poses no health risk'. For my level of wild shellfish and seaweed consumption (which is considerably more than most), this satisfies me, but you may feel differently. Whatever the statistics say, there is no fun in eating something you feel nervous about, so read the peer-reviewed scientific reports yourself (see page 265) and make your own mind up.

Rapid spoiling
Despite all these potential hazards, the main sources of illnesses from eating wild shellfish are poor handling, storage and cooking practices, all things that foragers can control. Shellfish deteriorate, die and begin to decompose faster than most other foods, so evaluating their condition, handling them hygienically, cooking them properly and eating them as soon as possible is critical. These processes vary a little between shellfish species, so check the details for individual species in the following pages.

Shellfish allergies
A shellfish allergy is an oversensitive response by the body's immune system to proteins in the flesh and/or shells of shellfish. Some people with a shellfish allergy react to all shellfish, while others react to only certain kinds. Crustaceans such as shrimp, prawns and crabs cause the greatest number of allergic reactions. Many shellfish-allergic people can eat molluscs with no problem. Reactions range from mild – such as hives or a stuffy nose – to severe and even life-threatening. If you are allergic to shellfish, you obviously won't be harvesting them, but be mindful also that most seaweeds are likely to contain shellfish fragments even after thorough rinsing – see page 157.

Minimum landing size

Where commercial fisheries exist, there is likely to be a minimum landing size (MLS) for shellfish. Shellfish sizes are measured across the widest or longest part of the shell or carapace. For quick measurement while foraging, gauges with marked minimum landing sizes for different species are commercially available, but finding a plastic ring of the same diameter as the MLS of your quarry is simpler – if the shell fits through, it goes back in the water.

There may also be a maximum landing quota for shellfish, limiting the number you can harvest from a particular location. Some locations may require you to have a permit to harvest certain shellfish, and local wardens might monitor popular locations at popular times. Recreational shellfish permits tend to be cheap and easy to obtain, and often come with lots of good safety and sustainability advice. Start by looking for notices at the beach and enquiring with local authorities. If no information is forthcoming, follow the common-sense guidelines I have provided for each species.

Opposite: A plastic hoop, or similar, is handy for quickly checking your harvest is above minimum landing size.

Shellfish safety checklist

- Avoid harvesting in urban areas, harbours, marinas, narrow estuaries and industrial sites.
- Avoid harvesting in summer months. This helps avoid algal blooms, spawning periods and hot weather when shellfish may bake in the sun between tides. In much of the North Atlantic, this is remembered by not harvesting unless there is an 'R' in the month, but the off-season may be longer in the south and shorter in the north.
- Depurate molluscs and gastropods in clean, cool, oxygenated, salinated water (see opposite).
- Do not store shellfish in fresh water.
- Ensure shellfish remain alive until they are cooked.
- Cook shellfish as soon as possible after harvesting/depuration.

- Always cook your wild shellfish, unless you are sure that they came from pristine waters.
- If you intend to store shellfish, cook them, then rapidly cool then refrigerate them, and use within two days.
- Research harvesting locations, paying particular attention to algal blooms, water discharge, sewage hotspots and any local minimum landing sizes:
  – Check websites of local authorities, environmental agencies and food standards agencies.
  – Visit sites and make personal observations: e.g. unpleasant films or solids in the water, obvious discharge pipes, etc.
  – Enquire in person with locals.

Depuration

Commercially traded bivalves, whether farmed or harvested wild, must be depurated before sale unless they are growing in pristine waters. This is done in giant tanks circulating temperature-controlled seawater through ultraviolet-irradiated chambers that destroy bacterial contaminants.

It is not possible to emulate these depuration systems at home without spending a small fortune. Domestic-scale depuration will help to purge the shellfish of sand and whatever they have been eating (including most microplastics), but without ultraviolet chambers there is no guarantee of removing bacteria. The main role of home-depuration is to reduce the amount of sand and grit in the flesh of the shellfish – *it is not a way to render unsafe harvests safe*. On the contrary, it may introduce further potential hazards if you don't do it correctly, so please carefully follow the directions below, being sure to use cool, clean, well-oxygenated water of the correct salinity.

Materials
- A large basin or roasting pan.
- A mesh tray that can fit inside your large basin (useful but not essential).
- Salt – any kind will do, but sea salt seems appropriate.
- Clean tap water.
- Fine oatmeal (optional).

Instructions

1 Thoroughly rinse your shellfish in clean tap water to remove excess sand and grit – this stops it from being absorbed back into the meat during depuration.

2 Place the mesh tray (if using one) inside the basin. This helps to keep the shellfish clear of any sediment they drop and aids aeration and removal, but it is not essential.

3 Place the shellfish in the basin (or on the mesh tray in the basin). The shellfish should be no more than two deep, with plenty of room for water in the basin.

4 Fill the basin with saline solution made by dissolving 35g (2 tbsp) of salt per 1L (2 pints) of clean tap water. Adding a handful or two of fine oatmeal to the water can improve depuration, but it is not essential.

5 Leave the pan in a cool place to depurate. The temperature should emulate the molluscs' usual ambient range, so set the tray outside in the shade, or in the fridge if the sea they came from is cool. Recommended depuration times vary between species – see below.

6 It is important to aerate the water during the depuration process or the shellfish will die of oxygen starvation. To do this, use a clean, empty squeeze bottle to hand-pump air through the water for a few minutes. If you are using a mesh tray, lift it high out of the basin a few times, allowing the water to splash down into the basin. Try to aerate the water every two hours. Use the shellfish soon after depuration.

RECOMMENDED DEPURATION TIMES

These times assume that you aerate the water every two hours and keep it near sea temperature.

MUSSELS	DEPURATION RECOMMENDED	6–8 HOURS
OYSTERS	DEPURATION RECOMMENDED	6–8 HOURS
COCKLES	DEPURATION RECOMMENDED	6 HOURS
CLAMS	DEPURATION RECOMMENDED	6 HOURS
WINKLES	DEPURATION MAY REDUCE GRIT	4–8 HOURS. PLACE A LID ON THE BASIN
LIMPETS	DEPURATION NOT ESPECIALLY HELPFUL BUT MAY REDUCE GRIT	
RAZOR CLAMS	DEPURATION NOT NECESSARY	

*Beards (byssus) are used
to attach to rocks.*

*Tiny female pea crabs
sometimes live inside
live mussels.*

Mussels

Mytilus edulis

Mussels often occur in vast colonies, providing food and protection for a multitude of other small animals in the intertidal zone. Their minute larvae are eaten by fish and jellyfish, and after they develop their shells they are still rich pickings for starfish, gulls, crabs and predatory whelks. One 5cm (2in) mussel can filter up to 50 litres (13 gal) of seawater per day, and colonies play a vital role in estuaries by removing bacteria and toxins. Like canaries in a coal mine, mussels are bio-indicators of the health of the seas they inhabit, which is why they should only be foraged from clean waters.

ALSO KNOWN AS Blue mussel.

EDIBILITY Excellent eating, but pay attention to safety and cleaning (see page 222).

IDENTIFICATION Distinctive black to blueish asymmetric hinged shells, often with pale concentric banding, especially in mature specimens. Fully grown at between 4cm and 8cm (1½–3in). Recommended minimum harvesting size: 5cm (2in).

DISTRIBUTION Very common within its habitat all around the world.

HABITAT Attached to rocks, piers and jetties in (often very large) colonies, between the mid-upper and subtidal range.

WHEN TO HARVEST September–April, best in autumn.

SIMILAR SPECIES *Mytilus edulis* is a species complex, with regionalized variants around the world. All variants are edible and abundant within their regions – foragers need not worry about their subtle differences.

Mussels use a small 'beard' of threads called a byssus to anchor themselves securely to rocks. It is made from iron deposits that the mussel extracts from seawater and secretes as a liquid from an adapted 'foot'. On contact with the water, the threads congeal into tough tethers that adhere to rocks using a strong glue. Some mussels have been observed using their byssal threads to hold predatory whelks at bay. This remarkable stuff has inspired all manner of glues and fibres, including biodegradable replacements for plastic fishing lines and nets.

Sustainable harvesting

Mussels generally grow in such numbers that foraging them for personal use is unlikely to make any impact on established colonies. If no local guidance or landing restrictions are available, gathering only those over 5cm (2in) in length (or from only the largest 25 per cent of a colony) and moving your harvesting location around (both within a season and from year to year) are good practices.

Safety notes

More people get sick from eating wild mussels than any other wild shellfish. This is no doubt because they are common and widely recognized, so more people eat them. But it's also because opportunistic foragers aren't always aware of best practice or don't take it seriously. Wild mussels are delicious and very good for you, but you should know the risks and how to minimize them, as detailed on page 223. Depuration can help to remove sand and impurities, and reduces microbial contamination, but it will not magically make contaminated mussels safe to eat.

Only cook live mussels. A live mussel will be tightly closed, or it will close when tapped or squeezed (they don't snap shut – gradual closing is normal). Trust your senses (especially your nose) before and after cooking: discard any with pale or shrivelled meat or unpleasant smells. Ensure your mussels are fully cooked. The meat of a healthy mussel once cooked should look opaque and orange, and smell pleasantly fishy. Un- or undercooked mussels look unappetizing: jelly-like, uncoagulated, somewhat translucent and with a strong tendency to split apart and stick to the perimeter of the shell.

There is an old, often-repeated rumour that mussels which do not open on cooking are dead and must be discarded. This is not a reliable way to evaluate mussels, as there is a good deal of variance in how they respond to heat. In lab tests, it was found that 1.9 per cent of mussels opened before they had been cooked long enough to kill all potential heat-sensitive pathogens; 11.5 per cent of mussels remained closed, but when forced open with a knife were found to be adequately cooked and safe to eat. So the 'rule' does not keep you safe and leads to a lot of wasted mussels – it has been calculated that it results in 370 metric tons (408 tons) of perfectly good cultivated mussels worth around $3 million being thrown away each year!

Cleaning and preparing mussels

Barnacles are a major nuisance. If you are lucky, your local mussel colony will be relatively free of them – exposed locations tend to have less. If you wish to cook and eat your mussels in the shell, moules marinières style, you will need to scrape the barnacles off first, otherwise they will fall off as the mussels cook, forming an unpleasant crunchy sediment in the cooking juices. Scrape them off under a gently running tap with a blunt knife. If you don't have the time or patience to do this, you could try cooking the mussels as normal, then sieving the cooking juices, but in my experience, pieces of barnacle remain caught within the mussels and can't be adequately removed without shelling and rinsing them.

Using a mussel shell to pluck other mussels from their shells is one of the great pleasures of eating seafood, so it is with a heavy heart that I have concluded that the delicious but barnacle-heavy mussels that grow near me are far too much work (or crunch) to serve in their shells. For these, my method is to cook them barnacles and all, then strain and reserve the cooking liquid (which is full of delicious juices that are an important part of any mussel recipe), remove the mussels from their shells, and thoroughly rinse them before use. Even then, I occasionally still find tiny-but-tooth-crunching pearls deep within the mussel flesh. There isn't much you can do about this, other than chewing gingerly.

Byssus threads are less troublesome. Remove them before cooking by holding the tuft between thumb and forefinger and firmly pulling it towards the narrow end of the shell. If you don't do this when the mussel is alive and closed, the threads will remain attached throughout the cooking process. They are not harmful, but neither are they pleasant to eat, and removing them from a cooked and open mussel usually pulls the mussel meat apart in the process.

Although mussels will stay alive in the fridge for up to 48 hours, I strongly recommend cleaning and cooking them as soon as possible after harvesting and depuration. If you are storing them, cover them with a damp cloth but do not keep them in water. Cooked mussels will also keep refrigerated in a sealed tub for a few days, but the sooner they are eaten the better. If you intend to keep cooked mussels for more than 24 hours, it is better to freeze them.

For converting recipes that call for cooking mussels in the shell, one de-shelled wild mussel usually weighs about one-third of its weight with shell.

Simple mussel cooking method

Mussels are generally steamed in a small amount of liquid. As they cook, their juices join the liquid at the bottom of the pan to make a delicious broth.

Heat 5cm (2in) of water (or white wine) in a large pan with a tightly fitting lid until it is boiling. Place the live, debearded mussels in the pan and replace the lid. Turn up the heat and leave to steam for 4 minutes.

Shake or stir the mussels, then replace the lid and steam for another 2 minutes. Inspect the mussels: if more than 80 per cent are open, remove from the heat and strain, retaining the cooking liquid; if not, leave to cook for another 2 minutes before inspecting again. Remove the mussels with a slotted spoon. Unopened mussels can be returned to the cooking liquid for further cooking, levered open and inspected as outlined above, or discarded. Strain the cooking liquid through a fine sieve or muslin.

Depending on how thoroughly you have depurated and cleaned them, it's your choice whether to use your mussels in their shells or remove them from their shells. Mussels prepared in this way can be used in stir-fries, salads, bouillabaisse, or pickled (see page 258). They can be used interchangeably, or mixed, with cockles and clams in most recipes.

Moules marinières and variants

This classic French dish can be easily made by adapting the simple cooking method above.

Use depurated, barnacle-free mussels. Gently fry finely chopped shallots (scallions), garlic, bay leaves and thyme in a little butter before adding wine at the beginning of the cooking process. Once you are happy that the mussels are cooked, add cream and freshly chopped parsley and continue to cook, stirring until the hot broth has coated the mussels.

For a twist, use beer or cider rather than wine as the steaming liquid. Another nice variation is to use onion and Thai green curry paste rather than shallots and herbs at the beginning, and finish with coconut milk rather than cream. Shredded wild garlic is great strewn over any mussel dish.

To open an oyster,
a knife should be inserted
and levered here.

Everything that
easily detaches from
the shell is edible.

Store oysters flat,
with the cupped side
on the bottom.

Oysters

Ostrea spp. *and Crassostrea* spp.

Oysters are natural reef builders, forming beds with 50 times the surface area of an unoccupied seabed, thereby making countless niches for algae, small beasties and the larger fish and shellfish that prey on them. Their tendency to build these huge beds in estuaries made them accessible to early humans: 10,000-year-old oyster-shell middens have been found in Australia, they have been cultivated in Japan for over 4,000 years, and the Romans were enthusiastic consumers. Oysters remained an important food well into the 1900s, when the Thames Estuary and New York Harbour provided millions of cheap wild oysters that fed the burgeoning urban working classes. Fecundity is their key to success – a single oyster can produce up to 100 million eggs annually, and equally as many sperm.

EDIBILITY Excellent eating, but pay attention to safety (see page 222).

IDENTIFICATION Two oval or teardrop-shaped shells, the lower cupped, the upper flat, hinged at their narrowest point. See below for species characteristics.

DISTRIBUTION Varies by species.

HABITAT Lower intertidal and subtidal range, with a preference for shallow estuaries, where they may form reefs.

WHEN TO HARVEST September–April.

HARVESTING RESTRICTIONS May apply, especially to native species – check local regulations (see page 265).

Similar species

Pacific oyster (*Crassostrea gigas* or *Magallana gigas*, illustrated on page 228). Introduced for cultivation to Europe and eastern North America in the early 20th century, the Pacific oyster has since escaped into the wild, where it is now considered a problematic non-native invasive species, especially as warming seas allow it to spawn more readily. It has elongated teardrop-shaped grey shells measuring up to 18cm (7in) long with many bumps and ridges, and attaches to jetties, rocks and other oysters in the lower intertidal zone. This is the oyster you are most likely to be served in restaurants. There are no restrictions on harvesting it from the wild in UK waters – in fact, you may be actively encouraged to remove as many as you can. Our local coastal ranger once delivered several dozen to me that he had removed from a sensitive site!

Portuguese oyster (*Crassostrea angulata* or *Magallana angulata*) is another introduced cultivated oyster in UK waters that is now considered a non-native invasive species. It is very similar to the Pacific oyster, though less able to naturally reproduce in colder waters.

European flat oyster (*Ostrea edulis*) was once an abundant native oyster of northern Europe but is now considered quite scarce, mostly restricted in the UK to localized fisheries in England and one in south-west Scotland. It is occasionally cultivated in North America, where it is known as the flat oyster, mud oyster or Belon. Wild colonies are mostly subtidal and tend to be protected either as controlled fisheries or for conservation reasons. The shells are flatter, rounder and less corrugated than those of other oysters, with a brownish hue. They grow up to 12cm (5in) long at their broadest point, with a minimum landing size of 7cm (3in), and are harvested between November and February. They have a stronger, more iodine taste than their cultivated cousins, and are generally more esteemed by gourmets.

Eastern oyster (*Crassostrea virginica*), also known as the Atlantic oyster, American oyster and East Coast oyster, the eastern oyster is native to the eastern seaboard of North (and South) America. It was once a prolific and important commercial species, but its distribution has been decimated by over-fishing and habitat degradation. While it isn't yet rare, it is now classed as vulnerable in the wild. It is similar in size and appearance to the pacific oyster, but with a smoother shell.

Racoon oyster (*Dendostrea frons*), also known as the frond oyster, this species likes to attach itself to mangrove roots and can be found along the east coast of North America, from North Carolina southwards. It is smaller and much folded at the edges.

Saddle oyster (*Anomia ephippium*) is not a true oyster but may be mistaken for a small one. It grows up to 6cm (2½in) long, is thin-shelled and pale brown, and usually has a hole in the lower shell which takes on the shape of its substrate. Common on both sides of the Atlantic, it tastes bitter and is not recommended for eating.

Sustainable harvesting

Unchecked exploitation and increased pollution has taken its toll on wild oyster beds and they have gradually moved from food for the masses to a rich person's indulgence. Commanding good money made them attractive for aquaculture, and it's now quite challenging to find an oyster that is any wilder than feral in many parts of the North Atlantic. Whichever side of the pond you are on, eating more than an occasional native oyster is hard to justify on ecological (and possibly legal) grounds. Fortunately, the opposite is true for non-native escapees from cultivation, and harvesting them is a chance to both gather gourmet food and support marine diversity.

Even feral oysters aren't an easy harvest, though: their shells are often so encrusted with barnacles, tubeworms and seaweed as to make them virtually indiscernible from the rocks or empty oyster shells to which they cling. Spotting the glistening mother-of-pearl interiors of empty shells (known in the oyster trade as 'boxes') washed up on beaches is a good prompt to explore nearby.

Oysters attach themselves by secreting a cement-like adhesive that is 90 per cent chalk and 10 per cent protein, making them extremely hard to dislodge. I recommend carrying something like a screwdriver or stout knife for levering off more stubborn ones. The edges of the shells can be sharp, so gloves are a good idea too.

Opposite: Fresh oysters with pickled dulse.

Preparing and eating oysters

You don't meet many people who have eaten an oyster and feel indifferent about the experience – most are either appalled by their saltiness and slippery mouthfeel, or in raptures about their creamy iron-rich umami. Eating wild oysters comes with many more risks than those that have been cultivated and processed to pass stringent health and safety regulations, and unless you are quite convinced you are harvesting them from pristine waters, I recommend you only eat them cooked. Cooked oysters are every bit as delicious as raw oysters, just in a different way.

Before harvesting wild oysters, refamiliarize yourself with the shellfish safety checklist on page 222. Much of my advice on handling mussels also applies (see page 226), but do not depurate oysters for more than four hours or they are likely to die.

Unopened oysters will clamp their shells tight shut, retaining moisture and staying alive in the fridge at 4–8°C (39–46°F) for up to a week, provided they are stored in the position in which they naturally grow (flat side up) and covered with a damp cloth. However, I recommend you go nowhere near that limit and cook them as soon as possible.

Shucking an oyster

Opening – or shucking – any oyster can be challenging, but wild oysters can be particularly stubborn. First, scrub them with a stiff brush to remove any external sand or critters that may fall in during opening. Next, place them on a solid surface, cup side down, hold them firmly with your weaker hand, insert a screwdriver or oyster knife into the small cavity at the narrow hinge end, then push and lever it until the top shell yields. Do not use good kitchen knives as their tips may snap, and their sharp blades make an already hazardous task positively dangerous. Please be warned: a lot of pressure is sometimes required, especially on older, larger specimens, and the shells can break, leaving the oyster knife or screwdriver to plunge into the oyster-holding hand. Wrapping the holding hand in a tea towel is a good precaution, and also protects you from the sharp ridges of the shell. Once the top shell yields, run a knife along its underside to cut the muscle. The hard work is now over. Discard the top shell and gently work your knife under the oyster to detach it from the bottom shell.

Everything in the shell is edible, though you may wish to check for broken shell fragments, sand and perhaps even the occasional tiny pearl. Provided your oyster is in good condition and you have opened it without too much spillage, there should be plenty of briny liquid in the shell. This is precious and when eating oysters raw is consumed along with the meat, but if you intend to cook them it should be strained off and used to flavour stocks and sauces. Opening your oysters over a bowl makes retaining this briny nectar easier.

If all of this sounds a bit challenging, and as you are likely to be cooking your wild oysters anyway, you can also just pop them (flat side up) in a hot oven until they open. Placing them on a tray on a bed of cheap salt is a good way to keep them level. The top shells can then be discarded, and you can either remove the oysters from their bottom shells to add to recipes, or leave them to grill further in the shells, perhaps with a knob of garlic butter and a few breadcrumbs sprinkled on. Utterly delicious.

Shucked oysters can be sautéed for a couple of minutes with butter and garlic, then served in their shells. A sprinkle of toasted or fried seaweed (sea lettuce or laver, ideally) sets them off beautifully. They also make an excellent addition to chowder, or they can be dipped in beaten egg then breadcrumbs and fried.

Oyster velouté with pepper dulse

This delicious recipe comes from Antonio Carluccio's book, *A Passion for Mushrooms*. Antonio finished it with shavings of fresh white alba truffle, but fresh pepper dulse (see page 191) makes a great substitute.

Ingredients

12 oysters, carefully opened and their brine and lower shell retained

30g (1oz) butter

Juice of ½ a lemon

Small glass of white wine

Salt and black pepper to taste

3 egg yolks

A handful of fresh pepper dulse or Dumont's tubular weed (dried and powdered also works)

Scrub the empty oyster shells and put them to warm in a low oven.

Filter the oyster brine into a pan and add the butter, lemon juice, wine and seasoning. Bring to a simmer, but do not allow it to boil. Drop the oysters into the pan and cook gently for 30 seconds. Remove the oysters and keep them warm. Ensure the contents of the pan are not boiling and briskly whisk the egg yolks into the liquid over a very low heat (you could use a bain marie for this). Beat until you obtain a firm, foamy consistency. Taste and adjust the seasoning if necessary.

Place the oysters in the warmed shells on a plate and spoon over the sauce. Scatter small fronds of pepper dulse on each oyster.

Limpets are protandry hermaphrodites, changing from male to female as they grow.

They grow taller in more sheltered locations.

Limpets

Patella spp. and near relations

Limpets are a type of marine snail that avoids predation and desiccation by clinging tightly to rocks. Though they appear to do very little, they are in fact dynamic and important players in coastal ecosystems, with a fascinating lifestyle. Once they are submerged, or when night has fallen, they slither into action, grazing microalgae and nascent seaweeds from the rocks using a rasping, file-like tongue called a radula, which is comprised of nearly 2,000 teeth that are so strong they leave tiny scratches on the rock. As the tide goes back out, they follow their own slimy trails back to where they started.

EDIBILITY Good flavour but need careful preparation to avoid becoming overly chewy.

IDENTIFICATION Conical shell with the apex central or slightly offset, greyish in colour (sometimes tinted yellowish), with coarse radiating ridges and contouring growth lines, up to 6cm (2½in) in diameter. Varying in height (up to 5cm/2in) according to species, location in tidal range, age and wave exposure. Individuals from higher up the shore generally have a taller shell relative to diameter when compared to lower shore dwellers. May be covered in barnacles and small seaweeds.

DISTRIBUTION Common and abundant all around the North Atlantic.

HABITAT Attached to rocks in the intertidal zone.

WHEN TO HARVEST September–April (spawning November/December).

HARVESTING RESTRICTIONS See local regulations in North America.

Individual limpets can live for up to 20 years, returning to exactly the same spot on every tide. Over time, the edges of a limpet's shell can grind out a 'home scar' on softer rocks, or on harder rocks their shell edge may become finely sculpted to the contours of their nest. A tight fit is essential to resisting attempts by starfish to prize them free. Limpets have been observed fighting off starfish by twisting their shell in such a way as to turn its edge into a cutting blade. They rarely stray more than 1m (3ft) from their home scar and jealously defend their territory from other limpets.

Similar species

Several similar species occur in the North Atlantic, all usable in similar ways.

Common limpet (*Patella vulgata*), the species described and depicted here. It is abundant around the UK and Ireland.

Blackfoot limpet (*P. intermedia*) is generally smaller, up to 3cm (1¼in) in diameter, with a flatter shell, a more angular footprint and more southerly European distribution.

Rough (or China) limpet (*P. ulyssiponensis*) has an off-centre apex with pronounced ridges that protrude noticeably beyond the edge. It is common around the UK except in the south-east.

Atlantic plate (or tortoiseshell) limpet (*Testudinalia testudinalis*) grows up to 3cm (1¼in) in diameter with an offset apex and brown and white vertical banding. It is found on both sides of the North Atlantic.

Slipper limpet (*Crepidula fornicata*) is not a true limpet. It has a more rounded shell, and individuals tend to attach to one another, often making large stacks, with a larger female at the bottom and males on top. As the female at the bottom dies, the next male up the stack transitions to female, and so on. They are native to North America and considered a problematic non-native invasive species in Europe, where they can overrun oyster fisheries. They can be eaten in the same manner as true limpets.

Sustainable harvesting

Far from being inert dozers, limpets are constantly alert, and you will need some stealth and savvy to harvest them. In their resting state they are quite firmly attached to rocks, but if they feel any sign of being tampered with, they tighten their grip rapidly, exerting a pull of up to 70lb per square inch, and it becomes almost impossible to remove them without smashing their shells. To harvest them, you need to surprise them either with an unheralded sideways kick from a rubber boot (but not one with a hard sole or you risk smashing the shell), or by firmly pushing the point of a short, stout-bladed knife under their shells. If you fail to dislodge a limpet with your first attack, move on to an unalerted one.

Resist the urge to go for only the largest limpets on any given rock as these are the females. The smaller males will eventually turn into females, but they may be lonely for a few years before they do! Although limpets are extremely common and abundant on all but the most exposed rocky shores, remember to just lightly thin them by not taking more than a couple of limpets from any given rock, and moving your harvesting area around throughout a season and from year to year.

Preparing and eating limpets

In North European and North American cuisine, limpets are generally considered the poor relations of most other shellfish, with a reputation for being tough and rubbery. While they certainly aren't as delicately flavoured as an oyster or as softly textured as a mussel, they can be delicious if you know how to handle them. They are highly esteemed in Portugal, where they are known as lapas and are a standard menu item in coastal restaurants.

The key to tasty limpets is brief cooking – certainly not the extended boiling recommended by some older foraging guidebooks. Freezing them before cooking helps to tenderize them, as can pounding their meat gently with a rolling pin, as you might tenderize a steak or abalone.

Cooked limpets are usually eaten from their shells in their entirety, including the dark stomach part. If you are squeamish about this, it can be removed, but it's not much different from eating the whole of a mussel or oyster. The only time I remove it is when I want to slice and marinade the limpet, as it breaks and discolours everything around it.

Limpet ceviche

If you can't cope with the chewy texture of limpets, this treatment makes them thin, soft and delectable. This is good served on, or mixed through, a leafy salad.

Ingredients

6 limpets per portion

Juice of 1 ripe lime

Sea salt

Finely shredded green onions (wild garlic/ramps are great for this, but spring/salad onions are good too)

Flakes of sea lettuce, pepper dulse, chilli, herbs (optional)

Remove the limpets from their shells by running a knife around their inner edges. Cut away the dark stomach and discard (don't worry about the small, dark tubes). Rinse the limpet meat, pat it dry and place in the freezer for a couple of hours. Remove the limpets from the freezer, and as they defrost, use a sharp knife to thinly slice them into thin discs. If they are still partially frozen, this will be easier.

In a bowl, mix the sliced limpets with the lime juice and a generous pinch of salt. Place in the fridge for one hour. Remove from the fridge and stir in the rest of the ingredients.

Limpets Portuguese style

This is delicious finger-food, best cooked over the glowing embers of open fire but also good done under a grill (broiler) or in a pan – it doesn't overly matter whether the heat comes from above or below.

Ingredients

12 limpets still in their shells per serving (shells scrubbed, then frozen and defrosted)

Butter, about ½ teaspoon per limpet

Garlic cloves, about 1 for every 2 teaspoons of butter, finely chopped

Parsley, finely chopped, to garnish

Lemon juice to serve

Salt and pepper, to taste

Fresh red chillis, finely chopped, or a little hot sauce (optional)

Fresh fronds of pepper dulse, or any seaweed powder or flakes, to garnish (optional)

Low-grade salt to hold the limpets level while cooking (optional)

Soften the butter and mix with the garlic (this can be chilled or frozen in small discs for future convenience). You could also use pepper dulse or wrack siphon weed infused butter here instead of making the garlic butter.

Place the limpets shell side down and add a little garlic butter to each, and the chillis or hot sauce if you are using them. Next put them, still shell side down, directly on the hot embers of a fire, or on a grill above the embers. If you are cooking indoors, place them under a hot broiler/grill; you may like to use a bed of low-grade salt to hold them level in the pan. The key is to keep them upturned so they don't spill their juices.

Cook until you see the liquid at the edge of the meat sizzle and the limpet detaches from its shell – no more than 5 minutes.

Arrange the limpets on a plate or in a bowl (a bed of seaweed or salad leaves will help keep them upright), sprinkle with parsley, add a squeeze of lemon juice and any other garnishes you fancy, and serve immediately.

*Topshells come in a
range of glamorous
colours and designs.*

*Winkles have alternate
light and dark banding
and a pale area around
the opening.*

*Predatory dog whelks
are pale shelled with
a red operculum.*

Winkles

Littorina littorea

Winkles have been a common food around northern Europe since prehistoric times, but weren't present in North America when the first European colonists arrived. They were first seen there around 1850, and a hundred years later they were abundant pretty much everywhere. Nobody knows whether they were deliberately introduced or made their way there themselves, possibly in the bilges of sailing ships, but they are now a common part of the marine landscape on both sides of the North Atlantic. Like limpets, winkles graze on intertidal rocks, feeding on fast-growing microalgae and immature seaweeds, with a particular fondness for sea lettuce and gutweeds. Their grazing habits are a significant factor in the balance of seaweed species in any given area.

ALSO KNOWN AS Common winkle, periwinkle, wrinkle/wrinklers (US), pennywinkle, whelk.

EDIBILITY An underrated but versatile and delicious shellfish.

IDENTIFICATION Marine snails with squat, cone-like, spiralling shells, with seven or eight whorls decorated with fine ridges, though older specimens are often worn smooth. Dark grey, olive or brownish in colour, looking almost black when wet and considerably paler when dried out. Shell opening and interior are white.

DISTRIBUTION Common and abundant on both sides of the North Atlantic, as far south as New Jersey in the west.

HABITAT On rocks, especially crevices and rock pools throughout the intertidal zone.

WHEN TO HARVEST September–April.

HARVESTING RESTRICTIONS Check for localized landing restrictions, which tend to be between 13mm and 16mm (½–⅝in), tip to tip.

Similar species

Topshells (*Gibbula* spp.) tend to be more glamorous looking than winkles, with colourful, patterned, conical outer shells, and a mother-of-pearl inner shell. They are similarly edible.

Dog whelks (*Nucella lapillus*) are white or pale yellow, occasionally with more elaborate colours and markings. Their shells have a more pointed spire than winkles, with a small groove running through the lip of the opening. They are fearsome predators of mussels and barnacles, deploying calcium-dissolving enzymes through a drill-like tongue (radula) to penetrate their shells before immobilizing them with narcotic saliva. Once their prey is helpless, they inject more enzymes that dissolve the victim, before sucking them up. Rock pools are tough neighbourhoods! They can be eaten in the same way as winkles but are generally considered less tasty.

Sustainable harvesting

Winkle picking is still a significant but largely unregulated commercial foraging activity around Western Europe and the less populous coasts of North America. Most often it is an accessible cash-in-hand enterprise, with local dealers buying sacks from local pickers and exporting them to countries where they are esteemed as a delicacy, such as Japan and Spain.

The key to efficient harvesting of winkles is to find the crevices and rock pools where they can be scooped up in numbers. Try not to gather them from sand or mud, as they will be more likely to be gritty. They are so ubiquitous and numerous that hobby foragers needn't worry too much about over-harvesting, provided they visit different areas throughout the season and from year to year.

Preparing and eating winkles

Winkles are the most underrated of North Atlantic shellfish in their native range. Perhaps it's their curious name, or the rather fiddly technique for removing them from their shells, or some deeper squeamishness about snails that puts people off, but those who go to the trouble with an open mind will find them deeply delicious morsels and come to love winkling them out of their shells.

Being grazers rather than filter feeders, winkles generally bring fewer safety concerns than bivalves – but you should nevertheless follow the safety checklist on page 222. Depurating them for four to eight hours, while not strictly necessary, can do no harm and reduces the likelihood of sand. Use a metal pan lid or baking tray to keep them submerged or you may find them exploring your fridge! Rinsing in several changes of water helps too.

The basic method for preparing winkles is to simmer them in salted water for 4 minutes. After this, extract them from their shells using a pin or unbent paper clip – it's best to have something that can be bent into a small hook at the end to pull out the shyer ones. It's a rather satisfying little job, and you'll soon develop a knack for hooking and twisting them out.

Once removed from its shell, all parts of a winkle are edible except for the small round door (known as an operculum) which it uses to keep predators (except humans) out and moisture in. It is easily flicked aside, and it is traditional to wear one as a beauty spot while winkling. Squeamish types sometimes remove the dark tapered end too, but this is an awful waste as it is as sweet and rich tasting as the rest.

The basic cooking method can be embellished by simmering them in stock – a nice court bouillon or seaweed dashi (see page 207) ups the umami, and there is no reason why steaming with garlic and wine, à la moules marinière, should be exclusive to mussels.

Personally, I think a warm and freshly evicted winkle is pretty much perfect as it is, but they are traditionally dipped in malt vinegar before being eaten, possibly with a sprinkle of white pepper. A little powdered wrack siphon weed is a nice wild alternative. Even more decadent is dipping them in warm (wild) garlic or seaweed butter.

If you have the patience and dedication to shell a lot of winkles, they are versatile and delicious, but I warn you, once you get a taste for them you will eat more than you set aside. They are good in omelettes and make an excellent risotto (substitute them for cockles in the recipe on page 253), or try chopping and mixing them through laver burger mix before frying (see page 185). They are also delicious stir-fried with ginger, garlic and black bean sauce.

Should you find yourself with a glut of winkles, they can be pickled, or they freeze well – either live in their shells or just the meat.

Ensis ensis:
*Up to 12cm (5in)
with a curved shell.*

Ensis siliqua:
*Straight-edged shell,
up to 20cm (8in).*

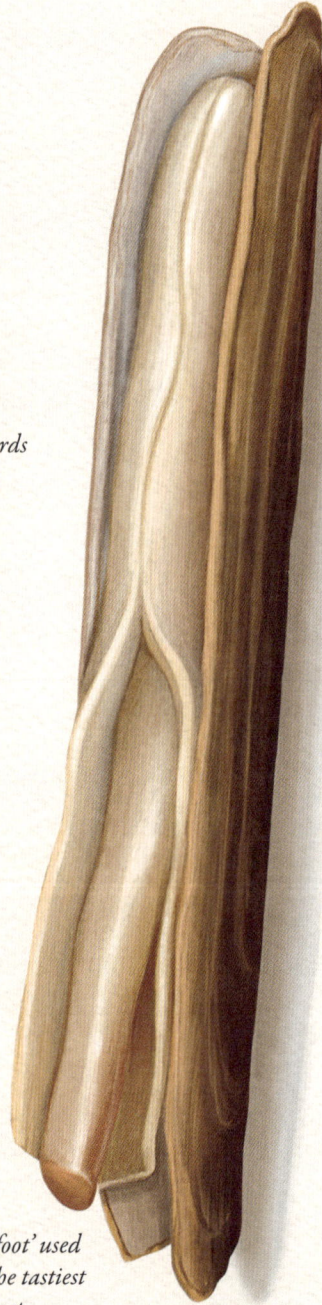

*Paler banded
section points towards
the 'foot' end.*

*Extendable 'foot' used
for digging. The tastiest
part to eat.*

Razor clams

Ensis spp.; *Siliqua* spp.

Razor clams ply their trade at and below the low spring tide line in near-vertical sandy burrows that they dig using an extendable 'foot'. This remarkable appendage can change shape, thrusting down in a narrowed pencil shape before swelling at the tip to allow them to pull themselves downwards, or reversing the process to move upwards. To aid this hydraulic motion, the clams siphon seawater into jets to loosen the sand, which can happen at both ends. They feed on sinking sediments, filtering plankton and organic materials from the water, thus contributing to the health of marine environments. Catching razor clams involves timing, stealth, observation and trickery that, when combined accurately, climax in a glorious reveal that has most folk squealing with delight.

ALSO KNOWN AS Jackknife clam (areas of North America), spoot (Scotland).

EDIBILITY Delicious – the main 'foot' section tastes like a cross between scallop and squid. The rest is chewier, but can still be used as food and flavouring.

IDENTIFICATION Distinctive hinged, elongated shells with openings at either extremity.

DISTRIBUTION Not uncommon within its habitat. Various species of razor clam inhabit different geographic regions and subtly different habitats – see similar species overleaf.

HABITAT At and below the low spring tide line in sand, silt or fine gravel.

WHEN TO HARVEST September–May, on low spring tides.

Similar species

There are a number of members of the *Ensis* and *Siliqua* families that may all reasonably be referred to as razor clams on account of their similar shell structure, lifestyle, ecological niche and gastronomy.

Ensis ensis Up to 12cm (4¾in) long, with two curved edges. Found in north-western Europe, as far south as Portugal.

Ensis siliqua (**Pod razor**) Up to 20cm (8in) long, with straight parallel edges. Found in north-western Europe, as far south as Portugal.

Ensis leei (**Atlantic jackknife clam**) Up to 15cm (6in) long, with two curved edges. Native to the West Atlantic from South Carolina to Canada, and colonizing some areas of north-western Europe.

Ensis terranovensis Up to 17cm (6¾in) long, with both edges curved. Native to the Newfoundland coast of Canada.

Siliqua costata Up to 7cm (2¾in) long, with wider shells (relative to their length) than any *Ensis* species, more oval and less like cutthroat razors. Native to the Atlantic coast of the United States and Canada. Adapt some of the cleaning and cooking methods on page 248 for this species.

Hunting for razor clams

Razor clams are common in sandy or silty tidal substrates around most of northern Europe and North America. Finding their empty shells around the high tide line is a good clue to their presence, but not infallible as shells can be moved around by tides and currents. Getting to them is as much about timing as location, as most are only revealed on the very lowest of low tides. Plan your razor clam hunt with a tide table or app and look for low spring tides around full moons, especially near the spring and autumn equinox.

Unsuccessful missions are almost always due to underestimating the importance of being at the sea edge exactly at the lowest point of low spring tides. But even when you get in the right place at the right time, you might still be unaware of them were it not for one giveaway. An undisturbed razor clam will have its non-foot end level with the seabed. On feeling the reverberations of your footsteps, it will vigorously dig downwards. In doing so it shoots a small jet of water out of both ends – the downward jet hastens its escape by loosening sand, but the upward jet betrays its burrow – a loosely defined oval hole in the sand.

Razor clams can usually 'outrun' digging by hand, so foragers have developed a number of techniques for extracting them. Which one works best is the subject of heated debate, but really depends on which species you meet and the texture of the sand they are burrowing in.

Mollusc wrestling

This may not be the most efficient technique, but I believe it is the most sporting, requiring no equipment and giving the clam a decent chance of escape. Thrust your forefinger down the burrow within about a second of seeing the water jet. If you are quick enough, your finger will catch the top of the shell (beware the potential cut hazard!). Press your fingertip sideways to stop the clam's descent. Next, work your thumb through the silt until you can pinch the top of the clam. Thus begins a mighty man vs mollusc wrestling match. Razor clams can pull pretty hard – you'll need good finger strength. Work the shell in a gentle circular motion to loosen the sand while pulling gently but steadily upwards. Do not yank it, as this invariably causes the swollen foot (the tastiest part) to snap off and be lost in the silt.

Spoot scoop

Being accustomed to intense wrestles in the fine silt of my home turf, I was shocked to see locals of the Outer Hebrides lazily scooping razor clams (known in Scotland as spoots) out by hand. A closer inspection of the substrate revealed it to be quite coarse sand, which is harder for the clams to tunnel through, but easier to push a hand through. Razor clams that live in coarser sands tend to have a tougher tip to their foot, making them slightly less tender than those that live in finer sediments.

Shetland knife dance

On the Shetland Islands locals take a long, thin kitchen knife to spoot beds, and walk backwards as they hunt. This is sound technique anywhere, as the clams often release their water jets as you lift your foot, meaning that most of the action is behind you. On locating a burrow, the knife is thrust in at an angle immediately beside the burrow and pulled until the blade digs into the edge of the clam's shell, arresting its descent. The clam is then dug out using the free hand.

Subtidal snatch

In calm and crystal-clear waters, it is possible to wade through the shallows and spot the feeding mouths of razor clams standing just proud of the sand, once you become accustomed to adjusting for the refracting illusions of water. Reach down and ease them up, benefitting from the extra lubrication of immersion. This technique is not suitable for silty estuarine waters.

North American clam gunning

Razor clam hunting is such a common pursuit in some areas of North America that a fancy bit of kit called a clam gun has become commercially available – often they have entertaining brand names like Claminator or Razor Vac. These devices are tubes with a T-shaped handle on top that are driven in around the burrow. As you drive the gun into the sand, a small vent allows air to be expelled; close the vent to lift out a core of sand, hopefully containing the clam. In locations where clam guns are commonly used, a shellfishing licence may be required to control overfishing.

Salting

This is perhaps the least sporting method, but it is often the most efficient. Razor clams (and other molluscs, for that matter) are highly sensitive to changes in salinity. When concentrated salt is introduced to a burrow (either as dry salt or a strong brine solution), the retreating clam changes direction, burrowing upwards until it flops dejectedly onto the sand. If you use this method, I recommend spreading out your salting – sea dwellers can be surprisingly perturbed by sudden increases in salinity.

Advanced 'spooting' tips

- Consider the angle of the sun – having the sun behind you will make water jets and holes easier to spot.
- Try to find a dry-weather window – razor clams are less active and their jets harder to spot in wind and rain.
- Mark the tide – it's easy to lose track of what the tide is doing on the gentle gradients of razor clam beaches: place a bucket on the sand so you can tell when it has turned.
- Arrive at least 30 minutes before low tide.
- Pair up – it's often easier to spot clam jets that others have triggered, but don't walk in single file.
- If you are using the salt method, recheck unsuccessfully salted burrows before you leave the area – occasionally, the clams emerge more slowly.

Sustainable harvesting

As the vast majority of razor clam colonies are underwater, it is unlikely, even on an extreme low tide, that catching domestic quantities will make any significant impact on established colonies. That said, on popular razor clam beaches in North America local catch restrictions may apply. Even where they don't, there is so much fun to be had in catching them that it's easy to get carried away and take more than you need, so try to have a plan in your head before you start.

Where there is no clear guidance on landing size, and as you can't tell the size or age of a razor clam before you catch it, I recommend putting the smallest 50 per cent back. This means you don't have to work out which subspecies you have been catching (each matures to a different size), and you can be sure you aren't catching immature specimens. Failing that, a minimum length of 10cm (4in) means you won't be taking juveniles of any species. Don't leave any clams that you are returning stranded and at the mercy of the birds and sun if the tide is still retreating – toss them just beyond the lowest low tide line near where you caught them and they will burrow back into the silt with a big sigh of relief.

Preparing and eating razor clams

Razor clams rank among the very finest of shellfish, with a taste and texture somewhere between scallop and squid – sweet and tender with ultra umami. As they live almost entirely below the mean low tide line, they carry less risk of contamination than the most other bivalves, and they do not tend to trap sand and grit in the same way as mussels, cockles and other types of clam, so depuration is not necessary. You should nevertheless familiarise yourself with the shellfish safety checklist on page 222 before harvesting and eating them.

Freshly caught razor clams can remain alive out of water for several days in the fridge, but like all shellfish, the sooner you eat them the better. Do not store them underwater as they will quickly die. They are best kept upright with the foot end down (the pale triangle shape on the shell points towards the foot). If stored on their side, you might open the fridge door to find them investigating the milk bottle! Securing bunches with elastic bands helps prevent gaping and retains moisture.

There are two ways to open razor clams (and one way to remove the foot without opening them – see below). Running a knife along the inside of one half of the shell leaves it still attached to the other side, which is ideal if you intend to grill or barbecue them. Alternatively, place them in a steamer until they open, then remove them from their shells. Keep cooking to a minimum, as they very quickly become chewy if overdone.

Everything inside the shell is edible except the dark stomach section, which should be cut out and discarded. By far the best eating is the foot section. If you are happy with the water quality at your harvesting location, I highly recommend eating it raw, as described in the recipe opposite. If you must cook them, try lightly poaching in seaweed dashi broth (see page 207), or tossing in a stir-fry at the last minute does justice to their tenderness. If you wish to grill them in their half shells, brush with a little garlic or pepper dulse butter and place face-up under a hot grill (broiler) for no more than 30 seconds, until the first signs of browning appear. A squeeze of lemon juice and perhaps a sprinkle of herbs or dried seaweed powder and they are good to go.

Other parts such as the siphons and shell seals can be more or less chewy depending on the exact species and the substrate you are harvesting from. These 'offally' bits can be used in chowder, to flavour fish stock, or fermented into garum – a salty condiment. The meat freezes well and is made even more tender by the process. Cleaned up, the empty shells are excellent for labelling garden beds and plants.

Razor clam sashimi

For seafood aficionados, the *Ensis* species of razor clams are at their best eaten raw. Eating their foot section live on the beach is one of the great gastronomic experiences.

If you intend to do this, be sure to harvest from good-quality water. You will not be eating the stomach contents, only the 'foot', so any risk of stomach upset is much reduced. I have eaten several dozen each year in this way for 20 years and never had an issue.

Your live clam will be tensed up with its foot fully retracted into its shell. To remove the foot, place the shell flat in the palm of your hand with the white banded arrow pointing away from you. Clenching your fingers from little finger to forefinger, progressively squeeze the clam towards the foot end (following the white arrow), and part of the foot will emerge from the end. Maintaining a firm squeeze, pinch this between the thumb and forefinger of your other hand and quickly ease it round the edge of the shell away from the hinge. Once 'around the corner', gently pull the foot until it is fully extended at a right angle to the shell (it will be about half the full length of the shell). The foot can only pull in line with the shell, so it will now dangle at your mercy, unable to retract. Cut it free by pulling it over the sharp long edge of the shell – it is a razor, after all! As a last act of resistance, the clam will eject a jet of seawater from the cut end. If you can't master this technique, you can simply run a knife down the inside of the non-hinge side of the shell, open it and cut off the foot.

Eat the foot while it is still wriggling, perhaps with a sprig of pepper dulse (see page 191) to take it to new levels of umami. If serving this at home, a twist of lemon juice or a dribble of soy sauce may further elevate it. Raw razor clam foot also makes a good centre to coastal sushi rolls (see page 145). The foot can also be marinaded ceviche style, as described for limpets on page 239. The non-foot parts aren't so good raw or marinated but can be retained for other recipes.

Razor clam offal garum

A great way to use the less appealing frills and gubbins of your razor clam is to ferment and autolyse them into a pungent salty umami garum.

This seasoning is similar to the fish sauce (nam pla) used in Asian cuisine, though it is actually an ancient preparation most associated with the western Mediterranean. In European cuisine, anchovy sauce is the closest you will find to it commercially.

Weigh your razor clam offal – including the stomach parts – then blitz them in a food processor with about 20 per cent of their weight in sea salt. Pour into a clean jar, seal the lid then leave at room temperature for about six months, stirring occasionally. Finally, blitz it again and re-jar. It's a smelly process, and the end result – a brown paste – is not for timid cooks. But applied judiciously it is superb for seasoning and adding umami to stews, stir-fries, miso soup and barbecued meat or shellfish. I also like to use it instead of salt in lacto-fermentation processes – it adds an extraordinary funky fruit note when used to precipitate lacto-fermented wild garlic (ramps).

*Heart-shaped
from the side.*

Cockles

Cerastoderma edule

In North America cockles are sometimes referred to as clams, and they are indeed a species of clam. In the UK they are known only as cockles and have a different enough place in the local cuisine to deserve a special focus. They are part of the Cardiidae family, which are more spherical and heart-shaped in profile than other types of clam, and have concentric growth lines (which indicate their age – one line per year) and prominent radial ribs. Cockle colonies can have locally distinct subspecies and phenotypes, some browner, some paler, some with slight banding. If you are very lucky, perhaps you might bump into the splendidly punk-looking spiny cockle *Acanthocardia aculeata*.

ALSO KNOWN AS European edible cockle, common cockle.

EDIBILITY Excellent for eating – cook only live cockles that close tight when tapped.

IDENTIFICATION Often confused with other clams, but they are all tasty. See also clams (page 255) and razor clams (page 245).

DISTRIBUTION Common within its habitat all around the North Atlantic.

HABITAT Sheltered intertidal zones of sandy, gravelly or muddy bays and estuaries, up to the high neap tide line.

WHEN TO HARVEST September–April, but best during September/October. Do not harvest May–August, as this is when they are spawning, underweight and perhaps baking in summer sun between tides.

HARVESTING RESTRICTIONS See local information. If not available, assume a minimum landing size of 2cm (¾in).

The natural posture – or resting beach face, as I like to call it – of a cockle is slightly open, as it siphons water for food, quickly clamping tightly shut when disturbed or tapped, perhaps also ejecting a small spit of disgust at being bothered. Discard any cockles that remain open, even if the flesh looks fresh – this is not a shellfish to take chances with.

Finding cockles

Cockles burrow just below the surface of mud or sand between high and low tide lines, occasionally stopping for a snooze at the surface when they are easy pickings for observant foragers. Look for them reclining where sand flats meet the upslope of the beach. They live for between two and five years, but their shells hang around for decades before being ground down by the sea, so you'll have lots of false alarms. With practice, you will learn to ignore empty shells (even when they are clasped around sand) by their lighter colour and develop a keen eye for the darker, grubbier look of a living cockle. There are whole beaches near me made of nothing but cockle shells, bleached white by sea and sun, a glorious sight and a lot of fun to walk over.

In well-established colonies, cockles can occur in high numbers and density, and are a rich source of food for crabs, fish, whelks and wading birds. In my local cockle bed I have observed a colony of rooks learning, over the course of a few years, how to drop cockles onto rocks to smash them open.

Sustainable harvesting

Although cockles are now cultivated in large quantities (especially in the shallow *zees* of the Netherlands), there is still an economically significant commercial fishery for wild cockles. Much of this is – scandalously – still done by dredging the seabed, while more benign hand harvesting takes place in large estuaries. This is potentially dangerous work, and stories of hapless cockle-harvesters being caught by rapidly rising tides, often with tragic results, are troublingly common. Take care to plan your cockling trips carefully, and spend time getting to know your local area.

If you spend some time learning the habits of your local cockle population, you may be able to harvest plenty without disturbing the sand, but some gentle excavation can help. On a fine sandy or muddy seabed this can be done by hand, though pros tend to use a rake. A nice middle way is to find an old scallop or oyster shell to scrape and dig with. There is no need to go deeper than a hand's width.

Check for any local regulations imposed to prevent over-collection. Minimum harvesting sizes are not uncommon, and sometimes cockle beds are officially closed to allow stocks to recover. Where restrictions are in place, they may be displayed on signs, but you might have to check with your local fisheries conservation authority. If no advice is available, make sure to minimize your impact by taking only domestic quantities of cockles sized over 2cm (¾in), or the largest 25 per cent of what you find.

Preparing and eating cockles

Not surprisingly, given where they live, purging cockles of sand and grit is the main challenge for foragers. Don't be tempted to take shortcuts when depurating cockles – it doesn't take much sand to turn a dish from delicious to unpleasant. See page 223 for guidance.

If your planned dish doesn't require your cockles to be served in their shells, they can be steamed until they open without the need for depuration. The cooked meat can then easily be removed by hand and thoroughly rinsed.

A less efficient but more fun way to extract cockles from their armour is to use one cockle to open another: hold a cockle in each hand and press them together, hinges facing one another at right angles. Push firmly together, twist, and one of them will unlock. By repeating this process, you will end up with a single unopened cockle – champion of your cockle sumo basho. I like to release the winner back into the wild to strengthen future cockle generations (though hopefully not passing on its trauma!). This method also allows you to eat a few raw cockles at the beach. This isn't for everyone, but personally I love their sweet, slightly metallic taste – like a teeny oyster.

Cockles can be cooked in the style of moules marinières, with wine, garlic, parsley and cream, though they are rather less satisfying than mussels – compensate for this by frying some chunks of bacon or chorizo in the pan first. They work well in (sea) spaghetti alle vongole (see page 257), though other clams are generally superior for that job. Their dainty size fits nicely with rice. Pickling is the traditional way to preserve them (see page 258).

Cockle and sea sandwort risotto

If you harvest your cockles in spring, you can usually find some sea sandwort on the same trip. Sea plantain, sea aster, sea campion tips and marsh samphire work nicely too.

Ingredients (Serves 4)

1kg (2lb 3 oz) cockles in the shell, depurated

1 courgette, finely chopped

4 shallots, finely chopped

275ml (9 fl oz) white wine

1 bay leaf

A few sprigs of (wild) thyme

500ml (¼ pint) of chicken, fish, vegetable or seaweed stock

50g (2oz) butter

300g (11oz) risotto rice

1 large onion, finely diced

1 garlic clove, finely chopped

200g (7oz) sea sandwort, or whatever coastal succulents you are using, thoroughly rinsed

Salt and pepper, or ground dried pepper dulse

Optional: a handful of fresh wild garlic, finely shredded

Lemon juice

Knob of butter to finish

Heat a pan on the hob and add the first six ingredients, retaining half of the wine. Place a lid on the pan and cook for a few minutes, shaking occasionally, until the cockles have opened – discard any that don't. Allow to cool, then remove the meat from the shells, tasting a few to ensure they are sand-free (give the meat an extra rinse if need be). Strain and reserve the cooking liquid. Combine the stock and reserved cockle liquor in a clean pan and heat to just below boiling.

To make the risotto, melt the butter in a large, thick-bottomed pan then add the onion and garlic. Cook gently and stir for 5 minutes then add the rice. Cook and stir for another 2 minutes then add the remaining wine. Continue to cook and stir until the rice has absorbed the wine.

One ladle at a time, gradually add the hot stock and cockle liquor, stirring steadily and allowing the rice to absorb each addition. Repeat until the stock is absorbed and the rice is soft, but with perhaps a hint of firmness in the middle, depending how you like it (you may not need all the liquid). When the rice is nearly cooked, add the sea sandwort shoots. They will need just a few minutes to soften a little – it's nice if they retain some bite.

Finally, stir through the cockles, wild garlic (if using), seasoning and lemon juice to taste, and a generous extra knob of butter. The finished risotto should slowly settle flat when spooned into bowls.

The risotto will thicken as it cools. Use any leftovers to make arancini by rolling the risotto into balls, dipping them in plain flour, then beaten egg, then breadcrumbs, and then deep frying. The sandwort can be replaced by or mixed with sea campion leaves (see page 113) for a traditional Italian dish (usually made without the cockles).

Grooved carpet shell clams have radial banding with distinct cross-cut grooves.

Sand gaper, soft shell or long-neck clams have more brittle shells that do not fully close, with a distinct protruding siphon.

Clams

There are so many species of clam around the North Atlantic that nobody is quite sure how many there are. This isn't helped by the fact that the word clam is used to refer to superficially similar but scientifically quite different families of bivalve. Fortunately, knowing enough to harvest them safely and responsibly is quite straightforward. I have already gone into some depth on two types of clam – the razor clam (see page 245) and the cockle (see page 251) – and the lifestyle of other clams falls somewhere between the athleticism of the former and the lethargy of the latter. Harvesting them involves a combination of all the skills I have described for their cousins.

EDIBILITY All clams are edible, but their flavour and texture vary depending on which species you have.

IDENTIFICATION It's easy to know you have a clam, but telling exactly which species can be difficult.

DISTRIBUTION All North Atlantic coasts have several species.

HABITAT Mostly in sheltered intertidal zones of sandy, gravelly or muddy bays and estuaries, though some species are adapted to more exposed beaches. Often buried to depths of 60cm (2ft).

WHEN TO HARVEST September–April.

Finding and identifying clams

Clams inhabit the lower intertidal and subtidal zones, buried in sand or gravel up to depths of about 60cm (2ft), though usually less. They feed through their siphons, which they poke towards the surface. Different species favour different substrates and levels of exposure to wave action. Locating them requires following clues like dead shells, holes in the sand, sudden fountains of seawater at low tide (though these are seldom as obvious as with razor clams), and a fair bit of experimental digging, by hand or spade.

It's best to think of clamming as something of a magical mystery tour, and you will enjoy it more if you embrace the uncertainty and treat clams like an opportunistic bycatch when you are on more focused forays for seaweeds or other shellfish. With experience, you will develop a feel for where clams like to hang out and you can revisit known colonies or recognize subtle signs in unexplored territory.

There is so much vagueness, regional variation and overlap in the common naming of different species of clam that it would take a very long and geeky book to even attempt to accurately catalogue them. But here is a (very simplified) 'clam primer' which should allow you at least an educated guess at what you are putting in your chowder. But don't be surprised if someone from 10 miles up the coast calls them something different!

Hard-shell clams

This is the name given to the group of roughly rhombus- or triangular-shaped clams, often concentrically banded, growing to around 6cm (2½in). As the name suggests, their shells are hard, and not at all brittle like razor clams or soft-shell clams. The key hard-shell clams are:

- **Carpet shell** (*Ruditapes* spp.). Rhomboid in shape and tend to live in coarse sand and gravel all around the North Atlantic. The best known and tastiest is the grooved (or cross-cut) carpet shell, also known as the palourde (*R. decussatus*), which is the clam traditionally used in the classic Italian dish spaghetti alle vongole.
- **Venus shell** (*Venus* spp.). Similar to the carpet shell but more triangular in shape, and prefers finer sand.
- **Quahog** (*Mercenaria mercenaria*). One of the most popular North American clams, with many common names, including hard clam, round clam and chowder clam. It is not common in the UK, with just a couple of non-native colonies in southern England. It has a thick, grey to off-white shell with concentric growth rings, up to 8–12cm (3–5in). They are often found in similar locations to razor clams, but also on the muddy bottoms of tidal streams where they are best raked up or perhaps groped for with bare toes. There are a host of different names for different sizes of quahog, including, from smallest to largest, countneck or peanut (tenderest, often eaten raw), littleneck, topneck, cherrystone and chowder. Chowder clams are the toughest and, as their name suggests, the variety most commonly used (chopped) to make chowder.

Soft-shell clams

These species have larger but more brittle shells than hard-shell clams. They are oval-shaped, with a long siphon that extends from the top. Once its tough skin is peeled off, the siphon is usually the best eating on them. The key soft-shell clams to know are:

- **Sand gaper** (*Mya arenaria*), known in North America as the soft-shell, longneck or steamer clam. It grows up to 15cm (6in) long, with a long protruding siphon. These are the clams traditionally used in chowder and clam bakes.
- **Otter shell** (*Lutraria lutraria*). Grows up to 12cm (5in) long. They are very similar to sand gapers but have a darker shell and a shorter, more tender siphon.

Trough-shell clams

These clams generally live subtidally and are beyond the reach of most foragers, but the best known and most accessible of them is the surf clam (*Spisula solida*), found in the eastern Atlantic, which grows up to 5cm (2in) long. A much larger North American variant is the Atlantic surf clam (*Spisula solidissima*), also known as the hen, bar or skimmer clam, which grows up to 20cm (8in) long. These clams like wave-exposed beaches and live just beneath the sand, but they may be found rolling around if you get lucky. The abductor muscle is tender and tasty, earning it the name beach scallop, but the rest is rather tough, best ground and added to chowders or sauce, or fermented into garum (see page 249).

In North America, wild clams may be managed as a commercial fishery, and some colonies are actively cultivated, so check local regulations and, if necessary, obtain a permit before harvesting. Commercial clamming is less common around the UK and Ireland, except for a few spots in the south of England.

Provided you follow the shellfish safety checklist on page 222, any wild clam you find will be edible and tasty, with the main culinary distinctions being where they sit on the tender–chewy spectrum. Generally, the larger they are, the chewier they will be, and they may be better chopped into smaller pieces. All my advice and recipes for cockles (see pages 252–3) applies here, though depuration is less important as most species of clam tend to trap less sand.

Spaghetti alle vongole

This is a classic Italian way to cook clams, and you can make it even wilder by using sea spaghetti (see page 199). The best clams to use for this are venus shells, but other species will still be delicious. It is served with the clams still in their shells.

Ingredients

1kg (2lb 3oz) clams in their shells, washed and depurated

300g (11oz) spaghetti, sea spaghetti, or a mixture of the two

4 tablespoons olive oil

4 garlic cloves, chopped

1 red chilli, deseeded and finely diced

125ml (4 fl oz) white wine

1 handful of parsley leaves, chopped

Salt

Bring a large pot of salted water to the boil and add the spaghetti. In another pan, heat the olive oil and add the garlic and chilli, sautéing until soft, but not browned. Add the clams and wine, pop a lid on and turn up the heat. With the lid held on, vigorously shake the clams every 30 seconds. They should be cooked and open after three minutes or so. Discard any that refuse to open and any empty shells.

Strain the spaghetti, retaining a cup of the cooking liquid. Toss the spaghetti and parsley through the clam and wine sauce, adding a little of the retained cooking water if you'd like things a bit wetter.

Italians will not approve, but you can tweak this dish by adding chopped onions, chunks of chorizo and chopped fresh (or even tinned) tomatoes.

Pickling your coastal harvest

Pickling – preserving food in an acidic solution – is a great way to store harvests of coastal plants, seaweeds and shellfish, as well as enhancing their flavours. This technique will help you pickle whatever you come home with competently and confidently.

The key to making good pickles is to achieve a pleasing balance of sharp and sweet, with the sharpness coming from vinegar. The strength of acids such as vinegar is measured on the pH scale, with 7 being neutral (water) and 1 being very corrosive acid. Moulds and bacteria that spoil food do not grow in acidic environments with a pH lower than 4.6. Most store-bought vinegars have a pH between 2 and 3 (2.2 is common). Pickling in undiluted vinegar is too acidic for most people, and can corrode what you are trying to preserve into mush, overpower the flavour and

be unpleasantly sour to eat. By diluting and sweetening our pickling vinegar, while keeping its pH below 4.6, we can make delicious preserves that keep well. Avoid strongly flavoured vinegars such as balsamic or malt, as they mask other flavours. More neutral vinegars such as apple cider vinegar, white wine vinegar or rice vinegar are generally best.

Opposite: Clockwise from top left. Egg wrack 'capers'; marsh samphire with spices; sea lettuce in ground ivy vinegar; sea sandwort with alexanders seeds; sea plantain; sea spaghetti with soy and chilli.

Basic 3-2-1 pickling recipe

For a tasty balance of acidity and sweetness in your pickles use a 3-2-1 ratio of dilution, which means 3 parts water to 2 parts vinegar to 1 part sugar. Salt can be added as seasoning and to improve keeping qualities.

Ingredients

300ml (11 fl oz) water

200ml (7 fl oz) apple cider vinegar (or other vinegar)

100g (3½oz) white sugar

1 teaspoon sea salt

About 1kg (2lb 3oz) of the plant, seaweed or shellfish you wish to pickle, thoroughly cleaned and cut to the size you require

Jars with tight-fitting rubber-sealed lids (or use plastic wrap)

Mix the water, vinegar and sugar in a pan, following the ratio of 3 parts water to 2 parts vinegar to 1 part sugar. Add the salt and heat, and stir until the sugar is dissolved. This is your basic pickling mix. This quantity of pickling solution will vary a little according to how densely your harvest fills the jar, but any surplus keeps well.

Now you can choose whether to cold pickle or hot pickle and what herb and spice embellishments you'd like (see page 261). I've noted my recommended method for each harvest on page 262 and in individual species guides.

Hot pickling

This method is recommended for harvests that benefit from a bit of softening up or need to be cooked. It improves keeping qualities but will diminish the crisp texture of succulent plants and seaweeds.

Make sure your jars and lids have been thoroughly cleaned. Add your prepared harvest to a pan of 3-2-1 pickle mix (see page 258) and bring to the boil. Turn the heat down to just below simmering for 5 minutes. Spoon your harvest into the jars. Top the jars up with the pickling solution while it's still very hot. Screw the lids on the jars while everything is still hot and leave to cool. If you don't have jars with glass lids and good rubber seals, fold a few layers of plastic wrap over the mouth of the jar, then screw on the lid. This will prevent the lid from corroding.

Hot pickles will keep for many months in the fridge, but eat them within a couple of weeks once opened. If not stored in the fridge, open and use within one month. Make sure your harvest stays submerged in the pickle solution, especially if you intend to keep it for a long time. A good way to do this is to take a very clean yogurt pot or small plastic tub, trimmed to size, and squeeze it into place on top of the harvest in the jar, where it should be held in place by the cap or shoulder of the jar.

Cold pickling

This method will keep the texture of your harvest crisp, but it may not keep as well. Allow the 3-2-1 pickle mix to cool. Make sure your jars and lids have been thoroughly cleaned, and ensure that your harvest is clear of debris. If in any doubt about this, plunge your harvest into boiling water for a maximum of five seconds, then immediately plunge it into iced water. Fill the jars with your harvest. Top up the jars with the cold pickling solution and screw on the lids. Store in the fridge for up to one month, or longer if you increased the acidity of the pickling solution.

Quick hot pickling

This is a middle way between hot and cold pickling. Pour the hot pickling solution into jars filled with an uncooked harvest. This works well to just slightly soften things, and increase keeping qualities.

Variations and embellishments

As you gain more confidence, don't worry about sticking exactly to the 3-2-1 ratio. Sample your pickling solution and tweak it to your taste as you make it. If you like a sharper-tasting pickle, you can equalize or reverse the 3 parts water and 2 parts vinegar in the basic recipe (2-2-1 or 2-3-1). You might vary this depending on what you are pickling, how you intend to eat it, how long you'd like to keep it and at what temperature you will store it. The sugar can be cut back, omitted altogether, or replaced with honey.

You can embellish by adding herbs and spices to your basic mix. Some work better cold-infused into the vinegar beforehand, while others should be added to the mix then simmered for 20 minutes or so to infuse. You can strain them out before filling the jars, or leave them in to infuse more flavour and add spicy flavour-bombs when eating.

Classic pickling spices include bay leaves, mustard seeds, coriander seeds, fennel seeds, star anise, peppercorns, chillies, juniper, horseradish (sliced thinly), garlic (sliced thinly), fresh ginger (sliced thinly), fennel (leaves or green seeds or dry seeds), dill, lemon peel, soy sauce and miso paste. Try adding about 1 tablespoon of each of these in any combination per 1kg (2lb 3oz) of harvest. You may wish to toast the hard spices in a dry frying pan first.

Wild herbs, spices and seaweeds also work well: alexanders (seeds), Scots lovage (seeds, leaves and stems), rock samphire (seeds), sea lettuce (dry flakes or pieces), pepper dulse (dried and ground), razor clam offal garum, and ground ivy (leaves and stems).

Eating your pickles

Here are some ideas for how to eat your pickles. Use the pickling solution too – it's great in salad dressing, especially if you have infused it with herbs and spices.

- With cheese
- Mixed through salads
- On the side of hot dishes (like a relish)
- On pizzas
- In sandwiches or on toast (under melted cheese)
- With charcuterie
- In or with wild sushi (see page 145)
- As antipasti
- By the jarful (for pickle addicts!)
- In/with a martini
- On laverbread/laverburgers (see pages 184–5)

What to pickle and how

Plants

Succulent coastal plants are versatile and forgiving when pickled. Below are my recommended pickling methods and embellishments, but please experiment!

PLANTS	PARTS TO PICKLE	HOT PICKLE	COLD PICKLE	QUICK HOT PICKLE	NOTES
Alexanders	Stems (peeled), flower buds			✓	Sprinkle salt over stems and leave overnight.
Sea sandwort	All harvested		✓	✓	Quick hot pickle if they are starting to become bitter. Try pre-infusing the vinegar with ground ivy.
Sea radish	Silques, leaf stems	✓	✓		Good with chilli.
Rock samphire	Leaves, green stems	✓	✓		Can take lots of spices. Blanch first if you like a milder flavour.
Sea aster	Leaves		✓		Try adding sea lettuce flakes to the mix.
Marsh samphire	All harvested	✓	✓		Great with lots of ginger and star anise.
Sea plantain/ buckshorn plantain	All harvested	✓	✓		Good with sand leek baubles.
Sea-blite	All harvested	✓	✓		Remove twiggy stems before pickling.
Sea purslane	All harvested		✓		Best not to heat as it can go slimy.
Sand leek	Bulbils, whole or broken up		✓		Great with pastrami

Seaweeds

Seaweeds will thicken the pickle mix with their alginates, especially if hot pickled. This does not affect their flavour but you may wish to give them a quick rinse before serving.

SEAWEED	PARTS TO PICKLE	HOT PICKLE	COLD PICKLE	QUICK HOT PICKLE	NOTES
Wrack	Tips and receptacles	✓	✓		Hot pickle if you wish to soften the tips. Receptacles are best cold pickled.
Sea lettuce and dulse	All harvested		✓		Fully dehydrate then pack into jars and press down the pickle solution until there are no air bubbles.
Sea spaghetti	All harvested	✓	✓		Cold pickle tender spring fronds; hot pickle fatter later harvests.
Mermaid's tresses	All harvested		✓		Especially good with lots of soy sauce.
Kelp	All harvested	✓	✓		Slice blades into thin strips first. Hot pickle to tenderize tougher blades.
Dabberlocks	All harvested		✓		Delicious with fresh garlic and ginger.

Shellfish

Mussels, limpets, winkles, cockles and some smaller clams all pickle well. Around the UK, pickling shellfish is a long-established tradition in coastal resort towns. If you want to do this at home, follow the shellfish safety checklist on page 222 and pickle only shellfish that are twitchingly fresh from clean waters.

Unadulterated malt vinegar is traditional for pickling shellfish and will preserve them for at least a month, but if you aren't intending to store them for a long period, or are susceptible to heartburn, I recommend the basic 3-2-1 pickle mix. A quick hot pickle works best – there is no need to simmer the cooked shellfish meat in the pickle mix.

Depurate the shellfish first (see page 223) then steam them in a little water for a few minutes until they open. Remove the meat, rinse thoroughly to ensure it is free of grit and sand, then pack in clean jars before topping up with pickling solution.

Resources

Although many of the resources below mention a geographic area, most of them are still useful beyond that.

Books

Stalking the Blue-Eyed Scallop, Euell Gibbons
A classic US-focused exploration of coastal foraging, with a strong emphasis on shellfish, written in a more carefree age.

The Wild Flower Key, Francis Rose and Clare O'Reilly
A well-structured book on wild plant identification (UK/Europe, but plenty of relevance to eastern North America).

Seaweeds of Britain and Europe, Francis Bunker et al
A comprehensive field guide to seaweeds (without foraging information). Helpful on both sides of the North Atlantic.

Field Guide to the Water Life of Britain, Reader's Digest
A beautiful and cheap illustrated guide covering all the weird and wonderful things you may encounter on the coast (and in fresh water).

Edible Seashore, John Wright
A fun introduction to coastal foraging around the UK.

Irish Seaweed Kitchen, Prannie Rhatagan
A comprehensive guide to healthy cooking with seaweeds.

Seaweed in the Kitchen, Fiona Bird
A ramble through seaweed uses and recipes.

Vegetables From the Sea, Seibin and Teruko Araski
An excellent source of nutritional information and recipes for seaweed.

Seaweeds – Edible, Available and Sustainable, Ole G. Mouritsen
A glossy deep dive into all aspects of seaweeds.

The Encyclopedia of Edible Plants of North America, Francois Couplan
A comprehensive run through edible plants of North America.

Edible Wild Plants, John Kallas
Not coastally focused, has good detail on wild spinaches and dock.

Field Guide to Edible Wild Plants: of Eastern and Central North America, Sam Thayer
An excellent exploration of edible plants.

Wildness: An Ode to Newfoundland and Labrador, Jeremy Charles
Not a foraging guide, but has wild inspiration in the form of recipes from one of Canada's leading chefs.

Learn to forage

Galloway Wild Foods: gallowaywildfoods.com
Most of the species covered in this book (and lots more non-coastal forageables) are explored in depth on my website. It also includes deep explorations of the legalities, politics, ethics and culture of gathering food from the wild. I also regularly share seasonal tips on Instagram (@markwildfood) and Facebook (Galloway Wild Foods). The best way to gain confidence with foraging is to go out with someone experienced. I run guided coastal forays covering most of the species in this book between March and September across Scotland, and further afield by arrangement – see my website for details.

Association of Foragers: foragers-association.org
An international professional foragers association, promoting considerate foraging, nature connection and ecological stewardship through teaching and harvesting wild plants, seaweeds and fungi. All members subscribe to clearly stated principles around the ethics of foraging. There is a directory of members so you can find a course provider that teaches coastal foraging in your area.

Wild Walks Southwest: wildwalks-southwest.co.uk
An excellent source of information and recipes on coastal (and other) forageables by foraging guide Rachel Lambert.

Forager Chef: foragerchef.com
Wild food tutorials, recipes and techniques from chef Alan Bergo.

Coastal ecology

Marine Life Information Network: marlin.ac.uk
Extensive information on the biology of species and the ecology of habitats found around the coasts and seas of the British Isles (but much also applies across the North Atlantic).

The Seaweed Site: seaweed.ie
A font of good, clear information on seaweed (Ireland-based, but relevant across the North Atlantic).

Go Botany: gobotany.nativeplanttrust.org
A great resource for researching plants and their distribution on the east coast of the US.

Survival of New England's salt marshes:
pmc.ncbi.nlm.nih.gov/articles/PMC6161497/#S5
An exploration of the challenges faced by salt marshes on the US North Atlantic coast – and relevant elsewhere too.

USDA Natural Resources Conservation Service PLANTS Database: plants.usda.gov/
An excellent resource for checking the distribution and abundance of plants in the US.

Foraging law

UK: *Negotiating the Non-negotiable: British Foraging Law in Theory and Practice*, Jennifer Lee and Supriya Garikipati, 2011, Journal of Environmental Law 23:3.
www.jstor.org/stable/44248787
Exploring the complexities and vagaries of UK foraging law.

US: *Food Law Gone Wild – The Law of Foraging*
ir.lawnet.fordham.edu/cgi/viewcontent.cgi?article=2740&context=ulj.
An excellent deep-dive into the history and current situation around foraging law in the US.

Water quality and shellfish harvesting restrictions

US States, Canadian Provinces and UK Regional Councils provide localized information on shellfish harvesting restrictions, water quality, etc. They are too numerous to list here, but see for example:
Maine Shellfish Identification and Recreational Limits
www.maine.gov/dmr/fisheries/shellfish/shellfish-identification

Canada – Shellfish Harvesting Map
www.dfo-mpo.gc.ca/shellfish-mollusques/cssp-map-eng.htm
A live map showing shellfish harvesting restrictions, algal blooms, etc. Other pages have excellent general information on shellfish harvesting that are helpful beyond Canada.

UK – Surfers Against Sewage: datahq.sas.org.uk
Safer Seas and Rivers Service (live map)
A good source of independent advice on water quality around the UK, including a regularly updated map of pollution hotspots.

UK – Food Standards Agency, Biotoxin and phytoplankton monitoring: www.food.gov.uk/business-guidance/biotoxin-and-phytoplankton-monitoring#closures

Sea and intertidal fisheries, guidance and services (Wales):
www.gov.wales/sea-intertidal-fisheries (Welsh government)

Radiation and shellfish

Health Risk to Seafood Consumers from Radioactive Particles in the Marine Environment near Sellafield: assets.publishing.service.gov.uk/media/5a75a63140f0b67f59fce864/PHE-CRCE-021.pdf

Radioactivity concentration measurements in fish and shellfish samples from the west coast of Canada after the Fukushima nuclear accident (2011–2018): www.sciencedirect.com/science/article/pii/S0265931X22001254

Tides and weather

Tides 4 Fishing (Website or App): tides4fishing.com/
A free service that gives tide times (and weather forecasts) for thousands of coastal stations, but only up to one week ahead.

Nautide (App): nautide.com/
Tide tables and weather for all North Atlantic coasts for up to one year ahead (requires subscription).

Index

About the author

Mark Williams grew up on the Isle of Arran on Scotland's west coast and has been teaching about foraging for over 35 years. He runs a wide range of guided events throughout the year on all aspects of wild food, from coastal foraging to fungi, healthy wild eating to drunken botany. On some trips he combines sailing or sea kayaking with foraging and wild gastronomy. He now lives in the forager's paradise of Galloway, south-west Scotland where, when not teaching or foraging, he can be found on his veranda 'researching' wild cocktails. He is a founder member of The Association of Foragers.

Acknowledgements

I am grateful for the patience of my wonderful wife and rock Cara, for tolerating my 'creative chaos', grumpy moments and a permanently hectic, often squelchy, fridge. I must also mention Gripper, my ever-present sidekick and joyful energy source on foraging missions. I'm particularly proud of how he has learned to interpret the nuances of tides and currents to help him forage his ultimate prize – balls!

This book wouldn't exist without my friend and foraging hero Liz Knight (surely you've read her foraging books!?) who introduced me to the great team at Skittledog:

Zara Larcombe, who believed me when I said that coastal foraging is about so much more than seaweeds, and let me have illustrations *and* photographs. This book would be a little more than a ramble without my brilliant editor Virginia Brehaut, who patiently and sensitively compressed the best of my massive draft into 272 elegant pages. Thanks too to Sofia Iva for accommodating all my tweaks to her fabulous illustrations and bringing out both the detail and personality of our cast of characters. I had a fantastic few days with photographer and daredevil Charles Emerson, whose eye for composition and head for heights really capture the beauty of the Galloway coast and its inhabitants.

Nothing comes from nowhere, and my thoughts and advice in this book are built on the knowledge, creativity and generosity of my foraging friends and fellow teachers and several thousand generations of foragers before them. In particular, thanks to David Labbe, whose advice on North American species and their distribution has been a huge help.

Above all I am grateful for this beautiful, generous world that has fed and taught me all my life, and in particular our great mother sea, who, despite our many abuses, continues to soothe and nourish us.

Skittledog

First published in the United Kingdom in 2026
by Skittledog, an imprint of Thames & Hudson Ltd,
6–24 Britannia Street, London WC1X 9JD

The Coastal Forager © 2026 Thames & Hudson Ltd, London

Text © 2026 Mark Williams

Illustrations © 2026 Sofia Iva

Senior Editor: Virginia Brehaut
Cover Designer: Alison Guile
Designer: Masumi Briozzo
Production: Felicity Awdry
Photographer: Charles Emerson

Additional photographs by Mark Williams: pages 39 (top
left and bottom), 43, 52 (right), 53, 69 (top left and top
right), 74, 94, 102, 116, 117, 118, 120 (top left and bottom right),
124, 141, 148 (top left and bottom right), 178, 183, 205 (right)
and 218 (middle and bottom left). stock.adobe.com, pages:
11 RTimages, 140 popovj2, 144 Tamara Kulikova, 204 (right)
Alena AV, 218 (top) AngieC and 227 magicbones. unsplash.
com: page 52 (left) Ram Kishor. Virginia Brehaut, pages:
98 (top right) and 106.

EU Authorized Representative: Interart S.A.R.L.
19 rue Charles Auray, 93500 Pantin, Paris, France
productsafety@thameshudson.co.uk
www.interart.fr

A CIP catalogue record for this book is available from
the British Library

ISBN 978-1-83776-072-5
01

Printed and bound in China by C&C Offset Printing Co., Ltd

FSC
www.fsc.org
MIX
Paper | Supporting
responsible forestry
FSC® C008047

Be the first to know about our new releases, exclusive
content and author events by visiting:

skittledog.com
thamesandhudson.com
thamesandhudsonusa.com
thamesandhudson.com.au